the BIG BANG THEORY™

The Official Trivia Guide

Adam Faberman

TOUCHSTONE
New York London Toronto Sydney New Delhi

Touchstone
An Imprint of Simon & Schuster, Inc.
1230 Avenue of the Americas
New York, NY 10020

First published in 2015 in Great Britain by HEADLINE PUBLISHING GROUP
Published by arrangement with Hodder & Stoughton Limited.

First Touchstone trade paperback edition October 2015

TOUCHSTONE and colophon are registered trademarks of Simon & Schuster, Inc.

For information about special discounts for bulk purchases, please contact Simon & Schuster Special Sales at 1-866-506-1949 or business@simonandschuster.com.

The Simon & Schuster Speakers Bureau can bring authors to your live event. For more information or to book an event, contact the Simon & Schuster Speakers Bureau at 866-248-3049 or visit our website at www.simonspeakers.com.

Interior design by Perfect Bound Ltd.

Manufactured in the United States of America

10 9 8 7 6 5 4 3 2 1

Library of Congress Cataloging-in-Publication Data

Faberman, Adam.
The big bang theory : the official trivia guide / Adam Faberman — First Touchstone trade paperback edition.
pages cm
1. Big bang theory (Television program)—Miscellanea. I. Title.
PN1992.77.B485F33 2015
791.45'72—dc23

2015033552

ISBN 978-1-5011-2715-1
ISBN 978-1-5011-2716-8 (ebook)

Contents

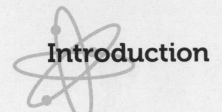

Introduction

Penny moved across the hall from Leonard and Sheldon on September 24, 2007, the same day *The Big Bang Theory* moved into my heart. Since you picked up this book, I'm guessing the show had a similar effect on you.

I have had the enormous privilege of being the script coordinator on this show since season 1. It's been the opportunity of a lifetime. It is such a joy to drive onto the Warner Bros. lot five days a week and work with tremendously talented, kind people who all put their heart and soul into every episode of this show.

One of the things I'm most proud about working on *The Big Bang Theory* is that it's a show the entire family can watch together. This means the world to me. After a long day of work or school, a family getting together, sitting in the same room and watching a television show is, quite frankly, a special thing. Families should do more things together—even if it is just to take a moment from their lives and laugh.

The other thing that makes me so proud to work on the show is that it's made science cool. I can't even begin to tell you just how many stories I've heard about young people who have been inspired to consider a career in the sciences because of *The Big Bang Theory.* I've learned more science working on this show than I did in all my time in school. This isn't an indictment of the American educational system, it's just—well, okay, it's a slight indictment. But that's the thing: growing up and becoming a scientist was never really something I aspired to. Which is probably for the best, because to this day I still have to count things out using my fingers.

Working on this book has given me a chance to reflect on the past eight years. It's been a wonderful but intense process. Last night, I woke up at 4:00 a.m. and remembered I forgot a quote from Sheldon: "Your 'check engine' light is on." I quickly grabbed my phone and typed a note so I wouldn't forget to add it to the book. I've been having these middle-of-the-night recollections a lot lately. So much so that for a while there I wondered if I was going insane. But that's okay; once I turn the book over to the publisher, I'm going to have my mother get me tested.

Adam Faberman
Warner Bros. Studios
Burbank, CA
May 2015

The Interrogation Stimulation

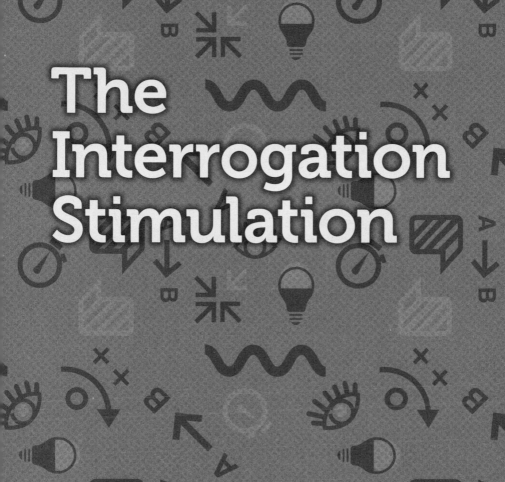

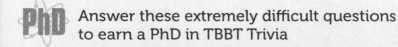

Master's Answer these bonus questions and get a Master's degree in TBBT Trivia

PhD Answer these extremely difficult questions to earn a PhD in TBBT Trivia

Season 1

1 Sheldon is proud to be the youngest winner of which award before Dennis Kim comes along?

2 What kind of engineer is Howard?

3 Germophobe Sheldon is concerned Penny may have brought some pathogens back from her trip home: "And having never been to Nebraska, I'm fairly certain I have no ___________ antibodies."

4 When Sheldon asks Penny who he should speak to about permanently reserving his table at the Cheesecake Factory, who does she suggest?

5 What "amazing" gift does Howard get Leonard for his birthday?

6 Sheldon, Howard and Raj are trying to persuade Leonard not to sell his collectibles. When Sheldon wields a toy sword, what line from *The Lord of the Rings* does he say?

7 Who does Sheldon recruit for his Physics Bowl team?

8 When Sheldon's twin sister, Missy, brags to her friends back home about Sheldon, what does she say he does for a living?

9 What kind of doctor is Raj's father?

10 Why doesn't Leonard celebrate his birthday?

11 What food is Howard allergic to?

12 Which "fairly savage preadolescent Jews" did the guys lose to at paintball?

Penny: I'm a vegetarian, except for fish, and the occasional steak. I love steak!
Sheldon: Well, that's interesting. Leonard can't process corn.

13 When Leonard and Sheldon fight at the Institute of Experimental Physics conference, who films it and posts it on YouTube?

14 *What is the name of the YouTube video?* **Master's**

15 In order to get his surprise party ready, Howard needs to keep Leonard in the ER and away from his apartment at all costs. When bribery fails, what does he do?

16 What does Sheldon accidentally call Leonard in Mandarin?

17 Howard and Raj are fighting on the floor: "I'm warning you, I was judo champion at __________ Camp."

18 Which of Sheldon's unlikely teammates correctly answers the final question of the 29th Annual Physics Bowl?

19 When Penny invites Sheldon into her apartment to tell him she is unsure about going out with Leonard, what does Sheldon do while she is talking to him?

20 While practicing her bartending skills, what drink does Penny make for Leonard?

21 When Leonard loses his glasses and is being guided through his apartment by Howard, what does Howard mean when he tells Leonard to "keep true"?

22 When Penny practices her cocktail-making, Raj discovers that he can talk to women after all. What cocktail is the secret to his newfound loquaciousness?

23 How old was Sheldon when he spent a summer at the Heidelberg Institute in Germany?

24 What is Leonard and Sheldon's combined IQ?

25 When Sheldon gets fired and refuses to apologize, who does Leonard call for help?

26 Why have the guys' rivals Fishman, Chen, Chaudury and McNair decided not to field a team in this year's Physics Bowl?

27 What condition does Raj have that means he can't talk to women?

28 What happened to upset Sheldon and lead him to learn Mandarin?

29 Which way does a sick Sheldon want Penny to rub VapoRub on his chest?

Howard: See a Penny, pick her up, and all the day, you'll have good luck.
Penny: No, you won't.

30 Sheldon decides to stop going to the Souplantation because the name confuses him. Why?

31 Sheldon explains why he is surrounded by fish in bowls: "I read an article about Japanese scientists who inserted DNA from luminous jellyfish into other animals and I thought, hey, __________ __________."

32 Penny walks into Leonard and Sheldon's apartment to ask them to turn the music down. Why are they so excited to have the stereo on?

33 *Penny asks the guys why they are doing that, and they reply in unison. What do they say?* **Master's**

34 When Penny tells Leonard grown men don't play with toys, who does he decide to sell his comic book collectibles collection to?

35 Why does Penny break up with her boyfriend, Mike?

36 Howard is frustrated that no one correctly identifies his costume for Penny's Halloween party. Who is he supposed to be?

37 How long is the *Planet of the Apes* marathon that Leonard, Howard and Raj go to to lie low while Sheldon is sick?

38 What is the name of the girl Raj's parents try to set him up with?

39 When Sheldon is fired and spends his days experimenting, how many eggs does he ask Penny to buy for his scrambled-egg research?

40 At Penny's Halloween party, what scientific principle does Sheldon's costume represent?

41 How many comic books does Leonard have?

42 What shift does Penny persuade the Cheesecake Factory to give her?

43 Who lived in Penny's apartment before her?

44 What musical instrument does Leonard play?

45 ***Which scientific principle does Sheldon explain to Penny as a way to help her understand her decision about whether or not to date Leonard?*** PhD

46 When Leonard is hooking up with Leslie Winkle, he confuses Sheldon by hanging a tie on the doorknob. Who has to explain what it means to him?

47 Penny has just met Leonard and Sheldon: "So, what do you guys do for fun around here?" Sheldon: "Well, today we tried ____________ for money."

48 When Penny helps Leonard find something to wear for his presentation, what comic book collectible does she find in his closet?

49 Who did Sheldon call a "glorified high school science teacher whose last successful experiment was lighting his own farts"?

50 How many times does Sheldon tell Raj's date he showers every day?

51 What does Penny's ex-boyfriend Kurt do to embarrass Leonard at Penny's Halloween party?

52 Who concludes a particularly vigorous dance session with the words "Grab a napkin, homie, you just got served"?

53 Why does Sheldon bring Leonard a cup of tea?

54 When Howard goes to Penny's apartment to ask Sheldon's sister for a date, how does he try to impress her?

55 What disappointing gift did Sheldon's parents get him for his twelfth birthday?

56 What time does Sheldon wake up every Saturday?

57 What costume does Penny find in Leonard's closet?

58 *When Penny asks why he didn't wear it on Halloween, what is Leonard's explanation?* **Master's**

59 Why does Sheldon cancel his membership to the Planetarium, despite having been a member since he was five years old?

Mary: He gets his temper from his daddy.
Leonard: Ah!
Mary: He's got my eyes.
Leonard: I see!
Mary: All that science stuff, that comes from Jesus.

60 According to his mother, the secret ingredient in Sheldon's favorite cobbler isn't love, it's ___________.

61 Penny's Halloween party starts at 7:00 p.m. What time do the guys show up?

62 ***Leonard tells Penny he can't attend her musical showcase because he is going to a symposium on ___________ in ___________.*** PhD

63 *Who does Sheldon say the imaginary symposium is going to be given by?* Master's

64 Why had Leonard stopped seeing his previous girlfriend, Joyce Kim?

65 When Sheldon spots Raj in the Cheesecake Factory with the girl his parents arranged for him to meet, which "beloved fictional character come to life" does she remind him of?

66 Why does Sheldon break into Penny's apartment in the middle of the night?

67 Sheldon tells Penny that Leonard cannot attend her showcase because he is taking Sheldon to an intervention for his cousin, who has escaped from rehab. What is his cousin's name?

68 Sheldon was disappointed by his twelfth birthday present. What was it that he had really wanted?

69 How does Penny's ex-boyfriend Kurt spell "confrontation"?

70 Leonard reassures Penny that there are plenty of people in the audience for his presentation: "In particle physics, twenty-five people in attendance is ___________."

71 According to Sheldon, Penny's costume at her Halloween party is a good example of what can go wrong when there's a lack of rules. What is it?

72 What one-night musical showcase is it that Penny invites Leonard and Sheldon to?

73 *What part does Penny get?* **Master's**

74 “Obviously, you’re not well-suited for three-dimensional chess. Perhaps three-dimensional Candy Land would be more your speed.” Who has Sheldon defeated?

75 What number apartment does Penny live in?

76 On the basis that “Teams are traditionally named after fierce creatures,” what does Sheldon think is a good name for a Physics Bowl team?

77 At the *Planet of the Apes* marathon, who is Howard talking to when he says: “Take your stinking paws off my popcorn, you damned dirty ape!”

78 Leonard explains to Sheldon that his system for organizing his groceries is a little unusual: “Hard as it may be for you to believe, most people don’t sort their breakfast cereal numerically by __________ __________.”

79 Who has to take Sheldon to pick out a birthday gift for Leonard, just as the party preparations are starting?

Sheldon: Oh gravity, thou art a heartless bitch.

80 When Leonard tells Sheldon he isn't sure whether he should go out with Penny or not, what common grammatical mistake does Sheldon point out?

81 What is the production error on Leonard's rare mint-condition *Star Trek: The Next Generation* Geordi La Forge action figure?

82 When we first meet Leonard's colleague Leslie Winkle, she is trying to see how long it takes to use a 500-kilowatt oxygen iodine laser to heat up what?

83 Leonard considers opening his presentation at the Institute of Experimental Physics conference with a physics joke about a spherical what?

84 When Leonard finally arrives at his surprise birthday party, what song is Raj singing?

85 Sheldon is unwilling to try Penny's cocktails, and prefers a Diet Coke. When she refuses, what does he request?

86 When the time machine is blocking Penny's way Sheldon suggests an alternate route: "Go up to the roof, hop over to the next building there's a small gap, don't look down if you're subject to vertigo—and use their stairwell." How big does Penny discover the small gap actually is?

87 ***How does Sheldon propose to solve the Middle East crisis?***

88 Who is Sheldon's mother talking to when she says: "I made chicken. I hope that isn't one of the animals that you people think is magic."

89 How much does Sheldon tell Missy to report back to his mother that he weighs?

90 At his introductory mixer, why does child prodigy Dennis Kim leave rather than tell everyone about his upcoming research?

91 When Raj suggests they need a "kickass team name" for their Physics Bowl team, what does Howard suggest?

92 How does Leonard describe Penny's job at the Cheesecake Factory?

93 When we first see Sheldon, what superhero T-shirt is he wearing?

94 Who's the only guy without a PhD?

95 What song does a drunk Sheldon sing at the Cheesecake Factory after Penny secretly puts rum in his Diet Coke?

96 Which "apparently very smart" TV actor does Raj suggest might make a good replacement for Sheldon on their Physics Bowl team?

97 When Sheldon is shopping for a birthday gift for Leonard, what is his first idea?

98 Who do Leonard, Howard and Raj ask to replace Sheldon on their Physics Bowl team?

99 What costume does Leonard wear for Penny's Halloween party?

100 When Raj first tells everyone he has been accepted to be a test subject for a miracle drug to overcome pathological shyness, what happens to his right hand?

101 How do Leonard and Sheldon get into Penny's ex-boyfriend Kurt's building?

102 When Penny invites the guys over for cocktails, what drink does she refuse to make for Howard?

103 ***Sheldon says his sandwich is "an unmitigated disaster." How has the restaurant gotten his order wrong?*** PhD

104 To which hotel are Leonard and Sheldon invited to present their paper on supersolids?

105 What gift does Leonard give Sheldon when he tells him the guys have decided to throw him off the Physics Bowl team?

106 Leonard wins a time machine in an online auction. What movie is it a prop from?

107 What song does Sheldon ask Penny to sing to him when he's sick?

Leonard: *Homo habilis* discovering his opposable thumbs says what?
Kurt: What?

108 Sheldon thinks Leonard's chances of a Nobel Prize are slim: "The day you win a Nobel Prize is the day I begin my research on the drag coefficient of tassels on __________ __________."

109 What instrument does Leslie Winkle play in the physics department string quartet?

110 Leonard and Sheldon's visit to Penny's ex-boyfriend's apartment ends in failure and humiliation. What does he take from them?

111 How old was Sheldon when he converted his sister's Easy-Bake Oven into "some kind of high-powered furnace"?

112 What food does Leonard offer Missy when she stays over at the apartment?

113 The time machine is owned by all four friends, but who gets to sit in it first?

114 When Sheldon decides none of the guys is good enough for his sister, who is he talking to when he says: "It's nothing personal. I just prefer if my future niece or nephew didn't become flatulent every time they ate an Eskimo pie."

115 What song is played when PMS wins the 29th Annual Physics Bowl?

116 What is the name of the research assistant from the particle physics lab who Sheldon recruits to pretend to be his drug-addicted cousin?

117 When Leonard, Howard and Raj all want to date Sheldon's sister, Missy, how do they decide to honorably fight it out?

118 It's not long after she has moved in that Penny gives Leonard and Sheldon a spare key. Why?

119 Having only just met them, Penny asks if it would be totally weird if she used what in Leonard and Sheldon's apartment?

120 What nickname does Raj give his next-door neighbor?

121 ***What's Tressling?***

122 What "awesome limited edition" does Raj give Leonard for his birthday?

123 When Howard seduces "the whore of Omaha" in Penny's apartment, what computer game does Penny have to take his place for?

124 What does Howard explain to Penny is the only way to make Sheldon get a gift for Leonard?

125 Who teaches Sheldon to speak Mandarin?

126 Penny asks Howard to get Leonard out of the apartment for a few hours so they can set up his surprise party. After all his attempts fail, what reason does Howard give Leonard to make sure he leaves?

127 Which fictional flesh-eating creatures does Sheldon encounter in his time machine dream?

128 *What is the name of their moving company?* **Master's**

129 When Sheldon's sister comes to visit, his friends all want to go out with her. But which of them does she want to go out with?

130 Who does Raj go to Penny's Halloween party dressed as?

131 What does Howard mean when he tells Sheldon that "the laundry is out of the hamper"?

132 What is "Sheldon's spot"?

133 What's on Leonard and Sheldon's shower curtain?

134 Remembering Sheldon's scientific explanation before their date, what does Penny say after Leonard kisses her?

135 The first time Leonard and Penny go to a restaurant, what physics principle does Leonard demonstrate by lifting an olive into a glass without touching it?

136 After insisting he's not a child, what does Howard ask his mother to give him for breakfast?

137 What is the name of Penny's friend she offers to introduce Howard to if he can successfully keep Leonard out of the apartment while she sets up the surprise party?

138 When Leonard pretends to travel to the future in the time machine, what do Sheldon, Howard and Raj do?

139 What number apartment do Leonard and Sheldon live in?

Leonard: You are not Isaac Newton.
Sheldon: No, no, that's true. Gravity would have been apparent to me without the apple.

140 What does Howard do when Penny falls asleep on his shoulder during Leonard's presentation about supersolids?

141 In Leonard's first attempt to impress Penny, what does he agree to try to retrieve from her ex-boyfriend?

142 Penny is not impressed by the guys' auction win: "Oh please, it's not a time machine. If anything, it looks like something ____________ ____________ would drive through the Everglades."

143 Growing up, Sheldon didn't have imaginary friends. He had imaginary ____________.

144 When Penny breaks up with Mike, she throws his iPod out Leonard and Sheldon's window. Who finds it on the street?

145 What is Leonard's middle name?

146 What does the "dumpling paradox" refer to?

147 What does Penny get Leonard for his birthday?

148 How does Penny know the Superman™ underwear she's found in the laundry room belongs to Leonard?

149 The guys talk about them each having the time machine on a time-share basis. Where does Raj want to kccp thc time machine when he has it in his apartment?

150 What is the receptionist doing when Leonard and Sheldon enter the sperm bank?

151 What battle is re-created using the condiments on the table of the Cheesecake Factory?

> **Sheldon:** Engineering. Where the noble semiskilled laborers execute the vision of those who think and dream. Hello, Oompa-Loompas of science.

152 What night is Halo night?

153 Having discovered that alcohol enables him to speak to women, what are Raj's first words to Penny?

154 What is printed on the back of PMS's T-shirts at the Physics Bowl?

155 What age was Sheldon when he went to college?

156 Why can't Leonard enjoy the *Planet of the Apes* marathon?

157 Raj's parents are eager to end their phone call with him and get back to their favorite show: "I'm sorry, darling, we have to go. __________ __________ is on."

158 How does Howard celebrate after his team wins the Physics Bowl?

159 When Leonard thinks about getting a cat to fill the relationship gap in his life, he's considering names: "I'm kind of torn between Einstein, Newton and __________ __________."

Penny: Why can't all guys be like you?
Leonard: Because if all guys were like me, the human race couldn't survive.

160 Sheldon's mom laments the trouble her son has caused her: "I love the boy to death, but he has been difficult since he fell out of me at the ___________."

161 Sheldon's friends know that no one wants to be around Sheldon when he's sick, so they use a code word to warn each other. What is it?

162 What kind of furniture do the guys struggle to put together for Penny?

163 Who is the "hot" girl the guys are shocked to see in Sheldon's office?

164 Why does Penny agree to go out to dinner with Leonard for the first time?

165 Why do Leonard, Howard and Raj kick Sheldon off their Physics Bowl team?

166 ***When Leonard and Sheldon first show Penny their whiteboards, what is the subject of the physics joke on Sheldon's?*** PhD

167 At the physics department party, who corners Sheldon for 45 minutes and speaks to him about spelunking?

168 ***Sheldon explains that Penny's favorite scene in the first*** **Superman** ***movie, where Lois Lane falls from a helicopter and Superman swoops down to save her, is scientifically inaccurate. What does he say would have happened to the falling Lois?*** PhD

169 What World of Warcraft weapon does Sheldon buy and then sell on eBay?

170 When the four guys are in the car with Penny for the first time, where does Howard suggest they go?

171 Who tampers with Sheldon's equations on his whiteboard and actually fixes a problem he was having?

172 After Sheldon cleans Penny's apartment in the middle of the night, he rewards himself with what kind of low-fiber cereal?

173 What does a shy Leonard do in order to fabricate a reason to talk to Penny?

174 Why does Sheldon throw away an invitation to Leonard and himself to give a speech on their supersolids work?

175 How does Leonard "fix" Penny's relationship with Mike after Mike blogs about their sex life?

176 Why does the gold-digging Christy break up with Howard?

177 Who follows Sheldon's twin sister, Missy, from the parking lot to his office?

178 When Leonard declares that he's done trying to pursue Penny, who does he ask out?

179 Where do Leonard and Penny have their first kiss?

180 Why does Leonard say he owes the Betty Crocker company a letter of apology?

181 What social convention does Leonard cite as a reason why he should intervene and help Penny when she splits up with Mike?

182 When Leonard and Sheldon are having difficulty moving Penny's furniture delivery up four flights of stairs, which superhero does Sheldon wish would help them?

183 When Leonard is depressed about seeing Penny with another guy, what kind of activity does Howard suggest as a way to cheer him up?

184 When Leonard asks who would sell a full-size time machine for $800, Sheldon refers to a Venn diagram. What two categories does he use to solve the query?

185 Why did Sheldon convert his sister, Missy's, Easy-Bake Oven into a powerful furnace?

186 On first meeting her, what language does Howard use to tell Penny she's pretty?

> **Sheldon:** A little misunderstanding? Galileo and the Pope had a little misunderstanding.

187 At the supermarket, what fun, interesting fact does Sheldon share with Penny about tomatoes?

188 At Penny's Halloween party, who do people *think* Howard is dressed as?

189 How does Sheldon's mother, Mary, reply when Sheldon asks her if Dr. Gablehauser will be his new daddy?

190 Why does Sheldon want to leave the sperm bank?

191 What is the name of the university that Leonard, Sheldon, Howard and Raj all work at?

192 What happens to Penny's laptop after she spills Diet Coke, yogurt and nail polish on it?

193 What character do Leonard, Sheldon, Howard and Raj all initially dress up as for Penny's Halloween party?

194 During their first meeting, Penny tells Sheldon and Leonard that she is which astrological sign?

195 What does Penny do when she finds out Sheldon broke into her apartment while she was sleeping?

196 What condition does Sheldon recommend Penny see an otolaryngologist about?

197 Before trying the Cheesecake Factory's barbecue burger, where did Sheldon's favorite burger come from?

198 At Penny's Halloween party, why does Cheryl hook up with Raj?

199 When Penny tries to help Leonard pick out a suit for his presentation, when does Leonard tell her he had his last growth spurt?

200 To test if he is sick, what does Sheldon use to make petri dishes?

The Roommate Agreement Legitimacy

Before Leonard could move in with Sheldon, they had to iron out a few details.

Sheldon: *(reading)* "Roommates agree that Friday nights shall be reserved for watching Joss Whedon's brilliant new series, *Firefly*."

Leonard: Does that really need to be in the agreement?

Sheldon: We might as well settle it now, it's going to be on for years. *(then)* Initial here.

Leonard does so.

Sheldon: All right, that's television and movies. "Section 9: miscellany. The apartment's flag is a gold lion rampant on a field of azure."

Leonard: We have a flag?

As Leonard initials, Sheldon waves a small apartment flag and gives it to Leonard.

Sheldon: Never fly it upside down. Unless the apartment's in distress. Next. "All haircuts or new items of clothing acquired during the cotenancy need not be acknowledged beyond this blanket waiver." Initial here for "nice haircut" and here for "new shirt."

Season 3, Episode 22: The Staircase Implementation

When Sheldon had difficulty with a grad student, he tried to get Leonard's help by citing three clauses.

Sheldon: I'm invoking the Skynet clause of our friendship agreement.

Leonard: That only applies if you need me to help you destroy an artificial intelligence you've created that's taking over the Earth.

Sheldon: All right. I'm invoking our Body Snatchers clause.

Leonard: The Body Snatchers clause requires me to

help you destroy someone we know who's been replaced by an alien pod.

Sheldon: Godzilla clause?

Leonard: Not unless she destroys Tokyo.

Sheldon: Rats.

Season 2, Episode 6: The Cooper-Nowitzki Theorem

When the university was going to send Leonard to Switzerland to attend a conference and see the CERN supercollider on February 14, he wanted to bring Penny. Guess what Sheldon pulled out.

Sheldon: I call your attention to the Friendship Rider in Appendix C: Future Commitments. *(reading)* "Number 37: in the event one friend is ever invited to visit the Large Hadron Collider, now under construction in Switzerland, he shall invite the other friend to accompany him."

Leonard: Oh, for God's sake.

Penny: You actually put that in an agreement?

Leonard: Yeah. We also put in what happens if one of us wins a MacArthur Grant, or one of us gets superpowers, or one of us gets bitten by a zombie.

Sheldon: He can't kill me. Even if I turn.

Leonard: You really expect to enforce this?

Sheldon: I've lived up to all my commitments under the agreement. At least once a day I ask how you are, even though I simply don't care. I no longer stage spontaneous biohazard drills after ten p.m. And I abandoned my goal to master Tuvan throat singing.

Season 3, Episode 14: The Large Hadron Collision

Sheldon: "Section 74C. The various obligations and duties of the parties in the event one of them becomes a robot."

Season 4, Episode 2: The Cruciferous Vegetable Amplification

Sheldon was upset with Leonard because he needed to use the bathroom when Leonard was taking a shower with Priya. Leonard took issue with the Roommate Agreement and hired Priya to be his lawyer.

Sheldon: Very well, count the first: On or about the twenty-eighth day of April, the accused did knowingly and with malice aforethought deny access to the shared bathroom in a time of emergency, to wit, my back teeth were floating. Count the second: The accused exceeded the agreed-upon occupancy of the shower, to wit, one. Unless we are under attack by water-soluble aliens.

Unable to get anywhere with Leonard and Priya, Sheldon turned to Captain Kirk for inspiration. In the *Star Trek* episode "Let That Be Your Last Battlefield," Kirk activated the self-destruct sequence and threatened to blow up the *Enterprise* and kill him and the alien (played by Frank Gorshin) unless the alien gave in. So Sheldon wrote a new Roommate Agreement that included a "self-destruct" sequence, whereby if Leonard didn't sign it in the time allotted, an email would be sent to Priya's parents informing them of her secret relationship with a white boy.

Season 4, Episode 21: The Agreement Dissection

Sheldon: Under Section 37B of the Roommate Agreement—"miscellaneous duties"—you are obligated to take me to the dentist. *(showing him the iPad)* See? It's right here after "providing a confirmation sniff on questionable dairy products."

Sheldon: Hold on, are you saying that you want to invoke Clause 209?

Leonard: I don't know what that is, but if it means I can go home and sleep, then yes.

Sheldon: Think carefully here. Clause 209 suspends our friendship and strips down the Roommate Agreement to its bare essentials. Our responsibilities toward each other will only be rent, utilities and a perfunctory chin jut of recognition as we pass in the hall. *(tossing a chin jut)* 'Sup.

Sheldon: We reinstate the full Roommate Agreement with the following addendum—in the spirit of Mother's Day or Father's Day, once a year, we set aside a day to celebrate all your contributions to my life, both actual and imagined by you. We could call it Leonard's Day.

Season 5, Episode 15: The Friendship Contraction

Sheldon: "Roommate Agreement, Section 27, paragraph 5—the Roommate Agreement, like the American flag, cannot touch the ground."

Season 6, Episode 15: The Spoiler Alert Segmentation

Season 2

1 What piece of kitchen equipment becomes the first victim of the killer robot?

2 When Sheldon's childhood pet died, what kind of faithful companion did he want to get to replace it, because he believed it would be capable of killing upon telepathic command?

3 Who would Howard be in Sheldon's *Star Trek* landing party?

4 When Leonard kisses Penny good night at the end of their first date, what does he notice over the door to his apartment?

5 When Penny says good-bye to Leonard before he goes on the North Pole expedition, she hugs him. She tells him "it was just a hug," but what does she say to herself after she closes the door?

6 When Sheldon goes to the bookstore to seek guidance about learning how to make friends, where does the bookseller tell him to look?

7 *What book does he pick up there?* **Master's**

8 What are Penny Blossoms?

9 How do Howard and Raj locate the house used on *America's Next Top Model*?

10 What's the first secret a drugged Sheldon reveals to Leonard when he returns to the apartment?

11 When Penny becomes hooked on Age of Conan, what is her character's name in the game?

Sheldon: I'm not insane. My mother had me tested.

12 When Howard builds a prototype of the space toilet in Leonard and Sheldon's apartment, what food does he use to test it?

13 *What happens to the food?* Master's

14 Sheldon's grant from the National Science Foundation was approved for him to go to the North Pole. What does he want to do there?

15 What's Kripke's first name?

16 What is Howard's theory about how Sheldon might reproduce?

17 How long is it going to take the dry cleaner to clean the paint from Sheldon's spot?

18 "What happens in costume at Comic-Con stays at Comic-Con." What does Raj want to forget about a girl he hooked up with at Comic-Con?

19 As he licks it from his cafeteria plastic spoon, what does Raj declare to be the best pudding?

20 *Sheldon tells Raj he is "axiomatically wrong, because the best pudding is ____________"*. Master's

Leonard: Sheldon lives in fear of the three-tined fork.

Sheldon: Three tines is not a fork. Three tines is a trident. Forks are for eating, tridents are for ruling the seven seas.

21 Why does Penny put her car key in her door lock?

22 How does Sheldon treat his laundered T-shirts to ensure they meet his exacting standards of neatness?

23 After drinking coffee to stay awake to finish making the Penny Blossoms, what superhero costume does Sheldon put on?

24 Why doesn't Sheldon celebrate Christmas?

25 A new neighbor, Alicia, moves into the apartment upstairs. Why does Sheldon think the people who moved out were the perfect neighbors?

26 Where does Sheldon think Leonard gets his cashew chicken on Monday nights from?

27 *Where does Leonard actually get it from?* **Master's**

28 When Leonard and Sheldon's TiVo fills up, what show does Leonard suggest they delete?

29 Raj doesn't know what he'd do without the assistant he gets after he's listed in a magazine as someone to watch. What's the assistant's name?

30 Sheldon makes a questionnaire to help him better understand why his current friends like him. How many questions are on it?

31 What does Raj say Leonard will be reborn as for sabotaging Stuart's date with Penny?

32 When Howard tells his mother he's going to the Arctic, where does she think he said?

33 What kind of Boggle are the guys playing when Penny comes over to watch their TV?

34 After Leslie Winkle dumps Howard, Leonard and Raj take him to Las Vegas. Where is Howard going to tell his mother he's going?

35 Why was Penny's ex-boyfriend Kurt arrested?

36 Raj's apartment used to be a factory making what?

37 *What "obvious hazard" does Sheldon seize on when Raj tells him the building's history?* **Master's**

38 Who's the only one who goes with Raj to the reception celebrating his "thirty under thirty" status?

39 After Sheldon tells Leonard Penny's secret, what does Leonard bring to her?

40 What does Howard try wearing to make himself "more distinctive and memorable" to women?

41 What does new neighbor Alicia do for a living?

42 What is Sheldon's character's name in the online multiplayer game Age of Conan?

43 When Penny prevents Sheldon from doing his laundry at his usual time, what does he do with her laundry in retaliation?

44 ***What are Sheldon's rules for Rock-Paper-Scissors-Lizard-Spock?*** PhD

45 What is Leonard's theory about how Sheldon might reproduce?

46 ***According to the Roommate Agreement, "a girlfriend shall be deemed quote living with un-quote Leonard when she has stayed over" how many nights?*** PhD

Howard: You know what? If it's "creepy" to use the internet, military satellites and robot aircraft to find a house full of gorgeous young models so that I can drop in on them unexpectedly, then fine, I'm creepy.

47 What happens that makes Penny finally admit she has an addiction to the Age of Conan video game?

48 What publication names Raj one of their "thirty visionaries under thirty years of age to watch as they challenge the preconceptions of their fields"?

49 In Leonard, Sheldon and Penny's building, what's the name of the woman on the third floor?

50 Leonard tries to help Penny beat her addiction to the online game Age of Conan. After he fails to get through to her in person, what does he do?

51 Growing up, Leonard never got love from his mother, so what did he do?

52 What does Sheldon do to Penny for the first time after they exchange Christmas gifts?

53 What is the name of the guys' fighting robot?

54 What pickup line, stolen from Howard, does Raj use on actress Summer Glau on the train to San Francisco?

55 What happens when Leonard drives Stephanie home after Howard brings her back to the apartment?

56 Where does Penny leave the emergency key for Leonard and Sheldon's apartment?

57 *Why did she leave it there?* **Master's**

58 How does Sheldon get Penny to sign up for online dating to distract her from Age of Conan?

59 What does Sheldon have for dinner every Friday night?

60 What does Raj call the little planetary object he spotted beyond the Kuiper Belt?

61 What was the name of the bully who picked on Leonard in third grade?

62 Having received Penny's Christmas gift, what does Sheldon give her in return?

63 Why is Sheldon excited when Stephanie tells him where she did her medical internship?

64 When Leonard finally gets the nerve to tell Stephanie he wants to spend more time at her place, how does he tell her?

65 With the other guys in Vegas, what does Sheldon order for dinner?

66 When Penny and Sheldon fall out, Leonard gives her something that will "shorten the war." What is "Sheldon's Kryptonite"?

67 ***Why does Sheldon persevere in befriending Kripke despite Kripke's reluctance?***

PhD

68 When Penny drives Sheldon to work, he is alarmed by her disinterest in a warning light illuminated on her dashboard. Which light is it?

69 When Stephanie tells Sheldon his larynx is inflamed and he needs to stop talking right away, what does she name the procedure?

70 Designed to be easily understandable to non-English speakers, what is Howard's username on www.anythingforagreencard.com?

71 What does Leonard find Sheldon and his mother doing in the apartment—something she could never do with her husband?

72 What kind of vehicle does Howard have?

73 How does Sheldon try to learn how to swim?

74 How does Sheldon try to communicate with Leonard when they're in their own bedrooms?

75 Why doesn't Sheldon like to go to the movies by himself?

76 Raj tells Summer Glau that the names of the constellations are different in India. According to him, what do they call the Big Dipper?

77 When Sheldon decides he needs to lose one of his friends to make space for Kripke, who does he tell "You're out"?

78 What was Penny's original plan when she moved to California?

79 *What was Plan B?* **Master's**

Sheldon: Thank you for letting me stay here.
Penny: You're welcome, sweetie.
Sheldon: Okay, I'm sleepy now. Get out.

80 When Penny starts dating Leonard, what secret does she ask Sheldon to keep from him?

81 What does Sheldon "borrow" to fashion historically accurate undergarments for the Renaissance Fair?

82 Penny finds many clues that Stephanie is living with Leonard, but what has Stephanie moved that makes him realize that she is, in fact, living with him?

83 When does Sheldon finally get fed up with his officious new assistant?

84 Who is Leonard excited to tell Penny is the keynote speaker at the "can't-miss symposium" in San Francisco?

85 How does Sheldon simplify the task of packing for their trip to San Francisco?

86 *How long does he anticipate this taking?* **Master's**

87 What's the name of Leonard's younger brother who is a tenured law professor at Harvard?

88 ***What is the Wolowitz Coefficient?*** **PhD**

89 When Howard and Leslie are hooking up in his bedroom, Mrs. Wolowitz comes home early because book club was canceled. Why was the book club canceled?

90 What does Sheldon discover Howard has drawn on his friendship questionnaire?

91 What does Penny give Sheldon for Christmas?

Sheldon: Penny, I'm a physicist. I have a working knowledge of the entire universe and everything it contains.

Penny: Who's Radiohead?

Sheldon: I have a working knowledge of the important things in the entire universe. Good luck.

92 How does Raj persuade Sheldon to go back to the Renaissance Fair?

93 While they are in Alicia's apartment, Penny tells a joke about a physicist. Where does the physicist go in the joke?

94 How does Sheldon try to establish Leonard as the alpha male in their relationship so he has a better chance of impressing Stephanie?

95 *Does Sheldon's ploy work?* Master's

96 Penny wants Leonard's help picking up a gift for her thirteen-year-old nephew. What does she want?

97 Why does Sheldon prefer Los Robles Avenue to Euclid Avenue?

98 What play is Penny going to star in above a bowling alley?

99 *How is the director going to incorporate the bowling sounds into the drama?* Master's

> **Sheldon:** Hot air blowers are incubators and spewers of bacteria and pestilence. Frankly, it would be more hygienic if they just had a plague-infested gibbon sneeze my hands dry.

100 When does Sheldon do his laundry?

101 What is the name of Stephanie's roommate?

102 ***Sheldon doesn't use more than half of his income. As well as putting some in his savings account, where does he hide it in the apartment?*** **PhD**

103 Why can't Sheldon eat dinner *after* they go to the movie theater?

104 When Leonard, Howard and Raj go to a bar to meet women, which one of them gets lucky?

105 Sheldon's new assistant catches him doing what in the shower?

106 What does Penny's character do to Leonard's character in Age of Conan?

107 What does Leonard give Penny for Christmas?

108 While Penny is looking for Sheldon's Japanese puzzle box, she finds another box with letters in it. Who are they from?

109 *How does the letter writer address Sheldon in the letters?* **Master's**

110 What is Leonard's password for Facebook . . . and everything else?

111 Sheldon is not impressed by Stephanie's medical advice: "It's not enough that she mocks me, but that isn't even the correct procedure for a ____________ shot."

112 When Sheldon goes to stay at Raj's apartment, why does Raj throw him out?

113 What does Penny do to Sheldon's takeout that he considers "strike two"?

114 When Sheldon was a kid, what was the name of the family cat?

115 When he's learning to drive on a simulator, Sheldon winds up in the Glendale Galleria and crashes into what sort of store?

116 What's the name of Howard's space toilet?

117 The keynote speaker at the conference in San Francisco is driven to ask Sheldon: "With all due respect, are you on ____________?"

118 Leonard isn't around to help Penny set up her printer because he's at Alicia's with Howard and Raj. What are they helping her do?

119 What game involves chess, lasers and aerosol disinfectant?

120 What pizza does Sheldon eat from Giacomo's every Thursday night?

121 How did Leonard and Sheldon first become friends?

122 Why does Sheldon go around the movie theater shouting "Ha!," "Ho-o!" and "Hmmmmmm-ah!" as he tries out each seat?

123 Howard makes a mistake on the specifications for what valve on his space toilet?

124 What's on Sheldon's schedule every Friday night?

125 Who orders a thousand Penny Blossoms from Penny's website?

126 How many servants did Raj have in India?

127 When Leonard sees Penny going on a date with Stuart, where does he ask Howard to take him?

128 Burdened with the knowledge that Penny has gotten him a Christmas gift, Sheldon feels bound to reciprocate. Why does he buy such a wide assortment of bath products?

129 What does Howard do to the Mars Rover when he's showing off the controls to impress Stephanie?

130 Sheldon thinks of the guys as a *Star Trek* landing party. Who's Leonard?

131 When Penny meets new neighbor Alicia in the hallway, what presidential candidate T-shirt is Penny wearing?

132 A grad student becomes obsessed with Sheldon and insinuates herself as his assistant. What's her name?

133 When Penny asks Sheldon to keep a secret from Leonard, he finds it agonizing, begging Penny, "Release me from my vow!" What way does he figure out to do it?

134 When Penny tells her date, Eric, about Schrödinger's cat, who does he think it is?

135 What TV show does new neighbor Alicia get a callback audition for?

136 What's the address of Leonard, Sheldon and Penny's apartment building?

137 On March 18, Penny got her first strike because she violated Sheldon's rule against forwarding email humor. What picture did she send him?

138 What kind of animal is pictured on the sweater Stephanie gets for Leonard?

139 Penny hopes her Penny Blossoms will turn into a new business. Who offers to help make her business more efficient so she'll make more money?

140 The third Thursday of every month is called what?

141 In the "How well do you know Sheldon?" section of the friendship questionnaire, what had Leonard and Howard put down for his favorite amino acid?

142 Howard is annoyed by Raj getting in before him and hitting on Summer Glau on the train. How does he stop him talking to her?

143 Where did comic book store owner Stuart go to college?

144 What modification does Kripke make to his robot before fighting the guys' robot?

145 What is the name of the MacArthur Grant winner who comes to the university to work on an experiment with Leonard and ends up going out with Penny?

146 *What puts Penny off him?* **Master's**

147 When Sheldon is staying at Howard's place and can't sleep, what does Howard give him?

148 In the comic book store, what's the name of the guy wearing the superhero T-shirt tucked into his sweatpants?

149 Having shaken off one obsessive grad student, Sheldon is approached in the cafeteria by another who wants to pick his brain. What is her name?

150 Howard tells Summer Glau that the word "pumpernickel" comes from the German words *pumper* and *nickel* and loosely translates as what?

151 On the train to San Francisco, what does Sheldon realize he's forgotten to pack?

152 In an attempt to cheer up Howard on their Vegas trip, Leonard and Raj hire a prostitute. What's her name?

153 *Leonard and Raj want the prostitute to pose as a Jewish girl who's interested in Howard. What does she tell him her name is?* **Master's**

154 How does Howard suggest adapting the Penny Blossoms to make them more appealing to men?

155 What does Sheldon draw on his whiteboard to try to explain his algorithm for making friends?

156 *There's a flaw in Sheldon's graphic, and he gets stuck in an infinite loop. Who fixes it?* **Master's**

157 Where does Season 2 begin?

158 Penny realizes the extent of Sheldon's new assistant's dedication to him when she enters their apartment to find her doing what for him?

159 Penny is so obsessed with Age of Conan that she doesn't notice she has a Cheeto in her hair. When Leonard points it out, what does she do?

> **Penny:** Your mom seems nice.
> **Howard:** People move away from her on the bus.

160 In Penny's apartment, Sheldon and Stuart get into a comic book argument. What's it about?

161 Where in Los Angeles do Howard and his mother live?

162 Why does Sheldon ask Penny if he can have access to the Cheesecake Factory's walk-in freezer?

163 Remembering Leonard's recent accident, what does Penny give Leonard for Christmas?

164 When Sheldon suggests that he and Kripke enjoy a recreational activity together, where does Kripke end up taking Sheldon?

165 *What happens to Sheldon during their time together?* **Master's**

166 Howard confides in Penny about the girl he dedicated his version of "My Girl" to in the ninth grade talent show. What was the girl's name?

167 What is Penny's "strike three" that makes Sheldon banish her from the apartment?

168 What gift does Penny give to Leonard for the North Pole expedition?

169 According to Sheldon, which part would Raj play in their *Star Trek* landing party?

170 When Penny goes back to Raj's apartment after the magazine gala, he welcomes her, saying, "Welcome to the __________ __________."

171 Which particular love of Sheldon's does Raj pretend to hate in order to dissuade Sheldon from staying with him?

Sheldon: *(to Penny)* You're the milk thief?! Leonard said I was crazy, but I knew the carton felt lighter.

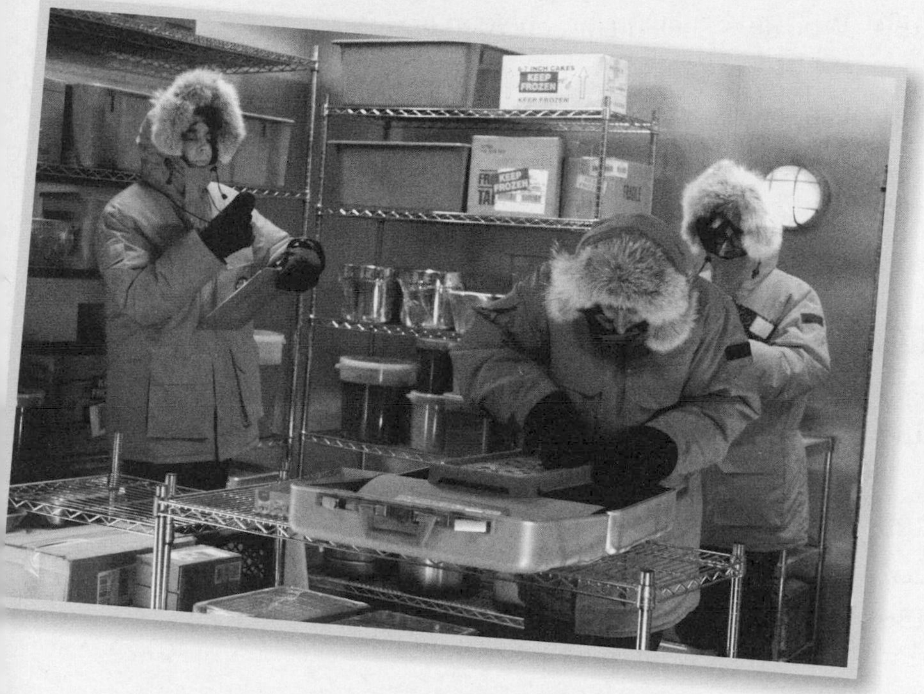

172 When an obsessed Penny wakes Sheldon up in the middle of the night to ask a question about Age of Conan, what does he say as he wakes up?

173 *Why isn't Sheldon wearing pajama bottoms?* **Master's**

174 How does Penny solve the Japanese puzzle box Sheldon asks her to open for him?

175 When Penny needs help paying her rent, who loans her money?

176 What is the name of Kripke's ultimately victorious fighting robot?

177 Which kindly relative bought Sheldon a stethoscope and blood-pressure cuff for his twelfth birthday?

178 In Sheldon's *Star Trek* landing party scenario, which character is he?

179 What do Howard and Raj wear to disguise themselves to get into the *America's Next Top Model* house?

180 Who does Sheldon discover Howard has a poster of over his bed?

181 What items of overstimulating bed linen did Sheldon have to return to Pottery Barn?

182 Leonard's mother is a woman with many academic interests, but she tells Sheldon: "My primary field is ____________."

183 ***What is the name of the fighting robot tournament?*** PhD

184 How does Leonard describe Sheldon's uncharacteristic reaction to receiving Penny's Christmas gift?

185 What pickup line does Howard use on Summer Glau when the guys meet her on the train?

186 What color paint does Penny accidentally shoot onto Sheldon's special spot?

187 Where does Stuart take Penny on their first date?

188 What sea shanty do the guys discover Sheldon and Penny singing to increase their productivity while making Penny Blossoms?

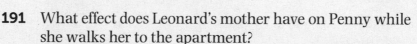

189 Who is Sheldon's favorite X-Man?

190 While in the Cheesecake Factory freezer dressed in Arctic gear, what game does Howard fail to complete?

191 What effect does Leonard's mother have on Penny while she walks her to the apartment?

192 When Leonard goes to see Kurt about the money he owes Penny, how does Kurt formally acknowledge the debt?

193 *Does Kurt pay Penny back?* Master's

194 What does Kripke decide to call Penny, as he thinks she needs a hotter name?

195 With their relationship developing, who updates Leonard's and Stephanie's status on Facebook first?

196 Why does Penny punch Howard when she visits him to apologize?

197 *How do Penny and Howard explain the bandage on his nose and his two black eyes?* **Master's**

198 Sheldon thinks Stephanie is the necessary addition to their *Star Trek* landing party. Who is she?

199 What is Penny shopping for when her laptop freezes?

200 According to the Roommate Agreement, how many times a week should the apartment be vacuumed, if the cohabitation clause is invoked?

The Culinary Corollary

The gang orders takeout a lot. Almost every single episode. I feel so bad for the delivery people who have to lug all that food up four flights of stairs. (The food used on the show is provided by the best prop department in the business, led by Prop Master Scott London.)

Sheldon: *(to Dr. Loris, played by Billy Bob Thornton, bringing flowers to Penny's apartment)* Deliverymen are the unsung foot soldiers of our nation's commerce. It's because of people like you, people like me can limit our human contact. I'd shake your hand, but, well, you know.

Season 8, Episode 8: The Misinterpretation Agitation

Sheldon: This sandwich is an unmitigated disaster. I asked for turkey and roast beef with lettuce and Swiss on whole wheat.

Raj: What did they give you?

Sheldon: Turkey and roast beef with Swiss and lettuce on whole wheat. *(from their looks)* It's the right ingredients, but in the wrong order. In a proper sandwich, the cheese is adjacent to the bread to form a moisture barrier against the lettuce. They might as well have dragged this thing through a car wash.

Season 1, Episode 13: The Nerdvana Annihilation

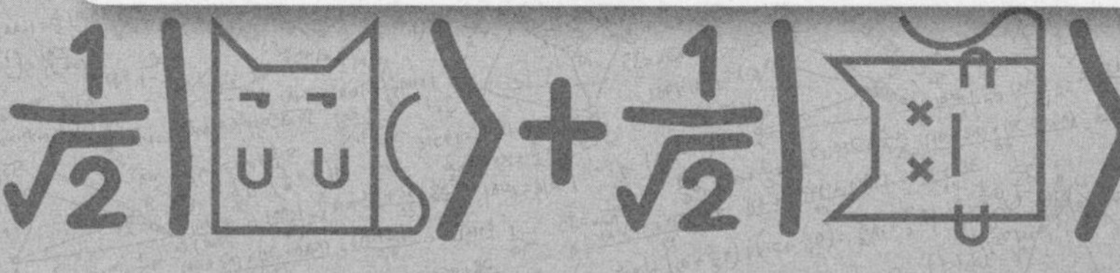

Leslie: I'm trying to see how long it takes a five-hundred kilowatt oxygen iodine laser to heat up my Cup O Noodles.

Leonard: I've done it. About two seconds. About two point six for minestrone.

Season 1, Episode 3: The Big Bran Hypothesis

Sheldon: *(sweetly)* Morning, old chum.

Leonard: What's going on?

Sheldon: I've made you breakfast. Juice, coffee and pancakes in the shape of some of your favorite fictional characters. See, here's Frodo.

Leonard: You made Frodo pancakes?

Sheldon: I used coconut shavings to do the hair on his feet. If you need to void your bladder before eating, I'll keep them warm with this beret I've thoroughly laundered and pressed into service as a pancake cozy.

Season 3, Episode 14: The Large Hadron Collision

Wolowitz made paninis in the hydraulic thermoforming press in his lab in The Infestation Hypothesis (Season 5, Episode 2).

Leonard: Just this morning, Sheldon wouldn't let me put almond milk on my Grape-Nuts because he said it was a theoretical nut conflict.

Raj: You should've told him to mind his own business.

Leonard: That's better than what I did say, which was, "Fine, I'll eat them with club soda."

Season 8, Episode 21: The Communication Deterioration

Wolowitz used molecular gastronomy to create cocktails:

Bernadette: What's going on in here?

Howard: I am making molecular cocktails.

He holds up a spoon with a large red sphere on it.

Howard: This sphere is actually a cosmopolitan.

He hands her one.

Bernadette: How do you drink it?

Howard: Just put it in your mouth and pop it like a zit.

Bernadette: I think I'll have a beer.

Season 8, Episode 21: The Communication Deterioration

Season 3

1 What are the names of the girls Sheldon and Raj meet at the science and humanities grad student and faculty mixer?

2 Leonard recalls a stressful moment for Howard: "He had a panic attack once when his head got stuck in a ____________."

3 What sort of facial hair does Sheldon have when he returns from the North Pole?

4 Apart from losing their virginity in cars, what other thing do Howard and Bernadette have in common?

5 When Penny slips in the shower, how does she hurt herself?

6 Leonard puts on a football jersey to see the game at Penny's apartment. On him it's oversize—what does Sheldon call it?

7 Penny told her friend Justin he could crash on her couch for a couple of weeks, but where does he end up sleeping?

8 Where does Marvel Comics legend Stan Lee take Leonard, Howard, Raj and Stuart after they meet him at the comic book store?

9 When Howard and Raj go to a goth club, what do they have on their arms?

10 Howard doesn't call Bernadette after their third date because she wants a commitment and he isn't sure if she's exactly his type. In his dreams, what kind of woman is his type?

11 Sheldon has hidden hot dogs under his clothes so Leonard won't know he's taking them over to Penny's for dinner. What happens when he goes out on the street?

12 Leonard, Howard and Raj think the trip to the North Pole was hellish. How does Sheldon describe it?

13 How do the guys acquire a prop ring from Peter Jackson's *The Lord of the Rings*?

14 When the guys find the cricket, what does Raj want to name it?

15 *What does Sheldon think is a suitable name for the cricket?* **Master's**

16 What 1980s movie baffles Sheldon every time he watches it?

17 Why does Sheldon get a summons to Pasadena Municipal Court, which clashes with the visit of Marvel Comics legend Stan Lee to Stuart's store?

18 What does Raj give Sheldon to bribe him to come with him to the science and humanities mixer because "Whether you split atoms or infinitives, this is the place to be"?

19 Penny sees the guys going out with their kites: "What'cha doin'? Going out to discover ___________?"

20 How does Sheldon describe a Christmas tree?

21 When we see how Raj dressed in 2003, he's obviously trying to look like which TV star of the time?

22 What is the name of the guy Howard knows "who deals with—shall we say—the seedy underbelly of the collectibles world"?

23 What prize does Sheldon offer Leonard for becoming the world's first winner of his board game Research Lab?

24 Sleep-deprived and unable to crack his physics problem, Sheldon breaks into a Chuck E. Cheese–style restaurant. When Leonard goes to pick him up, where does he find him?

25 When Leonard tells Penny that Sheldon has a kind of photographic memory, how does Sheldon correct him?

26 Howard gets the equipment for Leonard and Sheldon's new security system from a buddy of his who works where?

27 Sheldon invents a time of day that "better defines the ambiguous period between afternoon and evening." According to him, it should catch on, as it fills a desperate need. So what does he call 4:30 p.m.?

28 The gang offers to help Sheldon prepare his acceptance speech for the Chancellor's Award for Science. When Leonard suggests that Sheldon should think of himself as Professor Xavier and of them as his X-Men, what does Sheldon say they should be?

29 Why is Leonard's mother divorcing his father?

30 How was Howard's hair styled back in 2003?

31 Who told Penny if she cut her hair, she'd get a national commercial?

32 What's Sheldon wearing on his head when he and Penny come back from Disneyland?

33 Marvel Comics legend Stan Lee comes to Stuart's comic book store to do a signing. How does Stuart know him?

34 When Leonard, Sheldon and Penny are playing Pictionary, what does Sheldon draw on the whiteboard?

35 What's the name of Raj's cousin who's also his attorney?

36 Sheldon has vowed eternal hatred for Wil Wheaton because in 1995 he traveled ten hours by bus to a sci-fi convention and Wil Wheaton did not show up despite being advertised to appear. Where was the convention?

37 *Why had Sheldon gone to the sci-fi convention?* **Master's**

Penny: Anime. I knew a girl in high school named Anna May. Anna May Fletcher. She was born with one nostril. Then she got a bad nose job and basically wound up with three.

38 At the bowling alley, what, according to Raj, is the "magic elixir that can turn this poor shy Indian boy into the life of the party"?

39 After Penny has broken up with Leonard, how does she meet her "dumb" boyfriend Zack?

40 *When Leonard tells Penny that he and the guys will be bouncing lasers off the moon, why does Zack find this hard to believe?* Master's

41 After Sheldon and Penny get sick, who does Leonard end up taking to the conference at the CERN supercollider?

42 Sheldon hates it when people fight—it reminds him of his parents fighting. He remembers hiding in his bedroom "while my mom is shouting that Jesus would forgive her if she put ground glass in my dad's meatloaf." How would his dad retaliate?

43 Sheldon offers to hire Raj so he doesn't get deported, but rather than simply giving Raj the job, what does Sheldon want him to do first?

44 What is the name of Raj's authentic Indian fighting kite that his brother sent him from New Delhi?

45 Raj is prepared to surrender any interest he has in their *Lord of the Rings* ring in exchange for what?

46 What put the elevator in the apartment building out of service?

47 How does Penny try to help Sheldon prepare an acceptance speech for the Chancellor's Award for Science?

48 How does the security system Howard has installed in the apartment try to kill Sheldon?

49 What is Project Gorilla?

50 Where does Howard plan to take Bernadette for their first Valentine's Day?

51 Leonard, Howard and Raj are camping out to witness a meteor shower. Howard comes across some other campers—middle school teachers. What do they give him?

52 In the cafeteria Sheldon is about to tell the guys that he's going to be on the radio, but who beats him to it?

53 *What radio show is Sheldon going to be on?* **Master's**

54 After Leonard tells Sheldon that Penny stayed with him overnight because her bed broke, what does Sheldon call him?

55 Shortly after Leonard first moved into the apartment, Sheldon decided to send all his emails to his spam filter. Why?

56 Howard thinks he has three qualities that would attract a girlfriend: he's smart, he has a good job—and what else?

57 *How does Raj vouch for Howard's third quality?* **Master's**

58 When the guys go out kite fighting, what does Howard do to make Raj mad?

59 What prank does Kripke pull on Sheldon during his radio interview?

Sheldon: I grew up in Texas. Football is ubiquitous in Texas: pro football, college football, high school football, pee-wee football. In fact, every form of football except the original—European football. Which most Texans believe to be a commie plot.

60 When Howard and Bernadette are making out in his bedroom, why is he baffled by her bra?

61 While they were at the North Pole, how had the guys tampered with Sheldon's magnetic monopole experiment?

62 What are the names of the two girls Howard and Raj meet in the goth club?

63 After Raj falls out with Howard during the kite fight, what kind of kite does Howard bring to Raj as an apology?

64 Who's in Kripke's lab with him when Sheldon's rigged-up chemical concoction drops and the lab fills with foam?

65 Sheldon is sure the cricket the guys find isn't an ordinary field cricket. What does he agree to give Howard if it is?

66 Who thinks they should send *The Lord of the Rings* ring back to the film's director, Peter Jackson?

67 What does Leonard bring Penny back from the North Pole?

68 In the flashback to Leonard's early days living with Sheldon, why does Leonard have rocket fuel in the apartment?

69 When he's working at the Cheesecake Factory, Sheldon drops a tray of food, looks at the pattern of damage and solves his physics problem—"I've been looking at it all wrong. I can't consider the electrons as particles . . ." He announces his solution to the customers. What is it?

70 *Having made his announcement, Sheldon advises the customers that this would be a good moment to do what?*

Master's

71 Leonard recalls that when he was growing up, his family didn't so much celebrate ___________ as study them "for their anthropological and psychological implications on human society."

72 According to Leonard, what three things scare Howard?

73 Sometimes when Sheldon feels stifled and wants a change of scenery, he uses his imagination. Where does he go?

74 Raj has an opportunity to join the stellar evolution research team and stay employed at the university. How does he screw it up with Dr. Catherine Millstone, who heads up the data analysis team?

75 In the final round of Stuart's Warlords of Ka'a tournament, Sheldon and Raj are playing Stuart and Wil Wheaton. Why does Sheldon throw the game at the last minute?

76 When the guys go out to get Chinese food and come back without it, Penny asks them if they've traded it for what?

77 Raj is worried that he may get deported because his visa's only good as long as he's employed at the university, and his research testing the predicted composition of trans-Neptunian objects ran into a dead end six months ago. What does he say he's got to show for all his work?

78 *How does he revise this conclusion?* **Master's**

79 What does Sheldon think would be an appropriate outfit for his Chancellor's Award for Science acceptance speech?

80 When Howard and Sheldon make a bet about what kind of cricket the guys have found, who helps them determine the type?

81 What is Sheldon referring to when he says to Penny that "As a native Texan, I must say I've never heard the phrase 'yee-haw' used in quite that context"?

82 According to Sheldon, what three things are wrong with hotels?

83 Sheldon decides to moderate Penny's behavior by using positive reinforcement. How does he reward her good behavior?

84 When Leonard, Howard and Raj return from the North Pole, how havc their appearances changed?

> **Leonard:** The more the merrier.
>
> **Sheldon:** No, that's a false equivalency. More does not equal merry. If there were two thousand people in this apartment right now, would we be celebrating? No, we'd be suffocating.

85 Rather than giving each other conventional Christmas gifts, Leonard's family presented academic papers to each other. What did they do then?

86 ***What is Sheldon's "favorite Linux-based operating system"?*** **PhD**

87 Why does the world-weary judge throw Sheldon into jail when he appears in Pasadena Municipal Court?

88 According to Sheldon, what day of the week is Oatmeal Day?

89 Sheldon has been corresponding with Dr. Elizabeth Plimpton for years when he asks her to stay at the apartment. Why has Leonard heard of her?

90 Who does a drunken Beverly kiss at the end of her night out with Penny?

91 What is the slogan for Research Lab, a board game made up by Sheldon?

92 What typo on an Italian restaurant menu makes Sheldon remark that "Perhaps this restaurant is now a front for organized crime"?

93 When Sheldon, Howard and Raj hear a chirping sound in the apartment, it turns out to be a cricket. Where do the guys eventually find it?

94 What pact did Leonard and Howard make on June 30, 2004, opening day of *Spider-Man 2* at the AMC Pasadena?

95 What does Sheldon tell Penny the tattoo on her right buttock actually means?

96 *How has Sheldon seen it?* **Master's**

97 After their day at the La Brea Tar Pits, Howard buys Raj a souvenir, a peace offering. What is it?

98 Which of the guys does Sheldon consider to be only an acquaintance rather than a friend?

99 Why is Sheldon pleased to hear that Penny thinks they are still friends despite her no longer seeing Leonard?

100 To get back at Kripke for sabotaging his radio interview, Sheldon rigs up a chemical concoction that will foam up crazily. What does it consist of?

101 When Sheldon first showed Leonard the apartment, what had the previous roommate painted on the wall in red capital letters?

102 When Sheldon's houseguest, Elizabeth Plimpton, arrives, what choice of two particular products does he offer her, as a good host?

103 Sheldon is playing Traitors in the car with Leonard. In the first round he mentions three traitors—Benedict Arnold, Judas and ____________ ____________.

104 *Who are the three traitors in the second round?* **Master's**

105 Taking inspiration from Einstein, who had a lowly job in a patent office, why does Sheldon start working in the Cheesecake Factory without actually being hired?

106 When Sheldon returns from the North Pole, what does he say to his special spot?

107 How has going out with Leonard ruined Penny's chances of happiness with Zack?

108 What does Raj give Sheldon to convince him to go out with him and the two grad students again?

109 What is the name of the police officer's partner who comes to Leonard and Sheldon's apartment after it has been burgled?

110 While Howard and Raj are at the goth club, Leonard, Sheldon and Penny stay at home and watch some anime. What is it called?

111 How does Sheldon ask Raj to address him after Raj sneezes twice in the cafeteria?

112 After Penny slips in the shower, how does she get to the hospital?

113 What American food does Raj think he'll miss the most if he gets deported?

114 Raj explains to Sheldon why they had to tamper with his experiment at the North Pole: "It was the only way to keep you from being such a huge ___________."

115 When the guys are on the apartment building roof for their laser experiment, what does Sheldon notice that causes him distress?

116 When Marvel Comics legend Stan Lee visits Stuart's comic book store for a signing, how does Sheldon intend to differentiate himself from the "hoi polloi"?

Wil Wheaton: *(on Sheldon)* Did he just say "revenge is a dish best served cold" in Klingon?

Stuart: I believe so.

Wil: What's wrong with him?

Stuart: Everyone has a different theory.

117 Why has Penny's friend Justin come from Omaha to LA?

118 When the two goth girls take Howard and Raj to a tattoo parlor, where on his body does Howard want to get a tattoo?

119 When Sheldon appears in the Pasadena Municipal Court, what is the name of the judge?

120 Why does Bernadette tell Howard he's insane and walk away?

121 *How does Howard win back Bernadette's affection?* Master's

122 ***Leonard and Sheldon's apartment's flag is a gold ___________ rampant on a field of ___________.*** PhD

123 How does Raj try to help Sheldon prepare an acceptance speech for the Chancellor's Award for Science?

124 What does Penny offer to do to get Stuart to give her the address of Marvel Comics legend Stan Lee?

125 According to Sheldon, in their "ragtag band of scientists" he is the smart one, Howard is the funny one and Raj is the lovable foreigner who tries and fails to understand their ways. Where does that leave Leonard?

126 Following the burglary in the apartment, Sheldon no longer feels safe there. After much research, where does he want to move to?

127 What is Penny's nickname for Sheldon's guest Dr. Elizabeth Plimpton?

128 What argument do Sheldon and Howard have about Wolverine?

Sheldon: You see. People have been pointing and laughing at me all morning.

Kripke: Not true. People have been pointing and laughing at you your whole life.

129 Howard can't decide what tattoo to get. He considers a screaming devil or Kermit the Frog, but what does the goth girl he met in the club think is his best suggestion?

130 *What does Raj think he's likely to get at the tattoo parlor?* **Master's**

131 What did Sheldon's mother used to put in his spaghetti?

132 When Howard was eleven, what doll did his mother get him to help him sleep after his dad left?

133 When it goes public that Sheldon's experiments at the North Pole are flawed, where does he run away to?

134 What kind of car did Howard lose his virginity in?

135 When the guys find the cricket, Howard bets Sheldon it's just an ordinary field cricket. What does he agree to give Sheldon if he loses?

136 What animals are exempt from the ban on pets in the Roommate Agreement?

137 What does Leonard tell the guys he's done with the ring from *The Lord of the Rings*?

138 *What does Leonard actually do with the ring?* **Master's**

139 When Raj doesn't have a date for Valentine's Day, he says he'll do what he usually does: buy a rotisserie chicken at the supermarket, take it home and then do what?

Sheldon: What qualifies you to attempt to understand my mind?

Leonard: My mother's a highly regarded psychiatrist and I've been in therapy ever since she accused me of breast-feeding codependently.

140 Where does Penny take Leonard's mother, Beverly, for drinks?

141 What is Mrs. Wolowitz's famous tur-briska-fil?

142 Penny gets Stan Lee's address from Stuart and accompanies Sheldon to the home of the Marvel Comics legend. What does Stan get for Sheldon, after a few minutes of his company?

143 *Where does Sheldon plan to put it?* **Master's**

144 What qualifies Sheldon to teach Leonard about football?

145 In the game Mystic Warlords of Ka'a, every card beats Enchanted Bunny unless you have which card?

146 Sheldon wins the Chancellor's Award for Science, but has to make an acceptance speech. When he says he can't make speeches, why does Howard say he's mistaken?

147 After Leonard and Penny first have sex, they make a decision about their relationship. What is it?

148 *After Leonard and Penny have made this decision, what do they do?* **Master's**

149 How do Howard and Raj blackmail Sheldon into meeting Amy?

150 When Leonard has been invited to attend a conference at the CERN supercollider in Switzerland, why does Sheldon believe that Leonard must take him, not Penny, despite it being on Valentine's Day?

151 When Sheldon leaves home for a safer place, what happens to him when he arrives at the city's bus station?

152 When Sheldon is at the ceremony for the Chancellor's Award for Science, what does he do after saying: "Now for the astronomers in the audience, get ready to see the dark side of the moon"?

153 After the first time Leonard has sex with Penny, how does he describe it to the guys?

154 *How does Penny describe sex with Leonard to him?* **Master's**

155 What dish does Raj consider to be goth food?

156 When he's trying to persuade Leonard to take him to the CERN supercollider instead of Penny, Sheldon makes him a special breakfast with pancakes in the shape of what?

157 What does Penny do to prompt Leonard to say "I love you" to her for the first time?

158 *How does Penny reply?* **Master's**

159 Why did Sheldon once send flowers to Beverly Hofstadter?

160 What happened at the North Pole that the guys agreed to never speak of again?

161 As well as working at the Cheesecake Factory, what is Bernadette studying at grad school?

162 When Stuart asks Wil Wheaton to bowl with him, who is Wil a substitute for?

163 What do the guys have to do as a penalty after losing to Stuart's team at bowling?

164 *How does the penalty make Raj feel?* **Master's**

165 When Marvel Comics legend Stan Lee visits the comic book store, what question does Raj want to ask him?

166 When Howard is eating sweet and sour pork for dinner, Raj asks him if he'll go to hell as punishment. Howard says Jews don't have hell—according to him, what do they have instead?

167 Who wins Sheldon and Howard's bet about the cricket the guys find?

Penny: *(to Leonard)* Okay, just so I'm clear, the first piece of jewelry my boyfriend gets me is a prop from some movie and I don't get to keep it.

Howard: If you had gone out with me three years ago, by now you'd have my great Aunt Ida's brooch that she smuggled out of occupied Belgium in a cat.

Leonard: *(to Penny)* How'm I lookin' now?

168 When Dr. Elizabeth Plimpton is telling Leonard how she wrote about the Wilson-Bappu effect, what does she reveal that surprises him?

169 *How does she further surprise Leonard?* **Master's**

170 What was the name of the boy who lived down the street from Sheldon when he was a kid and put dog poop on the handlebars of Sheldon's bicycle?

171 What does Penny believe the Chinese character tattooed on her right buttock means?

172 What year did Leonard meet Sheldon?

173 When they're in a goth club, what does Howard tell Raj to remember that they are?

174 What did Sheldon want to put on the Christmas tree in the apartment?

175 In his early days in the apartment, where did Leonard get the couch?

176 *How much did Leonard pay for the couch?* **Master's**

177 In order to get out of jail, what makes Sheldon change his mind and apologize to the Pasadena Municipal Court judge?

178 How does Sheldon meet Amy Farrah Fowler?

179 When Sheldon's filling out Penny's paperwork at the hospital after she slips in the shower, what does he write down for "cause of accident"?

180 When Penny's dancing in the guys' apartment while listening to Shania Twain, what is she making for breakfast?

181 In Sheldon's dream, he cleans their *Lord of the Rings* ring in the bathroom sink. What does he see when he looks in the mirror?

182 When Leonard wants to spend time with Penny and her friends but doesn't know anything about football, who teaches him the basics?

183 How do the guys tell Penny they usually celebrate Columbus Day?

184 In Dr. Plimpton's foursome fantasy, what does she want Leonard and Howard to pretend to be?

185 *What part does she want Raj to play?* **Master's**

186 Sheldon is disappointed that his time at the North Pole has meant he's missed which two events?

187 What kind of car did Bernadette lose her virginity in?

188 When Leonard meets Sheldon's departing roommate, what does he tell Leonard to do as he walks out the door?

189 What was the name of Leonard's family dog?

190 Why do Leonard, Howard and Raj miss the meteor shower?

191 What does Sheldon give the police officer after his apartment has been burgled?

192 Sheldon doesn't want to give his acceptance speech for the Chancellor's Award for Science because he can't speak to large crowds. What's his definition of a large crowd?

193 When the guys are on their way to a Chinese restaurant, which celebrity do they think they see and follow?

194 Where do the girls Howard and Raj meet at the goth club work?

195 When Leonard met Sheldon for the first time, Sheldon had a series of questions to test his suitability as a roommate. What was the first, before Leonard could even set foot in the apartment?

196 When he finds that they are playing against Wil Wheaton, what does Sheldon name their bowling team?

197 What traumatic childhood experience means that Sheldon doesn't like chickens?

198 Where is Howard when he has his masturbatory fantasy about Katee Sackhoff?

199 *What does Katee ask Howard during his fantasy?* **Master's**

200 In Sheldon's car game Scientists, he names three scientists—what does Leonard then have to do?

> **Stuart:** You guys still on for bowling tonight?
> **Sheldon:** Oh, yes. In fact, I've prepared some trash talk for the occasion. You bowl like your mama, unless of course she bowls well. In which case, you bowl nothing like her.
> **Stuart:** Oh, ouch.

The Vehicular Diversion Principle

Sheldon: Leonard and I often use our commute time to exercise our minds with brain teasers like that. *(off Penny's silence)* We also play games. *(off Penny's silence)* Would you like to play one?

Penny: No.

Sheldon: Oh come on, it's fun.

They hit a speed bump.

Sheldon: Whoa, another speed bump. I'll say an element and you say an element whose name starts with the last letter of the one I said, okay? *(no reaction, then)* I'll start. Helium. *(no reaction, then)* Now you could say mercury. That would give me a "y." Very clever—that's a tough one. So I go with ytterbium, which gets you back to "m." *(a beat, then)* So you go molybdenum, and I say magnesium. And you say manganese, and I say europium, and you're left with mendelevium, and there are no more m's because I believe that meitnerium should still be called eka-iridium, so, congratulations. You win! *(beat)* You wanna go again?

Season 2, Episode 5: The Euclid Alternative

Sheldon: All right. This game is called Traitors. I will name three historical figures, you put them in order of the heinousness of their betrayal: Benedict Arnold, Judas, Dr. Leonard Hofstadter.

Leonard: You really think I belong with Benedict Arnold and Judas?

Sheldon: You're right. Judas had the decency to hang himself after what he did.

Leonard: Come on, Sheldon, can't you at least try to understand how much this means to me?

Sheldon considers.

Sheldon: Round two: Leonard Hofstadter, Darth Vader, Rupert Murdoch.

Leonard: Rupert Murdoch?

Sheldon: He owns Fox, and they canceled *Firefly*. Hint: he and Darth Vader are tied for number two.

Season 3, Episode 15: The Large Hadron Collision

Sheldon: You know, riding with Leonard has gotten a little tedious lately. The only car game he ever wants to play is the Quiet Game. And he's terrible at it; I always win.

Season 7, Episode 5: The Workplace Proximity

Sheldon: Would you like to play a physics car game I invented called I Can't Spy? It's all the nail-biting tension of I Spy but the added fun of subatomic particles and waves outside the visible spectrum.

Leonard: If it's half as fun as One Times Ten to the Fourth Bottles of Beer on the Wall, I'm in.

Season 8, Episode 19: The Skywalker Incursion

Season 4

1 How does Sheldon plan on strengthening his cardiovascular system?

2 For Howard's security clearance, his friends have to be interviewed. Why doesn't Raj want to talk to the FBI?

3 Who does Sheldon dress as for the New Year's Eve party at the comic book store?

4 What nickname does Howard tell Penny they call new couple Sheldon and Amy?

5 Who is Penny talking to when she says: "Oh my God, you're about to jibber-jabber about jibber-jabber"?

6 Where are Penny and Leonard when she says: "Sweetie, let me put this in a way you'll understand: from the waist down, my shields are up"?

7 Who visits Howard in a masturbatory fantasy?

8 Who is Sheldon referring to when he says, "Good grief, it's like trying to talk to a dolphin"?

9 Sheldon has created three new pieces for Three-Person Chess. One of them is Prince Joey, "the King's feeble-minded but well-meaning cousin." What are the other two?

10 *According to Sheldon, what's the fun thing about Prince Joey?* **Master's**

Sheldon: *(to Leonard)* I'm quite aware of the way humans usually reproduce, which is messy, unsanitary and—based on living next to you for three years—involves loud and unnecessary appeals to a deity.

11 After the guys are turned away from the movie theater showing *Raiders of the Lost Ark*, Sheldon sneaks in through a side door and steals what?

12 What was Sheldon planning to give himself for his 300th birthday?

13 What instrument that's been sitting in his closet gathering dust does Sheldon decide to play while Leonard, Howard and Raj work on Leonard's app?

14 What play do Leonard and Priya quote lines from?

15 What's the closest Amy's ever come to being invited to a slumber party?

16 What does Penny give Sheldon when he orders a Rosewater Ricky in the bar, claiming "every bartender makes it differently"?

17 Where does Howard imagine building his own home?

18 Someone has hacked into Sheldon's World of Warcraft account and stolen his enchanted weapons, his vicious gladiator armor, his wand of untainted power, all his gold—and even Glenn. Who or what is Glenn?

19 *Who tracks down the person who stole Glenn?* **Master's**

Sheldon: At my age, do you know how I'm statistically most likely to die?
Leonard: At the hands of your roommate?
Sheldon: An accident.
Leonard: That's how I'm gonna make it look.

20 When Raj and Priya invite everyone over for dinner, Sheldon fears Raj will serve haggis and blood pudding. What do they serve?

21 When the gang is invited to speak at a conference in Big Sur, what is Sheldon's self-appointed title for the trip?

22 How did Sheldon's Uncle Carl die?

23 Why does Penny exaggeratedly kiss Leonard in front of her father?

24 Where does Sheldon get the lock of flaming auburn hair that he wants Leonard to use as part of his alibi for the night he slept with Priya?

25 During Sheldon's orientation for the Big Sur trip, where is the first designated bathroom break on their route?

26 What is Penny referring to on the girls' night when she says: "All right, time to open bachelor number two."

27 Who says, "Hello, Maker of the Universe. I see what you did there. Good one," to the FBI agent investigating Howard?

28 ***What is the name of the game Sheldon and Amy invent where they "postulate an alternative world that differs from ours in one key aspect and then pose questions to each other"?***

29 What is Zack's last name?

30 Who does Penny leave the Big Sur symposium with?

31 What does the guy at the gas station make Leonard buy every time he uses their bathroom while the guys wait in line for the *Raiders of the Lost Ark* screening?

32 Why doesn't Raj want to go as Aquaman to Stuart's New Year's Eve party?

33 What is Raj referring to when he tells Sheldon that "Leonard's putting disgusting memories in my memory-foam mattress"?

34 What song do Kripke and Zack sing during karaoke in Sheldon's apartment?

35 *When Stuart returns from the shower in his towel, what song does he call dibs on?* Master's

36 What does Sheldon want to name Leonard's new app?

37 Bernadette catches Howard engaged in cyber sex with a troll while playing World of Warcraft. What's the name of the troll?

38 *Who is the troll in real life?* Master's

39 What did Amy name her electric toothbrush?

40 Sheldon assigns Raj the task of phone support for the development of Leonard's new app. What name does Sheldon want him to use?

41 When Priya tells Leonard to cut the cord with Penny, he tells her by beating around the bush and trying to explain Darwin's observations about what bird?

42 What has Bernadette done when Howard says: "Is it just me, or does she sound sexy when she's angry"?

43 What bar does Leonard visit to try to pick up women when he realizes all the other guys have girlfriends?

44 What is Sheldon's middle name?

45 When the gang is driving back from Todd Zarnecki's, the car breaks down and they call on Penny for help. Why does she turn her car around and say: "I'm gonna show ya how we finish a quest in Nebraska."

46 Howard isn't enjoying the cafeteria cobbler: "This is the worst cobbler I've ever eaten. It tastes like it's made of actual ground-up ____________."

47 What is Penny's idea for an app?

48 Leonard wakes up to find Sheldon surrounded by whiteboards. How many more years has Sheldon worked out that he'll live for?

49 What's the name of Sheldon's CPR dummy?

Mary: *(on Sheldon)* He thinks he's such a smarty-pants; he's no different than any man. Tell 'em not to do something, that's all they want to do. If I hadn't told my brother Stumpy not to clear out the wood chipper by hand, we'd still be callin' him Edward.

Penny: You want some Kahlua on your ice cream?

Amy: Ah, here's the alcohol and drug peer pressure mother warned me about. I was starting to think it was never going to happen. Yes, please.

50 When Howard claims to have never betrayed Raj's trust, where does Leonard reveal Howard once dropped Raj's iPhone?

51 When the guys take Zack to the comic book store, Stuart asks: "You guys finally chip in for a ____________?"

52 Penny is visited by her father. What's his name?

53 When Amy is out in a bar with Penny, Bernadette and Sheldon, who does she kiss?

54 Leonard's friends think it's a great idea when Mrs. Latham, a wealthy fund-raiser, hits on Leonard for a sexual quid pro quo to raise money for his department. What does Leonard say?

55 When Leonard invokes the girlfriend pact with Howard, what's the name of the girl Howard sets him up with?

56 What is Amy referring to when she says to Sheldon: "I'm glad you talked me into this. We work so hard, sometimes it's nice to goof off and do something silly"?

57 What happens when a drunken Raj leans forward to kiss Bernadette on the couch in the telescope laboratory?

58 In order to be on the team for the new Defense Department laser-equipped surveillance satellite, Howard needs security clearance. What's the name of the female FBI agent conducting the investigation?

59 What field of science does Bernadette get her PhD in?

60 What finally gets Sheldon to abandon his "mobile presence device"?

61 At the slumber party, Bernadette dares Amy to tell a dirty story as part of Truth or Dare. What story does she tell?

62 How long does it take Howard to unpack a takeout dinner using his robotic arm?

63 *What name has Howard given to the robotic arm?* **Master's**

64 Sheldon tells Leonard he can't tell Amy how he feels because he's "a physicist, not a ____________."

65 Howard once changed Sheldon's World of Warcraft character's name from Sheldor to what?

66 What technological visionary do the guys see at the Cheesecake Factory?

67 *How does Penny know who he is?* **Master's**

68 When is Raj's birthday?

69 Why does Kripke agree to hang out at Sheldon's apartment?

70 Howard tells his mother that he's asked Bernadette to marry him while Mrs. Wolowitz is in the ladies' room. How does she react?

71 Amy tries out some girl talk on her first girls' night: "So anyway, to make a long story short, it turns out I have an unusually firm ________."

72 In his effort to work out Howard's card trick, where does Sheldon try to find uranium-235?

73 Howard is relieved the robot arm has released its grip: "________ is out of the honey tree."

74 How does Sheldon's mother get him to resume his relationship with Amy?

75 When Sheldon apologizes to Howard for screwing up his interview with the FBI agent, Howard refuses to accept it. What does Sheldon give him?

76 Why is Amy "the ideal hotel roommate"?

77 What's Howard's ringtone for Raj?

78 During the girls' night, where does Penny say she got her manicure?

79 If "volunteering for a scientific study in which orgasm was achieved by electronically stimulating pleasure centers of the brain" counts, how many sexual encounters has Amy had?

Amy: Do you have any ethical qualms regarding human experimentation?

Sheldon: It's one of the few forms of interaction with people that I don't find repellent.

80 With the Indian food, the pizza, the Thai food, the tank of gas, the frozen yogurt and the rent, how much money does Penny owe Leonard?

81 After taking a pill to stop social anxiety, Raj gets naked while talking to Angela. Why is he disappointed when she leaves?

82 What are Sheldon's "bus pants"?

83 How does Sheldon refer to the geology department?

84 Who shows up late to the movie theater for the special screening of *Raiders of the Lost Ark* but is allowed to jump the lengthy line and is escorted inside?

85 *What does Sheldon say when this person turns up?* **Master's**

86 When Sheldon retracts his statement to the FBI agent investigating Howard, what secret of Leonard's does he reveal?

87 The guy who hacked into Sheldon's World of Warcraft account and cleaned it out is named Todd Zarnecki. Where does he live?

88 How does Sheldon get rid of the cats he bought after breaking up with Amy?

89 In order to live longer, Sheldon changes his diet. Instead of the regular pizza on Thursday, what does he have for dinner?

90 *When Sheldon wakes in the night with a bellyache, what does he think is wrong with him?* **Master's**

Bernadette: Gee, I don't know, I'm not a very good liar. They kinda whup that out of you in Catholic school.

Amy: Don't worry. I'll teach you. I did two years of Cub Scouts before they found out I was a girl.

91 While Penny and Priya are at the hospital, what do they talk about when they go for coffee?

92 On returning to the apartment, how does Sheldon describe the lecture he's just given?

93 Who drives Sheldon to his first date with Amy Farrah Fowler?

94 On Sheldon's list of Penny's annoying habits, what is number twelve?

95 Leonard sleeps with Priya. When Sheldon finds out, why does he think Leonard has betrayed Howard?

96 What was the name of Penny's ex-boyfriend who "mixed pig poop with a little water and pumped it into his mom's Camry" in the hopes of turning farm waste into biofuel and selling it to the government?

97 *Penny's father tells Leonard about another old boyfriend of Penny's who wanted what new game to be played in the Olympics?* Master's

98 What gossip does Amy share with Sheldon at Brian Greene's talk?

99 What is Sheldon referring to when he scorns "an evening talking about rainbows, unicorns and menstrual cramps"?

Penny: Sheldon, have you ever kissed a girl?

Sheldon: Other than my mother, my sister and my Mee-Maw, no. But in the interest of full disclosure, I was once on a bus and had to give mouth-to-mouth resuscitation to an elderly nun who passed out from heat exhaustion. Every year I get a Christmas card from her signed with far too many *X*s and *O*s.

100 Why does Sheldon say to Penny: "I just don't want to be yet another flip-flop fatality"?

101 How many *Star Trek* uniforms does Leonard have?

102 What's the name of the first cat that Sheldon gets when he and Amy split up?

103 Why does Sheldon tell Penny that he might have to let Amy go?

104 What does Raj's sister, Priya, do for a living?

105 What catcall for Sheldon "spread like wildfire" at his elementary school?

106 What kind of company hires Bernadette after she gets her PhD?

107 How does Amy tell Sheldon she paid for her lab?

108 For Stuart's New Year's Eve costume party at the comic store, the guys dress up as the Justice League of America. Leonard was going to be Superman until Sheldon decided Zack should do it, so what does Leonard go as?

109 What *Star Trek* uniform does Raj have?

110 What was the name of Leonard's aunt who had dozens of cats?

111 What sort of house does Penny's father want his grandkids to grow up in?

112 What kind of smartphone app does Leonard propose the guys make?

113 When Amy and Sheldon are talking over Skype, who does she say she wants Sheldon to meet?

114 On their girls' night, what's the first thing Amy does after Penny announces they are going to have a slumber party?

115 What is Sheldon playing with Leonard when he says: "What an elf I would have made"?

116 How does Amy find being "cast in the role of bad girl" by Sheldon's mother?

117 What costume does Zack get for Penny, which she's reluctant to wear for Stuart's New Year's Eve party?

118 Who is Amy's best friend?

119 What flavor snow cone does Sheldon make for Leonard in the Snoopy snow cone maker?

120 When Penny tells Amy she goes on a "few dates," how many dates does Sheldon say he has calculated Penny has gone on?

121 *How old was Penny when she started dating?* **Master's**

122 "It's not what it looks like." Who has Penny walked out of Leonard's bedroom with?

123 What is the name of the smoking research monkey Amy keeps in her apartment?

124 What does Amy say in the cafeteria that makes Sheldon move for their relationship to "terminate immediately"?

125 What *Star Trek* weapon does Sheldon take to confront Todd Zarnecki about hacking his World of Warcraft account?

126 *After the confrontation, why does Sheldon say Todd is "even more cunning than we thought"?* **Master's**

127 In the car going home from the Big Sur symposium, what makes Amy ask Leonard if he's concerned that Penny left with Glenn, "probably the most beautiful man I've ever seen"?

Sheldon: Look at you, getting me to engage in the social sciences. You're a vixen, Amy Farrah Fowler.

128 At the Cheesecake Factory, why does Sheldon order a seven-day course of penicillin, syrup of ipecac to induce vomiting and a mint from Bernadette?

129 ***What is the name of the one-act play Sheldon adapted from some* Star Trek *fan fiction he wrote when he was eleven?*** **PhD**

130 What was the name of Sheldon's elementary school?

131 What does Raj consume in order to talk to the FBI agent interviewing him for Howard's security clearance?

132 *How does he screw up the interview?* **Master's**

133 Howard tells Leonard that Sheldon once betrayed him by doing what to his food?

134 Amy persuades Sheldon to go to the university fund-raiser, as he is needed there to make the case for the physics department and prevent the money going to other departments, such as geology or where?

135 What do Leonard, Howard and Raj call Leonard's app?

136 When Penny is making conversation in the car with Sheldon and Amy, how does Sheldon describe growing up in Texas?

137 Amy thinks Priya has the smoldering sexuality of what kind of animal?

138 When recent events demonstrate that Sheldon's body is too fragile to endure the vicissitudes of the world, he makes a mobile presence device. What secure location does he control it from?

139 *Howard sees Leonard and robot Sheldon outside Sheldon's office: "Oh, look, it's Leonard and _____________."* **Master's**

140 In the limo, when Leonard asks the wealthy Mrs. Latham for funding, what does she do?

141 What does Howard call a contraption strapped to his calf that allows him to use the bathroom without going anywhere?

142 What does Sheldon tell Penny he and Amy are considering doing that makes Penny choke on her food?

143 With everyone spending more time at Raj's apartment, Sheldon invites a bunch of people over—Stuart, Kripke, Zack and TV's LeVar Burton. How has he gotten in touch with LeVar?

144 What did Sheldon send to the FBI Crime Lab for fingerprinting and DNA analysis, about which he still hasn't had a response eighteen years later?

145 What was Zazzles going to be called before Sheldon discovered he was "so zazzy"?

146 "Good news—the wildebeest is in the curry." What is Amy referring to?

147 How many sexual partners does Sheldon calculate Penny has had?

148 How does Sheldon screw up the interview with the FBI agent investigating Howard's security clearance?

149 Howard and Raj both think they'd be a superhero, not a sidekick. In order to determine who'd be the sidekick, what bravery test do they endure?

150 *Howard and Raj try to settle the question with a sports activity. What is it?* Master's

151 What's Howard's costume for Stuart's New Year's Eve party?

152 "Aw, he has the same look my little nephew gets when he can't figure out how I got his nose." What has confused Sheldon?

153 How does Sheldon describe the desk Raj puts in Sheldon's office when Sheldon refuses to get one for him?

154 What gift does Raj tell Sheldon he has bought him for Thanksgiving that makes Sheldon decide that they can still be friends?

155 What title does Sheldon bestow on Howard for the development of Leonard's new app?

156 After having problems with his new contact lenses, what does Leonard wear to bed?

157 As Sheldon is chased by the Indiana Jones fans, he asks: "Why is there never a ____________ ____________ when you need one?"

158 ***When Sheldon is calculating his life expectancy, what event is he disappointed to find he won't be alive for?*** PhD

159 Howard and his mother have their own Sabbath tradition. What is it?

Sheldon: Do you realize that teaching is the first thing that I've failed at since my ill-fated attempt to complete a chin-up in March of 1989?

160 Sheldon wants to play vintage video games with Zack, Stuart and Kripke. What does Kripke suggest instead?

161 In Sheldon's "ironclad" alibi for Leonard for the night he slept with Priya, what does he call the woman who Leonard supposedly met in a bar?

162 *In the alibi, in which bar did he meet her?* Master's

163 What does Amy name Bernadette's mission to learn more about Priya?

164 When Howard goes to the hospital to have the robot arm removed, what does the woman in reception announce through the hospital public address system?

165 *How does she get the robot arm off Howard's penis?* Master's

166 So Amy can't find him, after he's broken up with her, how does Sheldon try to change the address of the apartment?

167 In the argument about who has betrayed who, Leonard tells Sheldon that Raj once betrayed him by doing what?

168 ***According to Sheldon, what is the best number?*** PhD

169 What is the name of the ex-boyfriend Bernadette bumps into while checking in to the Big Sur hotel?

170 *Where did Bernadette meet him originally?* Master's

171 When the girls are playing Truth or Dare on girls' night, what excessively "personal or embarrassing" question does Amy ask Bernadette?

Amy: I find the notion of romantic love to be an unnecessary cultural construct that adds no value to human relationships.

Sheldon: Amy Farrah Fowler, that's the most pragmatic thing anyone has ever said to me.

172 What does Amy point out the first time she gets a ride with Penny?

173 What gossip about Raj does Priya tell Leonard?

174 *Why does Raj tell Penny to "Shut your ass"?* **Master's**

175 Who travels in the "lead car" on the way to Big Sur?

176 Why are the guys so excited about a midnight screening of *Raiders of the Lost Ark*?

177 Sheldon tells Raj that Howard lied to him about what Thanksgiving custom?

178 *What Fourth of July custom did he also make up?* **Master's**

179 When Penny is giving Sheldon acting lessons, in order to help get Sheldon out of his comfort zone, what role does Penny want him to read from his play?

Amy: I think you need to face the fact that Leonard is the nucleus of your social group. Where he goes, the group goes.

Sheldon: Leonard the nucleus? That makes no sense. I'm the whimsical elf that everyone looks to for a good time.

180 What does a drunken Amy do after kissing Sheldon for the first time that makes her say: "I hope you don't take what I'm about to do as a comment on what we just did"?

181 Why does Amy think Priya invited Bernadette and Howard to dinner with her and Leonard?

182 What is Leonard's ringtone for Priya?

183 When LeVar Burton sees drunken Stuart, Zack and Kripke doing karaoke, what does he say as he turns around and leaves the apartment?

184 *What does he say as he goes down the stairs?* **Master's**

185 "Oh, my metatarsals are barking." What is Amy doing?

186 ***Sheldon and Amy want to study how gossip spreads through their social group by fabricating two pieces of gossip. What are they?*** **PhD**

187 If Sheldon was a superhero, what does Raj reckon his name would be?

188 *What does Sheldon think his name would be?* **Master's**

189 When a lonely Raj comes over to see Sheldon because Leonard and Priya are having dinner with Bernadette and Howard, what hot beverage does Sheldon bring him?

190 After Leonard admits to Raj that he did sleep with Priya, how does he soften the blow?

191 During the game of Truth of Dare at the slumber party, what does Bernadette ask Penny?

192 When Bernadette says Raj is a cutie, he says, "Thank you, but cute is for bunnies. I want to be something with sex appeal, like a ____________."

193 How many doctorates does Sheldon have?

194 Why was Sheldon forced to take dance lessons when he was growing up in Texas?

195 How does Sheldon try to figure out Howard's baffling card trick?

196 *Leonard is shocked by the lengths Sheldon has gone to: "Okay, I'm leaving before the ____________ ____________ get here."* **Master's**

197 After waiting in line for hours to see the special screening of *Raiders of the Lost Ark*, the guys can't get in. What movie does Raj suggest they see instead?

198 When Mrs. Wolowitz is in the hospital and everyone's gone to support Howard, what happens to Sheldon?

199 Who prank-calls Sheldon while he's in line for the special screening of *Raiders of the Lost Ark*?

200 *What is Sheldon duped into saying?* **Master's**

The Shamy Chronology

Here's a look at some of Sheldon and Amy's milestones.

They first met in The Lunar Excitation (Season 3, Episode 23).

The first time we heard the term "Shamy" was in The Robotic Manipulation (Season 4, Episode 1).

They invented a game called Counterfactuals . . .

Amy: We postulate an alternate world which differs from ours in one key aspect and then pose questions to each other.

Sheldon: It's fun for ages eight to eighty.

Sheldon: *(reading)* "In a world where a piano is a weapon, not a musical instrument, on what does Scott Joplin play 'The Maple Leaf Rag'?"

Amy: Tuned bayonets.

Sheldon: Defend.

Amy: Isn't it obvious?

Sheldon: You're right, my apologies.

Season 4, Episode 3: The Zazzy Substitution

Also in this episode, Sheldon and Amy broke up. Sheldon tried to fill the void of her absence by buying 25 cats. Leonard called Sheldon's mother, Mary, and she met Amy for the first time. Mary used reverse psychology on Sheldon to get him to get back with Amy.

Sheldon met Amy's mother in The Desperation Emanation (Season 4, Episode 5).

They cuddled for the first time in The Isolation Permutation (Season 5, Episode 8).

They officially became boyfriend and girlfriend . . .

Sheldon: I present to you the Relationship Agreement. A binding covenant that in its thirty-one pages enumerates, iterates and codifies the rights and responsibilities of Sheldon Lee Cooper, here and after known as "The Boyfriend," and Amy Farrah Fowler, here and after known as "The Girlfriend."

Amy: It's so romantic.

Sheldon: Mutual indemnification always is.

Amy: *(reading)* "Section 5: hand-holding. Hand-holding is only allowed under the following circumstances: A) Either party is in danger of falling off a cliff, precipice or ledge. B) Either party is deserving of a hearty handshake after winning a Nobel Prize. C) Moral support during flu shots." *(then)* Seems a bit restrictive.

Sheldon: Feel free to retain a lawyer.

Season 5, Episode 10: The Flaming Spittoon Acquisition

We learned about their date nights . . .

Amy: Our Relationship Agreement specifies that the second Thursday of every month, or the third Thursday in a month with five Thursdays, is date night.

Season 5, Episode 12: The Shiny Trinket Maneuver

This was also the episode Sheldon gave Amy the tiara.

Amy: Jewelry? Seriously? *(opening bag)* Sheldon, you are the most shallow, self-centered person I have ever met. Do you really think another transparently manipulative—Oh, it's a tiara! A tiara! I have a tiara! *(to Penny)* Put it on me, put it on me, put it on me, put it on me, put it on me, put it on me.

Sheldon made his first episode of *Sheldon Cooper Presents: Fun with Flags* with Amy in The Beta Test Initiation (Season 5, Episode 14).

They had their first date night in Amy's apartment. They played *Star Trek* doctor—Amy wore a *Star Trek* Nurse Chapel uniform and took Sheldon's readings using a medical tricorder.

Leonard: What are you doing?

Amy: We're playing doctor. *Star Trek* style. *(she winks)*

Sheldon: I'm in hell, Leonard. *(then, to Amy)* Don't stop.

Season 5, Episode 23: The Launch Acceleration

On their second anniversary date, Sheldon invited Koothrappali to tag along.

Sheldon: I have a contractual obligation to provide Amy with conversation and casual physical contact, but nowhere is it specified that I can't outsource that to an Indian.

Sheldon: Amy, when I look in your eyes, and you're looking back in mine, everything feels not quite normal. Because I feel stronger and weaker at the same time. I feel excited and at the same time terrified. The truth is I don't know what I feel except I know what kind of man I want to be.

Amy: Sheldon, that was beautiful.

Sheldon: I should hope so. That's from the first Spider-Man movie.

Season 6, Episode 1: The Date Night Variable

Amy revealed her plan to marry Sheldon . . .

Amy: When I get married, I'm gonna register at the UCLA Cadaver Lab.

Penny: Ew, why?

Amy: 'Cause I've always wanted a whole human skeleton, and they are really spendy.

Bernadette: So you actually see you and Sheldon getting married someday?

Amy: Not just someday—in exactly four years. But don't tell Sheldon. He's still a flight risk.

Season 6, Episode 2: The Decoupling Fluctuation

Sheldon and Amy did their first couple's costume for Halloween. Amy was Raggedy Ann and Sheldon was Raggedy C-3PO.

Sheldon: It was a compromise. I lost.

Season 6, Episode 5: The Holographic Excitation

Amy directed an episode of *Fun with Flags* in The Habitation Configuration (Season 6, Episode 7).

Sheldon spanked Amy in The Fish Guts Displacement (Season 6, Episode 10).

Sheldon made Amy his emergency contact at work for Valentine's Day in The Tangible Affection Proof (Season 6, Episode 16).

They got extremely "intimate" in a game of Dungeons & Dragons in The Love Spell Potential (Season 6, Episode 23).

They had their Annual State of the Relationship Summit:

Amy: Which brings us to the final item of our annual State of the Relationship Summit. Item 29: Valentine's Day . . . We're going to have Valentine's Day dinner on a fully functioning vintage train.

Sheldon: Vintage? Be specific.

Amy: An Alcoa FA-4 diesel locomotive leading a train of meticulously restored 1915 Pullman first-class coaches.

Sheldon: Wow, I'm feeling the urge to hug you.

Season 7, Episode 15: The Locomotive Manipulation

And later in the episode they had their first kiss.

We learned more about the Agreement . . .

Amy: Our Relationship Agreement covers a wide array of scenarios, including career changes, financial instability, intelligent dog uprising—FYI, we plan on selling out the human race hard.

Season 7, Episode 18: The Mommy Observation

Raj: Wouldn't you be upset if you saw Amy out with someone else?

Sheldon: Can't happen. We have an ironclad Relationship Agreement that precludes her from physical contact with anyone other than me.

Season 7, Episode 23: The Gorilla Dissolution

Penny: You guys are going out two nights in a row?

Sheldon: I missed a number of date nights while I was on my train trip and I'm contractually obligated to make them up under the terms of the Relationship Agreement.

Penny: That's so hot.

Amy: It's better than hot, it's binding.

Season 8, Episode 3: The First Pitch Insufficiency

Sheldon told Amy he loved her . . .

Amy: Sheldon, there's something else I've been wanting to say—but before I do, I want you to know that you don't have to say it back. I know you're not ready, and I don't want you to say it just because the social convention dictates—

Sheldon: I love you, too.

Season 8, Episode 8: The Prom Equivalency

For Christmas, Sheldon gave Amy a photo of him sitting on Santa's lap. She gave him cookies she baked using his Mee-Maw's recipe:

Sheldon: They're perfect. It tastes like her hugs.

Season 8, Episode 11: The Clean Room Infiltration

Sheldon told Leonard that Amy taught him how to drive in The Space Probe Disintegration (Season 8, Episode 12). He said he didn't do it because "it's scary and sometimes I get the pedals mixed up."

They spent their first night together (in a blanket fort).

Amy: According to the codicil of the Relationship Agreement that you insisted upon, we're not allowed to pout or be moody on date night.

Sheldon: You know I just put that in because of *(whispering)* uterus stuff.

Sheldon was having such a good time with Amy in their blanket fort that he didn't want date night to end.

Sheldon: Well, wait. What if, just this once, we suspend the date night parameters and you stay later.

Amy: As long as we're suspending the parameters, I could stay really late and we could have our first sleepover.

Sheldon: That's a big step.

Amy: It's a big fort.

Sheldon: Very well. I will agree to a family-friendly, G-rated, boy-girl sleepover.

Amy: P.G. Some scenes may be too intense for younger viewers.

Sheldon: G-rated, with a warning for families with babies and toddlers.

Amy: You got yourself a sleepover.

Season 8, Episode 20: The Fortification Implementation

When they celebrated their fifth anniversary, Sheldon admitted to struggling with a major commitment issue—whether or not he should watch *The Flash* TV show. This infuriated Amy. At the end of the episode, Sheldon Skyped Amy and she told him that, while she loved him, she wanted to take a step back from their relationship. A stunned Sheldon hung up and turned to the Gollum statue on his desk.

Sheldon: Well, Gollum, you're an expert on rings . . . *(he takes a ring box out of his desk drawer and opens it, revealing an engagement ring)* * What do I do with this one?

Season 8, Episode 24: The Commitment Determination

** Knowing that Sheldon had the ring the entire time, watch the episode again. The scenes with Sheldon, Leonard and Penny kinda take on a whole new meaning!*

Season 5

1 What sword do Leonard and Sheldon decide to buy to start their fantasy sword collection?

2 What does Mrs. Wolowitz use to make two matching vests for Howard and Bernadette's magic show—plus half a dozen napkins?

3 Why does Stuart want to put Leonard's picture up on the Wall of Heroes at the comic book store?

4 What was the name of the boy band Raj tried to start when he was six?

5 What is the name of the character Amy creates to "help bring in some younger viewers" to Sheldon's online show *Fun with Flags*?

6 Sheldon is scared of birds because his first memory is of "a hummingbird dive-bombing my stroller to get at the apple juice in my sippy cup." What does he call hummingbirds?

7 When her sink's full of dirty dishes and glasses, what does Penny use to drink wine?

Amy: Kiss me where I've never been kissed before.
Sheldon: You mean like Salt Lake City?

8 What music does Amy play during their date night dinner at the beginning of her experiment with Sheldon?

9 Sheldon dreams that his Mr. Spock doll tells him in its Leonard Nimoy voice to open the mint-in-box transporter toy Penny has given him and play with it. What does he do when it breaks?

10 Where does Penny get her new chair, much to the horror of hygiene-conscious Sheldon?

11 After getting pranked by the guys, Sheldon shakes hands with Howard with a joy buzzer. What happens?

12 What nickname does astronaut Mike Massimino give Howard?

13 *What happens that makes Mike give him that nickname?* **Master's**

14 At the university, Howard is trying out the $175,000 hydraulic thermoforming press to do what?

15 When Sheldon finally allows Penny to cut his hair, he makes a sudden movement while she's using the clippers and she accidentally shaves a strip up the back of his head. What does she say to herself?

16 Who is Armen the miniature horse breeder?

17 When Leonard is despondent at Amy's colleagues' wedding, what sort of man does she tell him is the only kind in whom moody self-obsession is attractive?

18 Where is Howard's rocket launching from to take him to the International Space Station?

19 Sheldon finally gains possession of Professor Rothman's office: "Ah, the spoils. I see why victors love them." So why is he soon yelling: "Hey, gravel monkeys, if you need to shake rocks, try jiggling your heads around"?

20 What organism, according to Sheldon, would a human have to merge with to become fungus and algae as well as human?

21 What happened when Amy's mom paid her cousin to take Amy to her prom?

22 After NASA's Dave Roeger phones Howard to tell him that his mission's been scrubbed, why is Howard delighted?

23 When Sheldon conducts an experiment where he makes all trivial decisions with the throw of dice, what does he wind up having for dinner at the Cheesecake Factory?

24 When Amy's angry with Penny and Bernadette and Sheldon can't get hold of her via email, video chat, tweeting, posting on her Facebook wall or texting, what does Leonard suggest?

25 When Howard makes fun of Sheldon, a grown man, for being interested in toy trains, Bernadette says that's big talk for a man who has magic tricks in his mother's house. How does Howard correct her?

26 Who do Howard and Bernadette do a magic show for?

27 Who says: "For someone who has a machine that can travel anywhere in time and space, Doctor Who sure does have a thing for modern-day London"?

28 When Leonard and Sheldon see Wil Wheaton in the comic book store and Leonard accepts an invitation to his party, why does Sheldon tell him this is a "fiendishly clever" move?

29 Why is Sheldon unsettled by Howard's groomsman gift?

30 When Leonard and Penny get back together after a four-month break, what does Leonard say to Penny while they are having sex?

31 At Howard's magic show, Bernadette is not impressed by a heckler: "That's it. No cake for you. Anyone else want to join the No Cake Club?" What has one of the children pointed out is a fake?

32 Sheldon's mother, Mary, is going on a Christian cruise. What's it called?

33 *Christian Quarterly has given the cruise its highest rating. What is it?* **Master's**

34 How did Sheldon lose his hot dog on a Florida beach when he was a child?

35 When Leonard takcs a girl he's met in the comic book store back to his apartment, what character is he dressed as in an original sketch he shows her that he got two years ago at Comic-Con?

36 When they are both vying for Professor Rothman's vacated office, Sheldon and Kripke approach President Siebert in the men's room, where he gives them two reasons why they must sort it out for themselves. What's the first?

37 *What's the second?* **Master's**

Leonard: Why do I have to talk to Penny? She's not my girlfriend.

Sheldon: You invited her to lunch four years ago. Everything about her is on you. You make it so.

38 "Oh, internet, this is so going all over you." What is Wil Wheaton filming?

39 "You've taken a great evolutionary leap by abandoning human interaction and allowing yourself to romantically bond with a soulless machine. Kudos." How has Raj impressed Sheldon?

40 When Sheldon opens the window to shoo away a blue jay, it flies into the apartment. Where does it land?

41 Sheldon once tried having his hair cut at Supercuts. Why does he describe it as "Sodom and Gomorrah with mousse"?

42 What gift does Howard give to Bernadette before leaving for the International Space Station?

43 Leonard and Penny inhale from a canister of gas that he uses at work. What effect does it have?

44 Amy reckons that in the old way of marriage, when the groom would pay the bride's father in money and livestock, Bernadette would fetch at least two oxen and a goose. What would Penny fetch?

45 When Stuart sells the new Mystic Warlords of Ka'a expansion pack to Leonard, Howard *and* Raj, what does he say under his breath?

46 *What is the name of the expansion pack?* **Master's**

47 What kind of cookies do Leonard and Sheldon keep in the Batman cookie jar?

48 How does Penny fare in her first game of chess?

Sheldon: *(to Amy in her lab)* Boy, oh boy. This vacation is off to a wonderful start—the smell of formaldehyde, the whir of the centrifuge, the distant chatter of lab animals being dispatched for dissection—I can already feel my cares just melting away.

49 Professor Rothman is forced to step down because he's done something that theoretical physicists do all the time, according to Leonard. What is it?

50 Why does Howard take back the gift he buys Bernadette before he leaves for the International Space Station?

51 If Howard goes to space, what does Mrs. Wolowitz threaten to do?

52 When Leonard and Penny are considering getting back together, Leonard suggests that rather than seeing "Leonard and Penny" as a relationship, they could be like a new version of software. What does he call it?

53 What was the name of the girl who was always mean to Bernadette in school?

54 In his bachelor party toast for Howard, Raj reveals they once had a threesome at Comic-Con with who?

55 What's Sheldon's fun way of making young people more interested in science?

56 Howard tells the gang that NASA has picked his team's design for an important piece of equipment that's going on the International Space Station. What is it?

> **Penny:** I cannot believe you've never seen *Grease.*
> **Amy:** My mother didn't allow me to watch it. She was afraid it would encourage me to join a gang.

57 What nickname does Mary Cooper have for her son, Sheldon?

58 Howard is going to the International Space Station with Mike Massimino and one other astronaut. What's his name?

59 In order to assuage her guilt for being a bully in high school, Penny decides to donate some of her clothes to charity, but what does she do when she gets to the collection bin?

60 *What happens when she returns to the collection bin?* **Master's**

61 When Sheldon pranks Leonard and jumps out from under the couch dressed as a zombie, what does he say to Leonard?

62 When Penny and Leonard get together again, she gives him a heads-up that she's gotten a tattoo since the last time he saw her naked. What is it of?

63 What was the name of Amy's cousin who died in a horrific carbon monoxide poisoning accident the night before her wedding?

64 Why is Bernadette mad at Howard after his bachelor party?

65 In what way does Sheldon help Howard's mother as one of the humiliating tasks set by Howard when Sheldon wants him to show his paper to Stephen Hawking?

66 Raj is highly impressed by Howard's magic tricks: "I'm telling you, dude, there's a seat on the ____________ ____________ with your name on it."

67 ***What is the palindrome Sheldon makes with his Alpha-Bits?*** PhD

68 Frustrated by his lack of emotional attachment, Amy runs what kind of experiment on Sheldon?

69 When Leonard tries to persuade Sheldon to come to Wil Wheaton's party by telling him that one of his favorite actors from *Star Trek: The Next Generation* will be there, what is Sheldon's response?

70 What does Priya tell Leonard after he confesses to kissing Alice from the comic book store?

71 Sheldon has index cards with topics to turn a conversation into what?

72 Where do Howard and Bernadette have their wedding ceremony when they can't be fit in at City Hall?

73 *Why do they choose that particular place?* Master's

74 Suspecting that Raj's new girlfriend, Emily, is taking advantage of him, Penny and Howard confront her. Where?

75 ***What is the title of Leonard's mother's book?*** PhD

76 When Amy was fourteen years old, what operation did she perform on her feet?

77 When Raj tells his girlfriend, Emily, he is going to have to return the gifts he bought for her, what does she do?

78 How does Sheldon show Amy that she is officially his girlfriend?

79 When Leonard tells Sheldon he's having a dinner date with Priya via Skype, Sheldon points out it's morning in Mumbai. What does he think the date should be called?

80 What nickname did Howard use to call Raj but now reserves for his fiancée, Bernadette?

81 When Sheldon informs Leonard, Howard and Raj that he's decided on his rank for their upcoming paintball tournament, he thinks he is neither a general nor a sergeant, but instead they should call him what?

82 Penny, Bernadette and Amy are discussing possible girlfriends for a lonely Raj. Why does Penny say: "Okay, so future grief-stricken widow is the one to beat"?

Sheldon: Why are you waving a white flag?
Amy: I'm surrendering. To fun.

83 What was the name of Leonard's first girlfriend in high school?

84 What's Mary Cooper's secret to cooking great pancakes?

85 What does Penny tell Leonard are the acceptable responses to seeing her new tattoo?

86 Where does Sheldon finally ask Amy to be his girlfriend?

87 Raj has a new phone, and invites Howard to share in what Howard says is the best part of getting a new phone. But Raj warns him: "What's your hurry, cowboy? Savor the moment." What are they doing?

88 How does Bernadette make it up to Amy for not inviting her to go wedding shopping?

89 If Raj had a cool astronaut nickname, what would it be?

90 At his party, Wil Wheaton gives Sheldon an original mint-in-package Wesley Crusher action figure. What message does Wil write on it?

91 Who introduces the deaf girl Emily to Raj?

92 *How does Howard help when Raj meets Emily?* **Master's**

93 Howard wants "Rocket Man" to be his astronaut nickname. How does Raj suggest Howard get the other astronauts to think calling him that name is their idea?

94 During the paintball match, Leonard, Howard and Raj are too preoccupied with their own troubles to play the game. How does Sheldon inspire them to get involved?

95 What does Penny tell Bernadette is the best way of breaking bad news to a guy?

96 Why does Mary Cooper threaten to spank Sheldon in a sushi restaurant?

97 Who officiates at the wedding of Howard and Bernadette?

98 Sheldon is not impressed with the job Amy gives him while he is on "vacation" in her lab: "Excuse me, you have Dr. Sheldon Cooper in your lab, and you're going to make him do the dishes? That's like asking the Incredible Hulk to open a __________ __________."

99 What does Amy arrange for Sheldon to do that is usually only open to children but she got them to make an exception?

100 Sheldon explains to his mom why Penny has a revealing turquoise top in her laundry basket: "Penny has a lot of money tied up in __________ futures."

101 According to Leonard, there were only two obstacles that stopped him from being a great jockey. One is that he's too tall. What was the other minor consideration?

102 Who does Raj think should play Leonard's mother if someone makes a movie version of her book?

103 What does Bernadette's father try to presssure her to do before her marriage to Howard?

104 When Raj starts going out with Emily, it's not long before he gives her diamond earrings, pays all her credit card bills and leases her a car. What's the final gift he gives her?

105 Sheldon is scared by the blue jay hanging around the outside windowsill. Who does he call for help?

106 For the Bavarian-themed episode of *Fun with Flags*, what does Amy dress as?

107 When Amy and Sheldon are on a date and she tells him the news that she is getting a paper published, Amy is mad because he acts like it's no big deal. What is he more interested in?

108 When Sheldon and Kripke are competing to take over Professor Rothman's office, Sheldon thinks he deserves it because he arrived at the university first. What is Kripke's claim?

109 Why is Amy upset when Sheldon loses his fear of the blue jay that flew into the apartment and starts making a great fuss over it?

110 Amy wants to show her appreciation for everything Penny has done for her: "Before I met you, I was a mousy wallflower. But look at me now. I'm like some kind of downtown hipster party girl." What "little something" does she give Penny?

111 Sheldon and Kripke attempt to play each other at basketball to decide who will get Professor Rothman's empty office. After 45 minutes of fruitless dorky endeavor, Leonard no longer finds it funny and suggests they do what?

112 Sheldon discovers something new about one of his hobbies: "All these years I've been so wrong. The tinier the ____________, the more concentrated the fun."

113 What reason does Howard give for setting Sheldon a series of humiliating tasks before he agrees to show his paper to Stephen Hawking?

114 Sheldon boasts to Amy that he has plenty of experience in biology: "I bought a ____________ in 1998, and it's still alive."

115 Sheldon is horrified to learn that his regular barber is sick and one of the barber's relatives will cut his hair instead: "To paraphrase T. S. Eliot, 'This is the way the world ends, not with a bang, but with a ____________.' "

116 Why does Sheldon unfriend Leonard, Howard and Raj on Facebook?

117 At the wedding of Amy's colleagues, how does Leonard manage to pull his groin?

118 When Leonard's girlfriend, Priya, has moved back to India and he is frustrated by this long-distance love affair, what does Howard build so that Leonard can simulate love-making with her?

119 *Who does Howard demonstrate it with?* **Master's**

120 How does Bernadette's father crack walnuts?

121 Amy spent a lot of her childhood throwing coins into wishing wells hoping for friends. What did she start having to do to keep things interesting?

122 When Sheldon informs everyone that Raj can afford to spend lots of money on Emily, how does he reveal he knows that Raj's family is rich?

Leonard: Are you okay?

Sheldon: Am I okay? Leonard, I'm on a lifelong trajectory that includes a Nobel Prize and cities named after me. All four wisdom teeth fit comfortably in my mouth without need of extraction, and my bowel movements run like a German train schedule. Am I okay?

123 Once he's decided to have an arranged marriage, Raj's parents fix him up with Lakshmi. Why is she willing to go through with it?

124 *Lakshmi says there's a rumor around New Delhi about Raj. What is it?* Master's

125 Jimmy Speckerman, the guy who used to torment Leonard in high school, turns up and pitches a business idea to him. What's his idea?

126 When Sheldon was five years old, what did Billy Sparks put up his nose?

127 Amy tries to comfort Penny after her drunken night with Raj: "You can't blame yourself. When your pre-frontal cortex fails to make you happy, promiscuity rewards you with the needed flood of dopamine. We neurobiologists refer to this as the ____________ ____________."

128 Why doesn't Amy want to accompany Sheldon to the train store?

129 Howard is training for his upcoming NASA expedition. During his overnight survival training in the wilderness, he's starving—what does he eat?

Penny: Well, ladies, we killed the bottle.

Amy: I had half a glass.

Bernadette: I didn't have any.

Penny: Okay, don't judge me. So, what do you want to do? Go to the movies, go dancing, lay down for a little bit?

130 Howard and Bernadette don't want Raj to marry Lakshmi, but they don't want him to be alone either. What is their solution?

131 When Sheldon was six years old, who did he dress up as for Halloween?

132 When Amy feels left out because Penny and Bernadette went wedding shopping without her, she craves human intimacy and physical contact from Sheldon. After careful negotiation, what kind of physical contact do they agree on?

133 *As "a man of science, not someone's snuggle bunny," Sheldon feels put upon by this demand from Amy. What does he tell Leonard and Howard to do so it doesn't happen again?* **Master's**

134 On top of inflicting various cruelties on Leonard in high school, bully Jimmy Speckerman also called him what demeaning name for three years?

135 After Leonard goes to the wedding with Amy, he tells Sheldon, "Truth be told, my groin's a little worse for wear." What does Sheldon do?

136 ***What comic book does Alice try to take from Leonard in the comic book store?*** **PhD**

137 What souvenirs from his meeting with Stephen Hawking does Howard give to Leonard and Raj?

138 At Howard's bachelor party, Sheldon decides that in order to "participate in the social convention that is the stag night" he "must embrace all of its components." What does he try that makes him say: "Jeepers! That's yucky"?

139 What is the name of the guy Stuart puts in charge of the store when he goes on a date with Amy?

140 Why do Bernadette and Penny go wedding shopping without telling Amy?

141 In the gift bags for Howard's out-of-town relatives that the girls make, there are antihistamines, antacids and medicines for what?

142 After Priya moves back to India to pursue her career, Sheldon tells Leonard he should stop trying to continue the intercontinental long distance relationship and take up what hobby?

143 According to Raj, what kind of relationship is it where he buys gifts for his girlfriend and she gives him sex?

144 What Texan delicacy caused Sheldon's father to need an extralarge coffin?

145 When Leonard goes with Amy to her colleagues' wedding, what's the first dance they do?

146 When the guys are getting dressed up for Howard's wedding, Sheldon tells Leonard: "These rental tuxedos have been worn by hundreds of sweaty strangers. I don't like my own sweat touching my skin; how do you think I feel about theirs?" So what does he do about it?

147 How does Sheldon's mother thank Leonard when he offers to draw up a list for her of racist terms to avoid?

148 Sheldon has ordered a life-size cardboard cutout of Mr. Spock. Why is he disappointed when it arrives?

149 What does Sheldon name the blue jay that flies into the apartment?

150 When Amy tries out Penny's new chair, she gets bitten, and both girls see "something" moving under the cushion. What do they do?

151 *What happens to the chair?* **Master's**

152 How does Bernadette justify her decision not to return a pair of boots she takes from the charity collection bin?

Sheldon: Knock knock.
Leonard: Who's there?
Sheldon: Interrupting physicist.
Leonard: Interrupting phys—
Sheldon: Muon!

153 Amy's paper on how cooperative long-term potentiation can map memory sequences on dendritic branches makes the cover of which magazine?

154 When Leonard asks Sheldon's mom if she enjoyed her sushi, what does she say would've made it better?

155 The ever-studious Sheldon is worthless after what time of night?

156 As well as his mother, who does Amy think Sheldon formed emotional attachments with as he grew up?

157 Howard remembers the last time Sheldon found something so funny: "I haven't seen him laugh that hard since the day Leonard made that ___________ error."

158 Just as Penny is despairing of ever getting acting work, she lands a job on a TV commercial for what?

159 Who calls Raj's parents to tell them he is spending all their money on his new girlfriend, Emily?

160 When Amy asks Sheldon if he really does have a list of mortal enemies, he assures her he does. How many are currently on the list?

161 *How old was Sheldon when he started compiling the list?* **Master's**

162 Who is Sheldon's ninth-favorite person?

163 When does NASA reschedule Howard's space mission to?

164 When Sheldon has irritated Amy, Leonard advises him that the best thing to do is to "skip over any attempt to repair your emotional connection" and instead win her back with what sort of gesture?

165 Amy tells Bernadette that she finds Sheldon's eidetic memory sexy. What does she ask him to do to demonstrate it?

166 Amy tells Sheldon to overcome his fear of birds by interacting with the blue jay that flies into the apartment. How does Bernadette suggest he do this?

167 When his mother asks him when the landlord is going to fix the elevator, what does Sheldon say he wants to convert it to?

168 What marriage-themed groomsman gift does Howard get for Leonard, Sheldon and Raj?

169 In ninth grade, what did the mean girls put in Amy's hand lotion?

170 *When Amy used the adulterated hand lotion, what nickname did she get?* **Master's**

171 Who refers to himself as "the make-out king"?

172 Where was the specialist based who Sheldon's mom regrets not having taken him to in order to determine that he wasn't crazy?

173 Who was the only person who signed Amy's yearbook?

174 *What was the message?* **Master's**

175 Raj has always had a backup plan: "I keep telling you, if I wasn't an astrophysicist, I would have been a __________ __________. It was always a coin flip."

176 When Penny takes Sheldon to the jewelry store to buy a gift for Amy, what does Sheldon buy for himself?

177 *What does Sheldon eventually choose for Amy?* **Master's**

178 At Wil Wheaton's party, Brent Spiner spots the mint-in-package action figure that Wil has given Sheldon and rips it open. When Sheldon protests, Brent offers to sign a Mr. Data doll. Sheldon says he's already signed something. What is it?

179 When giving Bernadette's hand in marriage to Howard, what does her father say to him?

180 *What does Bernadette then say to her father?* **Master's**

181 Back at the apartment after his uncomfortable date night with Amy, where does Sheldon decide to go for a walk to clear his head?

182 Who said: "Handicapped people are nice, Leonard. Everyone knows that"?

183 When Sheldon's mother points out that Raj is hurting and "drunk as a skunk," what hot beverage does she want Sheldon to make for his friend?

> **Stuart:** Howard, when I think about you and Bernadette starting this wonderful life together, I can't help but get a little choked up. I mean, look at you—you have everything. Look at me. I'm thirty-seven, I sleep in the back of a comic book store and I have the bone density of an eighty-year-old man.

184 *According to Mary, what do "we" make this beverage with?*

Master's

185 What makes Bernadette's father change his mind and think Howard is the right guy for his daughter?

186 Who most recently told Amy she "overstays her welcome"?

187 Howard thinks he and Bernadette might not be right for each other because he wants kids and she doesn't. What solution does Bernadette come up with?

188 Leonard takes Penny to a gun range as a treat. What brings it to a premature end?

189 Why does Sheldon need anesthesia for a dental cleaning?

190 When Sheldon is having a "vacation" in Amy's lab, what happens when she asks him to remove the locus coeruleus from a brain sample?

191 Why does Penny buy both Sheldon and Leonard a vintage mint-in-box 1975 Mego *Star Trek* Transporter with real transporter action?

192 What was the name of the girl Penny and her friends blindfolded, tied up and left in a cornfield overnight?

$E=mc^2$

Howard: Hey, I was thinking, for our first dance at the wedding, what if we learn the final number from *Dirty Dancing*?

Bernadette: You're kidding.

Howard: No, come on. How cool would that be? Me running into your arms, you lifting me up in the air.

Mary: Now you listen to me. I know you feel like you can't find someone, but there's a lock for every key. Back home, there's a girl, works at the Walmart. Tall, tall girl. Woman could hunt geese with a rake. Thought she'd never find a man. Then one day, wouldn't ya know, Harlem Globetrotters come to town. Long story short, today that woman travels the world with a semiprofessional basketball player and two beautiful mixed-race babies.

Raj: I didn't get a lot of that because of your accent, but the general tone was soothing, and somehow I feel better.

193 When Leonard meets Alice at the comic book store, while still dating Priya long distance, who does he go to for dating advice?

194 When Amy finishes brushing Penny's hair, how does she describe it?

195 Where do Howard and Bernadette decide to have a trial run at living together?

196 Apart from having the bird carry messages to his enemies, how does Sheldon think he and the blue jay that flew into his apartment could have fun together?

197 What is Sheldon's favorite pink fluid, "narrowly beating out Pepto-Bismol"?

198 Sheldon thinks there's not much wrong with him, though he can be faulted for being overly fond of what animal?

199 According to Howard, who was the last Jew who did sit-ups?

200 What's the name of the train store Sheldon says he will never set foot in again?

The Wolowitz Harmonic Phenomena

When Wolowitz was fourteen, he had a crush on Marcy Grossman and sang a song for her at the ninth-grade talent show.

Sung to the tune of "My Girl" by the Temptations:

Howard: Marcy Grossman is sunshine, on a cloudy day
When it's cold outside, Marcy Grossman is the month of May
I guess you'd say, what can make me feel this way
Marcy, Marcy, Marcy
Talkin' 'bout Marcy . . . Grossman.

Season 2, Episode 12: The Killer Robot Instability

After not calling Bernadette for week, Wolowitz impulsively proposed to Bernadette and she said no. To show her just how much she meant to him, he surprised her at the Cheesecake Factory and sang the following song, saying "I wanna dedicate this number to a great gal who I've done wrong."

Sung to the tune of the Four Tops' song "Bernadette":

Howard: Bernadette!
I am so sorry for trying to propose to you,
Bernadette! You found it creepy but that's just the kind of thing I do
Ahhhh! *(bridge)*
I know now it was too soon to talk of love,
it was just a crazy idea that came to me in my tub
But Bernadette, if you give me one more chance
(Sweet Bernadette!)
I'll get the hang of this thing they call romance
(Sweet Bernadette!)
I dream to once again kiss your lips
(Sweet Bernadette!)
Sincerely yours, Howard Wolowitz . . .

Season 3, Episode 9: The Vengeance Formulation

Howard plays the instrumental section, during which Penny said to Bernadette, "I am so sorry." Bernadette replied, "Are you kidding? That's the most romantic thing anyone's ever done for me."

On the anniversary of their first date, Wolowitz performed a song he wrote with help from the gang to Bernadette while she was in a hospital quarantine room. The song was written by musical comedy duo Garfunkel and Oates—Kate Micucci (who played Raj's girlfriend, Lucy, in Season 6 and one episode of Season 7) and Rikki Lindholme (who played Ramona Nowitzki in The Cooper-Nowitzki Theorem).

Howard: If I didn't have you
life would be blue
I'd be Doctor Who without the TARDIS

Sheldon: *(about Bernadette)* Is it me or does she not look so good?

Amy: Shh.

Howard: A candle without a wick
a Watson without a Crick
I'd be one of my outfits without a dick-ie
I'd be cheese without the mac
Jobs without the Wozniak
I'd be solving exponential equations that use bases not found on your calculator making it much harder to crack
I'd be an atom without a bomb
A dot without the com
And I'd probably still live with my mom

Everyone: *(singing)* And he'd probably still live with his mom.

Howard: Ever since I met you
you turned my world around
you supported all my dreams and all my hopes
you're like uranium-235 and I'm uranium-238
almost inseparable isotopes
I couldn't have imagined
how good my life would get
from the moment that I met you, Bernadette

Bernadette: *(tearing up)* Howie . . .

Howard: If I didn't have you
life would be dreary
I'd be like string theory without any string
I'd be binary code without a one
a cathode ray tube without an electron gun
I'd be *Firefly*, *Buffy* and *Avengers* without Joss Whedon
I'd speak a lot more Klingon
HEGHLU'MEH QAQ JAJVAM

Everyone: *(singing)* And he'd definitely still live with his mom.

Howard: Ever since I met you
you turned my world around
you're my best friend and my lover
we're like changing electric and magnetic fields
you can't have one without the other
I couldn't have imagined
how good my life would get
from the moment that I met you, Bernadette

Everyone: *(singing)* We couldn't have imagined how good our lives would get from the moment that we met you, Bernadette.

Season 7, Episode 6: The Romance Resonance

Season 6

1 What does Amy describe as looking like "something used by Tinkerbell's gynecologist"?

2 What punishment do Sheldon and Amy agree on after he catches her pretending to be sick?

3 When the girls discuss how comic books are such an important part of the guys' lives, who suggests they should read some?

4 When Howard is angry at Sheldon for reading the letter in his closet and telling everyone what was in it, Sheldon comes up with a plan to keep Howard forever in "a state of epistemic ambivalence." What's the plan?

5 Amy tells Penny that she once tried bleaching her upper lip when she was in high school—"I dozed off and woke up with second-degree chemical burns on my face." What cover story did she have to stop the other kids from making fun of her?

6 If Raj gives Cinnamon any more foie gras, what does his vet warn him will happen to her?

7 When Raj ends up spending the evening with Mrs. Wolowitz after Howard asks him to check in on her while he and Bernadette are in Las Vegas, what does he watch on TV with her?

8 *What does he have to drink?* **Master's**

9 When Leonard admits he was pushed into a life of science by his parents, what does he say he really wanted to be?

Sheldon: FYI, secret-keeping? Hate it. Hand-holding? Not a fan. Hammerhead shark? I love that thing. It's another fish with a tool on its head.

10 Of the three Valentine gifts bought on his behalf for Amy, Sheldon doesn't like two and keeps the third, a drawing of a brain cell, for himself. What does he give her instead?

11 What did Bernadette mistake for a towel when she took a shower at Howard's mother's house?

12 As dungeon master for Dungeons & Dragons, which three actors does Howard impersonate?

13 Raj wants to introduce Lucy to his friends. She is uncomfortable with meeting too many people at once, so who does she agree to meet first?

14 Bernadette describes Howard as "a sexy ___________ ___________."

15 When Howard and Bernadette go to Las Vegas, why does Howard ask Raj to come by the house and check on his mother on Saturday night?

16 When Penny and Leonard go on a Valentine's double date with Howard and Bernadette, who does Penny see at the restaurant?

Sheldon: Yes! That is the reason. My work is suffering because of all the laid I'm getting.

Kripke: You lucky bastard.

Sheldon: What can I say? Y'know, she enjoys my genitals, and I am giving them to her on a nightly basis.

17 When Howard looks at his old school locker, what does he remember Scott Kapinski did?

18 What startles Leonard so much he knocks the Giant Jenga tower over?

19 As a child, what "time-suck" activity did Sheldon have to cut out in order to hit his academic stride?

20 What did Sheldon's father mean when he said that "a woman is like an egg salad sandwich on a warm Texas day"?

21 Sheldon says that if science is to advance, people should have chips implanted in their heads that do what?

22 What Jewish prayer does Howard recite when his Soyuz capsule returns to Earth?

23 What does Leonard suggest would be a good name for a *Star Wars*–themed coffee shop?

24 At Disneyland, who does Penny dress as at the princess makeover?

25 *Who does Amy dress as?* **Master's**

26 After Amy's car has been towed from Howard's parking spot, how does Sheldon use Howard's spot?

27 What brings the guys' *Star Trek* photoshoot to a sudden end?

28 What happens after Raj makes a heartwarming speech to all the single people who come to the Valentine's party at the comic book store?

29 How does Lucy break up with Raj?

30 What is the final challenge at the guys-versus-girls game night?

31 When Raj finds a website making personalized action figures, why doesn't Sheldon want one?

32 When Howard gives Stuart a signed NASA portrait of himself, what does he write on it?

33 Bernadette's father is warming, very slightly, to Howard, and says he can call him by his first name. What is it?

34 What is Sheldon's primary fear if he gets tenure?

35 Penny invites the guys to a production of a play her acting group is putting on. Which American classic is it?

36 What online game does Sheldon invite Professor Stephen Hawking to play with him?

37 What costume does Leonard wear for Stuart's Halloween party?

38 What does Amy suggest she and Sheldon do on Valentine's Day that he says is "the most thoughtful gift that anyone's ever given me"?

39 What happens for the first time when Penny checks in on Raj after Lucy dumps him?

40 Which favorite sci-fi drama is Sheldon upset has been canceled after a Season 2 cliffhanger?

41 How much do Howard and Raj pay for their personalized action figures?

42 When Sheldon starts his online game partnership with Stephen Hawking, what nicknames does he come up with for the two of them?

43 *When Stephen Hawking doesn't like it, what alternative does Sheldon suggest instead?* **Master's**

44 What does Stuart call the coffee liqueur he's drinking from a Chewbacca mug?

45 When Raj and Lucy are on their first date at the coffee shop, what does Lucy do when she goes to the bathroom?

46 What would Lucy love to be able to tell the lady who cuts her hair that she doesn't like?

47 Penny compares having tenure, a job for life, with what?

Raj: Disneyland? I don't know. With all the crowds and the weird characters walking around—just reminds me too much of India.

48 Who comes up with the idea for a Christmas-themed Dungeons & Dragons quest?

49 Which special guest on Sheldon's show *Fun with Flags* does Amy criticize for being "wooden"?

50 Whose team is conducting Leonard's expedition to the North Sea?

51 "Let's see, this is about two thousand dollars. Um, I think she likes monkeys and the color gray." Sheldon is asking his assistant, Alex, to buy what?

52 How old is Arthur Jeffries when Sheldon meets him?

53 When Amy wants to pretend to still be sick, what does she put in her nose to make her seem congested?

54 *How does Sheldon figure out Amy isn't sick after all?* **Master's**

55 When they are trying to get tenure, where do Leonard and Kripke attempt to kiss up to Mrs. Davis, a member of the tenure committee?

56 What complaint has Sheldon made that means Sheldon's assistant, Alex, has to go and find "quieter pants"?

57 Bernadette is playing Dungeons & Dragons with the guys: "Come on, mama wants a pair of __________ __________."

58 ***What is Sheldon's "wormhole generator test"?*** **PhD**

59 What does Sheldon clean that he describes as "like cleaning out the entire building's belly button"?

60 The first time Penny got a bikini wax, what did her sister use to do it?

61 Arthur Jeffries tells Penny that it is possible to power a clock with a potato. When he feels unwell, what does she suggest he plug into the potato?

62 Howard is his middle school's most famous alum, if you don't count who?

63 Where do Raj and Lucy have their first kiss?

64 Howard makes a Valentine's gift for Bernadette: using the atomic force microscope in the materials science lab, he writes their initials in a heart one one-thousandth the sizc of a grain of sand. How does he describe it to Leonard?

65 *What is Leonard's response?* Master's

66 While driving to the Bakersfield Comic-Con, what popular *Star Trek* filming location do the guys decide to visit so they can take pictures in their costumes?

67 ***What will Leonard be testing while on his expedition to the North Sea?*** PhD

68 When Amy's sick, what does Sheldon suggest he rub on her chest?

69 According to Raj, Howard is "staring down on our planet like a tiny Jewish Greek god" named what?

70 When Sheldon and Kripke are working together on the grant proposal for a fusion reactor, what explanation does Kripke suggest for Sheldon's work being below par?

71 Raj tells Lucy that Cambridge totally looks like where?

72 Amy asks Bernadette about Howard's clothes: "Question—do you think your husband's fondness for turtlenecks is an expression of longing for his missing ____________?"

73 The guys' contracts oblige them to serve on a university committee encouraging women to pursue careers in the sciences. Whose old middle school do they visit to talk to girls about it?

74 What misleadingly named drink does Penny make for Sheldon when he visits her at the Cheesecake Factory to talk about his problems with Amy?

75 *Where does Sheldon get a bus to after getting drunk on the drink?* **Master's**

76 When Sheldon hasn't seen Raj for a few days, he wonders if he's still part of the group: "Should we be interviewing for a replacement? Perhaps, this time, we go ____________."

77 Who unsuccessfully tries to teach Howard to fish?

78 What grade does Penny get on her first paper for her history class at Pasadena Community College?

Raj: I think the next time I have to speak to a call center in India, I'm going to try using an American accent.

Howard: Why?

Raj: Because when I use my regular voice I feel like I'm making fun of them.

79 When the girls blow off work and head for Disneyland, Bernadette wants to go to the place that gives you a princess makeover—"hair, makeup, the works." In the car she calls first dibs on which princess?

80 What happens when Howard and Bernadette take Cinnamon to the park?

81 When we first see Howard on the International Space Station, who is he talking to on the phone?

82 What does Sheldon think is the best-tasting jelly?

83 *And the worst-tasting?* **Master's**

84 What does Amy do during security check-in that means the girls are not allowed to get on the plane to Las Vegas?

85 After telling Howard to return the expensive 3D printer, what does Bernadette do so he can't buy anything else?

86 Sheldon doesn't like the scent of Penny's new shampoo: "Coconut? What were you thinking? Are you a hula girl?" What scent does he want her to go back to?

87 While talking to Bernadette via videophone from the Space Station, why does Howard ask her to drop something so he can watch it fall?

88 When his assistant, Alex, hits on Leonard, Sheldon decides to bring Penny, Bernadette and Amy together to give him advice about this "delicate workplace situation." What does he call them?

89 *What has he had made specially for the occasion?* **Master's**

90 What does Amy do that makes Sheldon finally get the guts to tell her he doesn't want to live with her?

> **Leonard:** My dad was an anthropologist. The only father-son time he spent was with a two-thousand-year-old skeleton of an Etruscan boy. I hated that kid.

91 What's the title of the grade school project Alex finds among Sheldon's childhood papers, which he thinks could be his ticket to winning the Nobel Prize?

92 Why did Howard learn to sew when he was a little boy?

93 When Leonard and Penny spend a night together watching football, what phrase does Leonard paint on his stomach?

94 Sheldon is called to see Mrs. Davis in Human Resources after Alex has filed a complaint about him. What does she say he's done?

95 In Sheldon's office, why does Amy rub Sheldon's phone under her armpit, then lick his stapler?

96 When the guys are creating fight poses in their *Star Trek* costumes, why does Sheldon, as Mr. Data, keep the same pose throughout?

97 What does Bernadette say to a glum Howard dressed as Papa Smurf, which she thinks is the funniest thing she's ever said in her life?

98 When the guys give a talk to a group of schoolgirls about getting into science, why aren't the girls impressed that Howard is an astronaut?

Sheldon: All games are made up. They're not found in nature. You don't just dig in the ground and come across a rich vein of Rock 'Em Sock 'Em Robots.

99 After reading the *Thor* comic book, what do the girls argue about?

100 *In another comic book argument, how does Bernadette defend Red Hulk?* Master's

101 At the guys-versus-girls game night, what does Penny do to Sheldon after she has wrestled him to the floor and pinned him down?

102 *When he calls on Amy for help, what does she do?* Master's

103 What is Stuart's costume at his Halloween party?

104 Howard and Raj order personalized action figures, but what's wrong with them?

105 *Leonard says there must have been a shipping problem and the figures were intended for two other customers. Who?* Master's

106 During a game of Dungeons & Dragons, who casts a love spell on Sheldon and Amy?

107 Professor Proton—Arthur Jeffries in real life—tells the gang he's a real scientist. Where did he get his PhD?

108 To improve his chances of getting tenure, what does Raj send to committee member Mrs. Davis?

109 *What gift does Sheldon bring Mrs. Davis?* Master's

110 Raj tells the gang that on last night's video date with Lucy, he spent twenty minutes just staring into her eyes until he realized what?

111 What does Sheldon reveal to Leonard about the Harry Potter books that makes Leonard throw out the Roommate Agreement and announce he's going to live with Penny?

112 What name does Raj give the themed menu he prepares for Stuart's Halloween party?

113 When Sheldon is invited to Howard and Bernadette's dinner party, what does he bring with him?

114 *Why is Bernadette annoyed with Sheldon?*

115 When the other astronauts are mean to Howard, what does Bernadette suggest he say to them?

116 After Leonard tells Sheldon he talks in his sleep, Sheldon decides to record himself in case he says something that is "pure gold." What does he call the recording?

117 Why, according to Howard, will his mother not let Bernadette help with the dishes?

118 Why does Amy think Sheldon is so upset when his favorite TV series is canceled after a season-ending cliffhanger?

119 Why is Leonard alarmed to hear that the guy Penny is working on a project at college with is English?

120 How does Penny spoil *Harry Potter and the Half-Blood Prince* for Leonard?

121 When Howard's asleep on the International Space Station, one of his fellow astronauts goes for a space walk and glues a big-eyed rubber alien mask to the outside of his window. What does Howard say you need to google to find it?

122 Why are Howard and Bernadette having an argument when they arrive at the restaurant to meet Leonard and Penny for a Valentine's Day meal?

123 When Penny takes a history class at Pasadena Community College, Leonard sneaks a look at her first paper and thinks it's terrible. What does he do?

124 "I have a contractual obligation to provide Amy with conversation and casual physical contact, but nowhere is it specified that I can't outsource that to an Indian." So what has Sheldon asked Raj to do?

125 When he's preparing for Stuart's Halloween party, why does Raj ask Howard if he can borrow his bullwhip and fedora?

126 When Penny and Sheldon are playing Dizzy Long Division, which involves making themselves dizzy and then trying to do a problem on the whiteboard, how does Sheldon fare?

127 When Raj gets dumped by Lucy, he decides he'll be a monk and denounce all worldly pleasures except what?

128 What is Mrs. Davis in Human Resources first name?

129 Playing the game of Dungeons & Dragons, Sheldon knows another name for Svaty Vaclav. What is it?

130 Penny asks Sheldon if he'd ever have sex with Amy. What does he say?

131 When the guys play Christmas-themed Dungeons & Dragons, Raj is the first to "die" in the game, so what does he do?

132 Bernadette suggests that Howard and her father have a fishing weekend together, to get to know each other better. Where do they end up going?

133 What does Sheldon google in order to learn how to spark the interest of school children?

134 In the fight over Sheldon's parking spot, what does Howard do on Sheldon's spot on the couch?

135 Howard hears Bernadette in the bathroom, hacking, coughing and spitting up phlegm, and asks, "Did you get a ____________ while I was gone?"

136 Sheldon doesn't enjoy Amy's consoling hug: "I feel like I'm being strangled by a ____________ ____________."

137 When Penny, Bernadette and Amy go to the comic book store, what "female-friendly" book does Stuart recommend they read?

138 When the guys fail to connect with the girls they are supposed to be inspiring in the middle school, what does Sheldon suggest?

139 Sitting in the cinema with Amy, what does Sheldon find "preposterous"?

140 Why does Raj need Howard and Bernadette to watch his dog, Cinnamon, for the weekend?

141 When Bernadette tells Howard that his messy closet has to be sorted out, why does he want to show it to Sheldon?

142 What is the first thing Howard and Raj make with their new 3D printer?

143 *How long does it take to make?* **Master's**

144 What does Sheldon put in his egg salad to make it so tasty?

145 Raj tells Howard and Bernadette that Cinnamon has an egg-white frittata for breakfast, plus one of which two options?

146 *What two dinner options does Raj suggest they feed her?* **Master's**

147 If Raj had a "white name," what does he think it would be?

148 In the argument over the parking spot, Sheldon gets back at Howard by "breaking in" his new car. How does he do this?

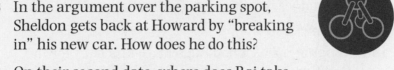

149 On their second date, where does Raj take Lucy for a picnic where they can talk via text?

150 After *Inspector Gadget* and *Teenage Mutant Ninja Turtles*, what is Sheldon's third-favorite cartoon theme song?

151 What was the name of the robot girlfriend Howard was working on before he met Bernadette?

152 When Penny goes to the comic book store with Bernadette and Amy, which comic book does she pick?

153 Amy tells Leonard that she's no longer associated with the addiction study she'd been working on: "You can get animals addicted to a harmful substance, you can dissect their brains, but you throw their own ____________ back at them and suddenly you're unprofessional."

154 Who helps Penny write the history paper she ultimately turns in for her history class?

155 Whose discovery inspires Sheldon to ask his mother to send him the journals and research papers he wrote as a child, to check whether he's already hit on an idea that could win him a Nobel Prize?

Sheldon: Penny, all my life I have been uncomfortable with the sort of physical contact that comes easily to others—hand-shaking, hugging, prostate exams. But I'm working on it. Y'know, just recently I had to put VapoRub on Amy's chest. A year ago that would have been unthinkable.

156 What gift does Sheldon plan to get for Professor Wu, one of the members of the tenure committee?

157 What does the photo booth that Raj gets for Stuart's Halloween party look like?

158 What happens when Raj tries to kiss Lucy for the first time?

159 What does Leonard tell Penny is a perfect TV show for the two of them to watch?

160 When Howard enters the LAX baggage area, why are members of the paparazzi yelling, "Howie!"?

161 What does Sheldon want Professor Proton, the host of his favorite science show from his childhood, to do?

162 How does Leonard try to warn Penny's college friend Ryan off her?

163 Sheldon disappears every day at work between 2:45 and 3:05 p.m., so Howard and Raj follow him to a university storage room. How do they find out what he does there?

164 What does Amy show Sheldon in the back of the car that makes him say: "I think you're high on paint fumes. And boy, that's a lot of Band-Aids"?

165 When the guys hear the girls arguing about comics in Sheldon and Leonard's apartment, what, according to Sheldon, is the only logical explanation?

166 What is Kripke's nickname for Mrs. Davis?

167 Why does Sheldon open and read the letter addressed to Howard that he finds in Howard's closet?

Sheldon: *(on Penny)* How can she remember all those lines, but as a waitress she can't remember "no tomato" on my hamburger?

168 According to Sheldon, what drink do you make for someone who's "angrier than ever and filled with despair"?

169 Sheldon hates Santa Claus because when he was five he didn't bring him what he asked for but instead brought him Lincoln Logs. What had Sheldon asked the mall Santa for?

170 What is the name of Professor Proton's puppet on his TV show?

171 Howard was five years old when he hid under the desk in his bedroom and ate some peanut M&Ms—with what result?

172 What does Howard always like to eat at the movies?

173 What is Mrs. Wolowitz doing when Howard shows up at her house after returning to Earth from space?

174 When Sheldon tells Penny, Bernadette and Amy that Alex hit on Leonard, what pseudonym does he use for Leonard?

175 *Who is Tondelaya della Ventimigilia?* **Master's**

176 When the university reassigns his unused parking spot to Leonard, what does Sheldon take from Howard in return?

177 How does Raj discover that Lucy thought he was "a little feminine" when they first met?

178 *How does he try to counteract this impression?* **Master's**

179 In the hospital, what favor does Arthur ask of Sheldon?

180 "You said you told her, but you never did!" Why is Bernadette angry on the phone with Howard on the International Space Station?

181 Who does Sheldon use gas money and the promise of free food to persuade to be his second guest on *Fun with Flags?*

182 How much does the 3D printer cost that Raj and Howard buy so they can make action figures that look exactly like them?

183 Howard puzzles over the number 43 written on the whiteboard in the university storage room wall: "Forty-three. What is forty-three? Besides my mom's ____________ ____________."

184 *What is the significance of the number 43?* **Master's**

185 Leonard realizes that he and Sheldon find it difficult to actually talk to each other, and suggests a way of managing a conversation: “We each get five minutes to talk about our problems. We’ll take turns. Each turn will consist of a statement and a helpful response from the friend.” What does he buy to facilitate this procedure?

186 How does Raj offend Amy on the girls’ night out?

187 After she’s walked out of the Christmas-themed Dungeons & Dragons game, Amy tells Sheldon that she wants a more intimate relationship with him. What does he do?

188 For Stuart’s Halloween party, Amy wants to go as Raggedy Ann with Sheldon as Andy. Sheldon favors C-3PO and R2-D2. What do they actually go as?

189 When Sheldon and Kripke have to work together on a grant proposal for a new fusion reactor, what does Sheldon think of Kripke’s work?

190 *Why is Kripke disappointed with Sheldon’s work?* **Master’s**

191 Sheldon is complaining to Penny about the female sex: “Someday scientists will discover that second X chromosome contains nothing but __________ __________ __________.”

192 How long will Leonard’s expedition to the North Sea last?

193 What did Sheldon have engraved on the gravy boat he gave to Howard and Bernadette as a wedding gift?

Howard: We were worried about you.

Raj: Oh, just because I’ve stopped going to work and answering my phone, you think something bad has happened. Maybe something good happened.

Bernadette: Did something good happen?

Raj: Of course not. Nothing good ever happens.

194 Leonard explains to Sheldon why he couldn't find Waldo in the guys-versus-girls *Where's Waldo?* game: "Because he's hard to find! If he was easy to find, the books would be called ____________ ____________."

195 What is Penny's costume for Stuart's Halloween party?

196 What does Howard do with the letter Sheldon finds in his closet?

197 When Amy parks her car in Howard's new parking spot, who has it towed?

198 When Amy demands one reason why Sheldon doesn't want to live with her, what does he say?

199 What is the name of the professor at the university who has died, opening up another tenured position?

200 What does Amy have in the handbag she accidentally hits Penny with?

Sheldon: I don't want another parking space, I want *my* parking space. It's perfect. It's a corner spot, cutting the risk of door-dings in half. It's a mere twenty-eight steps from the building entrance. The nearby tree provides shade on hot days and is also home to a delightful squirrel, which is fortuitous because most squirrels are real jerks.

The Little Time Machine on the Prairie Interpretation

Amy: I love *Little House*. It made me want to live on a farm so much I tried to milk my cat. That tangy bowl of Cheerios was not worth the stitches.

Season 7, Episode 4: The Raiders Minimization

Penny: *(reading)* "It was just past dawn on the prairie, and like every morning, Amelia prepared to do her chores. Except something about this morning felt different."

Bernadette: Why? Why did it feel different?!

Penny: *(reading)* "Maybe it was the first whisper of winter in the air. Or maybe it was the unconscious handsome man with porcelain skin and curious clothing she was about to discover lying in the field. A man who would open her mind to new possibilities . . . and her body to new feelings."

A beat, then—

Penny and Bernadette: Ahh!!!!

Penny: *(reading)* " 'Time travel, I don't understand,' said Amelia. Cooper stared at her. 'Which word don't you understand, time or travel?' "

Bernadette: Wow, even in your fantasies Sheldon's kind of exhausting.

Amy: He's like that in the beginning so she can change him. It's called good writing—and wishful thinking.

Penny: *(reading)* "It stung Amelia when he spoke to her this way. In her little one-room schoolhouse, she was always the smartest student, regularly besting the boys in her class. But this was no boy in front her—this was a man."

Bernadette: Here we go!

Penny: *(reading)* "Cooper told Amelia about all the strange and incredible things the future would hold, like computers and living past thirty. He asked her if she had any questions. All she longed to ask was if his heart was beating as fast as hers, but she was too afraid to hear the answer."

Bernadette: *(feeling for her)* Oh, Amelia.

Penny: *(reading)* "So instead she asked if, in the future, Montana ever became a state."

Amy: *(off Bernadette's look)* Hey, in the 1800s, that was considered flirting!

Penny: *(reading)* "With a heavy heart, Amelia stood before the newly repaired time machine. She regretted giving Cooper the part he needed."

Bernadette: Because she wanted him to give her the part she needed.

Amy: *(reading)* "As Cooper prepared to depart, tears filled Amelia's eyes. He took her hand in his and said, 'I can't stay, but I will never forget you.' He brushed his fingers against her cheek, then quickly stepped into the machine. 'Please don't go,' she whispered, but it was too late. The engine hummed to life."

Bernadette: *(caught up in it)* But they didn't even kiss.

Amy: *(reading)* "She turned away, wiping her eyes—she couldn't bear to watch her one chance at true love disappear forever. Then she felt a strong hand on her shoulder spin her around. It was Cooper."

Penny: Yes!

Amy: *(reading)* " 'What about the future?' asked Amelia. He looked deeply into her eyes and whispered, 'There is no future without you.' He pulled her in close. She began to tremble all over. She felt his warm breath—"

Leonard enters.

Leonard: You will not believe what Stephen Hawking just—

Penny and Bernadette: Get out! Not now!

A shocked Leonard quickly exits.

Season 8, Episode 14: The Troll Manifestation

Season 7

1 What is Mrs. Wolowitz's first name?

2 What does Raj say is his best feature on his online dating profile?

3 What kind of monkey is Amy experimenting on to measure its response to visual stimuli?

4 What do Sheldon and Mr. Rostenkowski bond over at Thanksgiving?

5 After Leonard has disproved Sheldon's discovery of a new element, Sheldon retracts his paper. What nickname does Kripke give him?

6 Why does Raj want to watch *House of a Thousand Corpses* with Howard before watching it with Emily?

7 What is Leonard doing when Penny calls him on the North Sea expedition, which makes her think he isn't missing her?

8 At the murder mystery dinner, where does Raj's future fact about Leonard say he will work as a professor?

9 Why doesn't Leonard tell Sheldon he is returning from the North Sea a couple of days early?

10 When Sheldon decides to keep the original welcome-home gift he got for Leonard, what does he end up getting for him?

11 *How much does he pay for this gift?* **Master's**

Amy: Scavenger hunts at Harvard were really tough. I always got stuck on the first challenge—trying to find someone to be on a team with me. I guess that story's more sad than funny.

12 What does germaphobic Sheldon fear he will catch from 3D glasses, which means he always brings his own to the movies?

13 With Sheldon away in Texas, the gang is imagining how their lives would be different if they hadn't met him. In Raj's fantasy, what would Leonard be like?

14 Leonard comes back from the funeral of Arthur Jeffries, aka Professor Proton, and starts to tell Sheldon about it. What does Sheldon do?

15 *At the funeral, Leonard and Penny talk about regret. What regret does Leonard share with her?* Master's

16 ***What kind of quartz does Bert from the geology department bring Amy?*** PhD

17 What gifts does Penny get Leonard for Valentine's Day?

18 How do Howard and Bernadette help Stuart out after the fire at the comic book store?

19 In Amy's made-up language, what does "tweepadock" mean?

20 ***Trying to book celebrities for his own version of Comic-Con, Sheldon tracks down James Earl Jones. How did he know where to find him?*** PhD

Sheldon: So we're just randomly choosing a restaurant without researching it online?

Penny: Yes.

Sheldon: Great. This is how Anything Can Happen Thursday turned into It Won't Stop Coming Out Friday.

21 Why does Amy say that she doesn't mind Sheldon's repetitive knocking?

22 Raj comes up with the idea to do a scavenger hunt, where the teams have to find a hidden gold coin. How do the teams pair up?

23 What day is Arthur Jeffries's funeral on?

24 What is the sex of Sheldon's sister's new baby?

25 What is the title of Beverly Hofstadter's book that Penny picks up as recommended reading for her psychology class?

26 Why is Raj upset that Howard crashed the jewelry-making girls' night?

27 Since Raj is so intimidated by talking to attractive girls, Howard suggests he go to the mall to practice by talking to regular people. Who goes with him?

28 Who does Penny turn to for career advice when she doesn't know whether or not to accept the role in the *Serial Ape-ist* sequel?

29 *Penny is getting paid less for the sequel than she was getting at the Cheesecake Factory. What does she tell Leonard that her agent is thinking of doing?* **Master's**

30 When the guys fail to buy tickets online for San Diego Comic-Con, Sheldon decides to start his own convention, with its own celebrities. Whose agent do we see him call?

31 Why does Eric, the enthusiast Sheldon meets on a train, collect disability and ride trains?

32 When the guys are imagining life without Sheldon, who would Penny have ended up with in Leonard's fantasy?

33 ***When Amy goes to work at CalTech, the study she's leading is investigating whether a deficiency in the monoamine oxidase enzyme leads to what characteristic in monkeys?***

34 In Raj's future fact during his murder mystery dinner, where will Penny be living as a famous actress?

35 After Arthur Jeffries dies, Sheldon watches an old clip from one of his Professor Proton shows. What animal is featured?

36 How did the fire start in the comic book store?

37 Sheldon tells Leonard to find the winning Skee-Ball tickets from when they went to the arcade three years ago. When Leonard looks through the junk box in the apartment, he finds a DVD they rented on Sheldon's card that he forgot to return, and what else?

38 Why does Sheldon agree to do yoga with Penny?

39 With the guys "acting like teenagers" over San Diego Comic-Con, what do the girls decide to do that's a bit more grown-up?

40 *Why does the girls' idea turn out to be "a bust"?* **Master's**

41 In an effort to be a better friend to Sheldon, Howard invites him to accompany him to NASA in Houston. Why is Howard going?

42 During the scavenger hunt, Howard and Amy realize they both like which musician?

43 How does Howard ensure he fails his physical exam when NASA asks him to go back up to the International Space Station?

44 When Amy won't drive Sheldon home from work, he falls asleep on the bus. Where does he wind up?

45 To celebrate the anniversary of his first date with Bernadette, what special thing does Howard want the gang to help him with?

46 After they fail to get tickets for San Diego Comic-Con, Leonard, Howard and Raj decide to buy scalped tickets from "our friendly neighborhood scalper." What happens when he turns up at the apartment?

47 ***What does Arthur Jeffries ask Leonard to help him work on a paper about?*** **PhD**

Sheldon: Hey, Los Angeles, I'm on a Ferris wheel with Darth Vader, and he's nicer than you think!!!

James Earl Jones: I am!!!

48 What does Sheldon bring to the scavenger hunt, which he thinks proves that "my brain is better than everybody's"?

49 What kind of cake do Bernadette and Amy make to try and cheer up Sheldon after Arthur Jeffries dies?

50 When Penny and Leonard tell Sheldon that Amy has changed him, how does he react?

51 What gift does Leonard get Penny for Valentine's Day and give to her in a jewelry box?

52 Why can't Leonard return the *Super Mario Bros.* DVD he finds in the junk box to the video store?

53 Where does Bert from the geology department ask Amy to go with him on a date?

54 *What philosopher, according to Sheldon, said it's funny when a human being behaves like an object?* **Master's**

55 When Sheldon is having difficulty picking a new field of study after leaving string theory, why does Leonard suggest officially reinstating Anything Can Happen Thursday?

56 On Sheldon and James Earl Jones's night out, whose doorbell does Jones ring before running away?

57 What does Arthur Jeffries hopefully ask Penny when he's in Leonard and Sheldon's apartment?

58 When a girl named Emily contacts Raj on the online dating site he's been using, what does he do?

59 When Leonard is away on the North Sea, Sheldon has a dream that he's talking to him on the phone. What happens to Leonard in the dream?

60 *Sheldon starts his phone call to Leonard with a complaint about which DVDs he put in the wrong boxes?* Master's

61 How does Stuart answer the question about his best feature on his online dating profile?

62 When Penny and Zack got married in Las Vegas, who performed the ceremony?

63 After Sheldon appears to have discovered a new element by accident, he's interviewed by Ira Flatow on his *Science Friday* radio show. What does Flatow say some people in the science community are calling Sheldon's discovery?

64 *What kind of new stable element does Sheldon appear to have figured out a way of synthesizing?* Master's

65 What drinking game do Leonard and the other members of the North Sea expedition play?

66 How much does Sheldon spend on a "pretty rare" Aquaman statue as a welcome-home gift for Leonard, which Sheldon winds up keeping for himself?

67 On *Star Wars* Day, Raj is preparing appropriate food and drink in the apartment: "Admiral Ackbar's Snack Bar is open for business." There's R2-Decaf on the menu, and what other drinks?

68 When Sheldon is out with James Earl Jones, what song do they sing at karaoke?

69 What movie inspires Sheldon's friends to imagine how life would be different if they'd never met him?

70 *Who brings over the movie to watch?* **Master's**

71 "Attention all shoppers—my business is open for business!" What has Raj just done?

72 When Raj spends the week with Howard and Bernadette, why do they get mad at him?

73 Why does Raj slip gold coins into everyone's pockets at the start of the scavenger hunt?

74 What is "Rice Sheldon"?

75 At jewelry-making girls' night, Howard says he was going to make a necklace for his mom, but she doesn't have a neck. What does she have?

76 ***How does Sheldon incorrectly read a table from* The Handbook of Chemistry and Physics *that leads to him accidentally discovering what seems to be a new element?*** **PhD**

77 What does Leonard do for Penny after her car breaks down and she can't afford to fix it?

78 Penny tells the gang that she's gotten a part on the TV show *NCIS*. What part does she play?

79 When Sheldon and Raj bump into Emily, the girl Raj met online, at the movies, why are they surprised?

> **Sheldon:** I saw my mommy with a naked man—and she was trying to be a mommy again!

80 What cheers up Wil Wheaton when he's feeling down?

81 On his second—uninvited—appearance on Ira Flatow's *Science Friday* radio show, Sheldon informs the host, "I don't just say smart things about science." What else does he say he does?

82 How does Bernadette accidentally destroy one of Howard's comic books?

83 *What was the comic book?* **Master's**

84 Where did Emily go to college?

85 Why does Sheldon ask Amy: "You're sure your mothlike personality won't be drawn to this blazing fire that is myself"?

86 When Raj and Emily are on a double date with Howard and Bernadette, where does Emily tell Bernadette she works as a dermatology resident?

87 *What does Emily like doing that made her decide to specialize in dermatology?* **Master's**

88 When Leonard finds an unreturned DVD in the junk box, what does Sheldon make him do until he returns it, because unresolved issues make him uncomfortable and he wants Leonard to know how he feels?

89 The final item on Amy and Sheldon's annual State of the Relationship Summit is Valentine's Day—"the worst for last." How does Amy want to them to celebrate it?

90 Sheldon has a lot to drink while he's trying to choose a new area of work. Who does he prank-call when he is drunk?

91 Who makes a video audition for the new *Star Wars* film?

Bernadette: Thanks for saving the day.
Raj: No problem. It wouldn't be Thanksgiving without an Indian providing the food.

92 What does the university make Sheldon do, which he refers to as "an outrage"?

93 What does the pizza delivery guy smell of that makes Sheldon say to him: "Oh, that's a rather earthy cologne. My uncle used to wear that"?

94 When the guys thought they were going to San Diego Comic-Con, they all prepared costumes for the same character. Which one?

95 *The same character, but in the guise of which four actors?* **Master's**

96 How does Amy say claw-foot bathtubs make Sheldon feel?

97 When Wil Wheaton stands up for Penny on set, what happens?

98 Sheldon explains to Raj and Howard that Leonard is trying "to walk a mile in my metaphorical shoes." What does Leonard have that means he couldn't walk in Sheldon's actual shoes?

99 Having tried and failed to ruin Amy's favorite book for her, what TV show does Sheldon try to ruin for Amy instead?

Sheldon: Leonard, prepare to be humbled and weep at the glory of my genius.

100 *What comic strip does he also try to ruin for her?* **Master's**

101 When Leonard and Penny are looking after Cinnamon, why do they have to take her to the vet?

102 Why is Sheldon so calm when Leonard tells him he wasn't able to return the *Super Mario Bros.* DVD that he found in the junk box?

103 According to Sheldon, his feud with Howard began ten years ago at their first meeting. What did Howard call him?

104 What reason does Penny give Leonard for asking him to marry her that makes him feel "like a bran muffin"?

105 In Howard and Bernadette's apartment, Howard and Raj have taken their shirts off. When Bernadette walks in on them, what are they doing?

106 When Raj introduces Howard to Emily, the girl he met online, Howard realizes that he had a disastrous date with her four years ago. What happened?

107 *What did Emily's friends call Howard afterward?* **Master's**

108 Why does Amy say Sheldon won't let her play music in the car?

109 When he can't go to San Diego Comic-Con and decides to start his own convention, Sheldon invites Wil Wheaton, who, he says, thinks it's a great idea. "He was just concerned that he wasn't a big enough celebrity to headline such an amazing event." What was his other excuse?

110 Item number 28 on Sheldon and Amy's State of the Relationship Summit is his pet name for her. He says she's impossible to please, as she's rejected all his options: Gollum, Flakey, Princess Corn Cob and which other one?

111 When Raj is wondering whether to date two women, how many does he say is his "sweet spot"?

112 Sheldon goes to Texas because his sister is having a baby. According to him, why does she want to have a home birth?

113 What has caused Howard to get "all bloated and moody and a giant pain in the ass"?

114 On her first day at CalTech, Amy has lunch in the cafeteria with a Swedish professor. What is his name?

115 *When Sheldon joins them and fails to amuse the professor with his attempts at humor, what alternative name does he suggest for him?* Master's

116 Who does Stuart think are the best couple he knows because they "make each other better" and together "make one awesome person"?

117 When Arthur Jeffries doesn't want to work with Sheldon, which beloved children's TV science personality does Sheldon bring to Leonard's laboratory?

118 When Sheldon has tracked down James Earl Jones for his convention, Jones suggests they "go have some fun"—"I got a *Lion King* residual check burning a hole in my pocket." Where do they go first?

119 *When they go to a fair, what kind of stuffed animal does Sheldon win?* **Master's**

120 When Sheldon questions his work in string theory, what advice does Penny give him?

121 What does Howard's new TV remote control look like?

122 Penny had what she thought was a "silly, fake" wedding to Zack three years ago in Las Vegas. When she learns it was actually for real, what does Leonard do?

123 *Why does Penny invite Zack to the Thanksgiving dinner at Mrs. Wolowitz's house?* **Master's**

124 Amy is good at Kinect Sports Season Two: Skiing because she has an extremely low center of gravity: "I'm like a ___________."

125 Bert from the geology department starts to tell a joke to Howard and Raj: "What do geologists and Bon Jovi have in common?" Howard jumps in with the punchline—what is it?

126 When Sheldon falls asleep on the bus home from work, what takeout dish does he bring home?

127 Why does Leonard tell Penny, "It's like seeing a unicorn and Bigfoot at the same time" about Sheldon?

Amy: I propose we spend a weekend at a bed-and-breakfast in Napa Valley.

Sheldon: I hate every word in that sentence, including "in," "at," "we," and "a."

128 Why doesn't Sheldon like reclaimed wood?

129 What does Raj make for Howard because he feels bad about sulking at the jewelry-making girls' night?

130 Who confesses to being the murderer at Raj's murder mystery dinner?

131 What name does Sheldon choose for his scavenger hunt team?

132 When Howard suggests Raj go to the mall to talk to regular people to help get over his fear of talking to girls, who does he end up talking to?

133 What's Stuart's last name?

134 Sheldon has had what he calls the perfect day with Leonard, going to the barbershop, the dentist and, to cap it off, where?

135 When Leonard reruns the tests on the new element Sheldon apparently discovered, he finds it doesn't exist. How come the Chinese research team found it?

136 After the death of Arthur Jeffries, Sheldon dreams about him. What does he admit to Arthur?

137 *How does Arthur respond?* **Master's**

138 Bernadette tells the gang that an animal virus has crossed the species barrier and can infect humans. What saying is there in the pharmaceutical business that means it's great news?

139 Penny is not impressed with her lines for the *Serial Ape-ist* sequel: "I don't think ___________ ___________ ever had to say, 'Must keep gorilla hands from killing again!' "

140 Raj tells Howard that India doesn't have Smokey the Bear, but it does have Mun-Mun the Mongoose. What does Mun-Mun teach children not to play with?

141 When Bernadette destroys Howard's comic book, Stuart finds a replacement at Capitol Comics. When he goes there with her, which of his regular customers does he see?

142 *What reason does the customer give Stuart for going there?* **Master's**

143 What traumatic event during their Houston trip causes Sheldon and Howard to put their feud aside?

144 *What does Sheldon say he'd have in his life if Howard wasn't his friend?* **Master's**

145 While Penny is returning her uniform to the Cheesecake Factory, Sheldon waits in her car, listening to guided meditation. When he's told to "picture yourself in a peaceful environment," where does he choose?

146 Emily describes to Raj the whereabouts of her tattoos: "One on my ___________, one not on my ___________ and one really not on my ___________."

147 Why does Emily like watching movies like *House of a Thousand Corpses?*

148 *When she tells Raj, who's holding the TV remote, what does he say?* **Master's**

149 During the murder mystery dinner, Raj writes up facts about the players in the future. What does he say Amy will win a Nobel Prize in?

150 ***Sheldon tries to use science to construct the perfect joke: "So a sandwich, a rabbi and __________ __________ walk into a bar . . ."*** PhD

151 *What sort of sandwich does Sheldon tell Leonard it is?* Master's

152 Leonard notices something when he goes to put the engagement ring on Penny's hand: "This would have been so much more romantic if you didn't have __________ __________ on your finger."

153 When Penny and Sheldon are both missing Leonard, Penny asks Sheldon to share something about himself he's never told anyone. What does he tell her?

154 Sheldon's world is falling apart. The university is forcing him to continue with string theory, and his favorite comic book store has burned down. What else is pushing him to the edge?

155 *What is Sheldon's solution?* Master's

156 Why do Leonard and Penny get in a fight during Raj's murder mystery dinner?

157 While filling out his online dating profile, what does Stuart put down as a one-word description of himself?

158 In his office, Sheldon is telling Howard about what he's working on and says it's great Howard's there, as he'd love an engineer's opinion. On what?

159 What does Sheldon do when Amy tells him she deserves romance on Valentine's Day?

> **Bernadette:** Well, Stuart's cute in his own way.
> **Stuart:** When I was a baby my mother called me her little possum.

160 Why is Mrs. Wolowitz upstairs for all of the Thanksgiving dinner at her house?

161 *Who's in charge of the cooking instead of Mrs. Wolowitz?* **Master's**

162 Bernadette wrote a message on what she thought was a retirement card for a colleague: "Hey, Vivian! You deserve this. And at least with you gone no one will steal my yogurt out of the fridge. LOL. ☺ P.S. Good luck wherever you wind up." What kind of card was it really?

163 When Leonard tells Sheldon that he's been working on string theory for years and has gotten nowhere near proving it, how does Sheldon defend himself?

164 *What does Kripke call himself rather than a string theorist?* **Master's**

165 Sheldon says that if he develops a unified theory of comedy, he'll be able to elicit laughter from anybody except whom?

166 When Sheldon's away in Texas, Raj sits on his spot despite Leonard warning him that Sheldon has a "very sensitive ____________".

167 What did Sheldon once do that made Leonard need to know his password so he could track his phone and his whereabouts?

168 After Amy ruins *Raiders of the Lost Ark* for Sheldon, he tries and fails to ruin what favorite book of hers?

169 When Leonard can't return the *Super Mario Bros.* DVD he found in the junk box, he tries to reimburse the owner of the video store instead. Why can't he?

170 What had Leonard promised to bring Sheldon back from the North Sea if he took care of Penny while he's away?

> **Sheldon:** I just vomited on a lot of clowns.

171 On Anything Can Happen Thursday, Penny takes Sheldon to a psychic. According to Amy, what does he think psychics are?

172 *What does the psychic tell Sheldon?* Master's

173 Who "dies" at the start of Raj's murder mystery dinner?

174 Penny confides to Sheldon that when she first moved to Los Angeles, she did a topless scene in a low-budget horror movie called *Serial Ape-ist*. How does Sheldon already know?

175 How is Leonard able to get Penny an audition for the new *Star Wars* movie?

$E=mc^2$

176 What is Wil Wheaton dressed as in his scene in the *Serial Ape-ist* sequel?

177 On the set of the *Serial Ape-ist* sequel, why does the director tell Penny she should be happy that the movie is garbage?

178 *When Leonard stands up for Penny, the director snaps at him, and Penny snaps back. With what result?* Master's

179 Who tells Leonard's mother that he and Penny have gotten engaged?

Amy: The last time I got dressed up and had tea was when I was five. It was me, my teddy bear, Raggedy Ann and my hamster.

Bernadette: That's cute.

Amy: It was, until my hamster ate all her babies. It got less cute really fast.

180 Sheldon was so well behaved when Howard took him to NASA that Howard bought him a bobblehead figure of which astronaut?

181 Where do Sheldon and James Earl Jones finish their evening of fun?

182 Where does Sheldon see Chinese food containers in Penny's apartment that make him think she is cheating on Leonard?

183 When he was six, Leonard walked in on his parents when they were naked. What does his mother remind Leonard she was doing to his father?

184 What does Sheldon tell Penny is the only car game Leonard wants to play with him?

185 What piece of exercise equipment does Howard get for his mother?

186 *What happens when he and Raj are bringing it up the stairs in her house?* **Master's**

187 Having wound up in the hospital quarantine room, Bernadette has some advice to give: "Well, let's just say the next time you have to move a dozen vials of ____________ virus to the fridge, make two trips."

188 What "glaring story problem" does Amy point out in *Raiders of the Lost Ark*?

189 Who comes up with the idea of making jewelry on girls' night?

190 How does Sheldon try to prevent Leonard putting a dining table in the apartment?

191 What early Christmas present does Leonard give to Amy?

192 When Penny asks Leonard to marry her, what does he reply?

193 When they're thinking about Anything Can Happen Thursday, Sheldon says, "What can we do that's fun?" Leonard says, "What can we do that's different?" What does Penny say?

194 Why does Penny quit her job at the Cheesecake Factory?

195 ***What is the name of the institute in China that seems to endorse Sheldon's new synthesis?*** PhD

196 What happens when Sheldon and Howard drop in to see Sheldon's mother on their Houston trip?

197 After Arthur Jeffries dies, which *Star Wars* character does he appear as in Sheldon's dream?

198 *In the second part of Sheldon's dream, what* Star Wars *location do he and Arthur have a discussion in?* Master's

199 What's the title of the *Serial Ape-ist* sequel?

200 During Raj's murder mystery dinner, what's special about the receipt for a cup of coffee that Bernadette finds?

The Carol Ann Susi/ Mrs. Wolowitz Appreciation

Howard Wolowitz and his mother had an "interesting relationship." Lots of yelling, lots of nagging, but one can't deny lots of love.

According to Wolowitz, his mother's famous tur-briska-fil is "a turkey stuffed with a brisket stuffed with gelfite fish. It's not as good as it sounds."

Season 3, Episode 4: The Pirate Solution

When Wolowitz was eleven, his mother got him an ALF doll when his father left them.

Season 3, Episode 17: The Precious Fragmentation

Howard and Mrs. Wolowitz's Sabbath tradition was to light the candles and watch *Wheel of Fortune*.

Season 4, Episode 19: The Zarnecki Incursion

Mrs. Wolowitz: *(offscreen)* You should have seen me when I was young, Sheldon. The fellas used to line up and bring me boxes of candy. *(crying)* Why did I eat it all?!

Season 5, Episode 21: The Hawking Excitation

We got our first partial glimpse of Mrs. Wolowitz when Wolowitz and Bernadette got married on the roof of Leonard, Sheldon and Penny's building with an overhead shot showed the top of her head.

Season 5, Episode 24: The Countdown Reflection

Mrs. Wolowitz: *(on the phone, voiceover)* Wives don't take boys from their mothers!

Howard: They do! That's why we marry them!

Season 6, Episode 1: The Date Night Variable

We got our second (and third) partial glimpse of Mrs. Wolowitz when Raj was at the dining room table and Mrs. Wolowitz asked him if he was ready for dessert. In the kitchen, we see a large woman walk by wearing a muumuu. At the end of the episode, Koothrappali tried to sneak out of her house through the window and two big hands with muumuu sleeves pulled him back in.

Season 6, Episode 15: The Spoiler Alert Segmentation

Carol Ann Susi died on November 11, 2014. Mrs. Wolowitz died in The Comic Book Store Regeneration (Season 8, Episode 15). In this episode, we learned that Mrs. Wolowitz gave Stuart some furniture from her den for him to put in his newly refurbished comic book store. She also gave him money to help him reopen it.

The following is from the final scene of the episode:

Stuart: I still can't believe she's gone. I mean, that woman took me in. If it wasn't for her, I would have been homeless.

Raj: Yeah, Mrs. Wolowitz was pretty special. When I first came to America, Howard was my only friend, and she made me feel so welcome in her home. Which says a lot, because those first few years she thought I was the gardener.

Penny: Whenever I saw her, she'd say I was too skinny and try to feed me.

Amy: She did that to me, too.

Penny: Don't take this away from me.

Sheldon: I didn't care for her yelling, but now that I'm not going to hear it again, I'm sad.

Leonard: *(gently)* If you want, I can yell at you later.

Sheldon: It won't be as good.

Leonard: *(to everyone)* All right, let's have a toast.

Leonard raises his glass, and they all follow.

Leonard: To Mrs. Wolowitz. A loving mother . . . to all of us. We'll miss you.*

** And so will everyone involved with the making of the show, Carol Ann's family, friends and anyone who ever came into contact with her. She was a remarkable human being. Every time I saw her on set, I'd ask her how she was doing and she'd always say the same thing: "Groovy."*

When the power went out in The Leftover Thermalization (Season 8, Episode 18), Wolowitz took all the remaining food from Mrs. Wolowitz's refrigerator and threw a dinner party for the whole gang so it'd be like she was feeding them all one last time.

Howard: Hey, guys. I just want everyone to know, tonight's not a sad occasion.

Bernadette: Yeah, we want to have the kind of dinner we've all had here so many times.

Howard: Good food, good friends, and sometime around midnight, heartburn that makes you pray for death.

At the end of Season 8, Wolowitz and Bernadette decided to move into Mrs. Wolowitz's house. They slowly began bringing in all their things from their apartment. I can't wait to see what the future holds for them!

Season 8

1 Who did Leonard take to his school prom?

2 Why does Sheldon decide to stop making his internet show *Fun with Flags*?

3 During the love experiment, when asked if he could wake up tomorrow having gained one quality or ability, what does Sheldon choose?

4 Where do Sheldon and Raj go to re-create the conditions of a salt mine?

5 When Mrs. Wolowitz dies, what comforting words does Sheldon offer Howard?

6 Why do Beverly Hofstadter and Mary Cooper clash?

Leonard: Thank you for wearing your flats.
Penny: Thank you for wearing your heels.

7 When Sheldon tries to run into Skywalker Ranch, the security guard calls for "Code A-A 23." What is the significance of this to *Star Wars*?

8 Why did Sheldon never leave a train station on his "railroad journey of healing" across the country?

9 When Sheldon is hallucinating on the bus, what does he call the man next to him?

10 In order for Sheldon to become a junior professor, what does the university require him to do?

11 In Sheldon and Amy's blanket fort, which blanket is a load-bearing blanket?

12 Why does Dr. Koothrappali come to America to visit his son?

13 *What does his father's visit mean Raj is too busy to do?* Master's

14 Who does Mrs. Wolowitz go to visit in Florida?

15 ***What field of physics does Sheldon pick after leaving string theory?*** PhD

16 While waiting in the shop for Penny and Amy to try on dresses, what do Leonard and Sheldon talk about that makes them both start crying?

17 When they are driving to Las Vegas to get married, what secret does Leonard tell Penny?

18 What does Sheldon call the new clothing size he's made up between medium and large?

19 What is Sheldon's P. R. K.?

20 ***What does Sheldon tell Leonard is the ranking of relationships in their social circle?*** PhD

21 Which journal publishes an article about the paper that Leonard and Sheldon wrote, but only mentions Sheldon?

22 What game does Kripke play during the final episode of *Sheldon Cooper Presents: Fun with Flags*?

23 How many fava beans can Amy stick in her mouth?

24 What is the theme of Amy's Christmas dinner?

25 Who teaches Beverly that there's more than one way to raise a child?

26 What is the "escape room" that Emily invites Raj, Leonard and Amy to?

27 *What danger do they find in the escape room?* **Master's**

28 Why does Stephen Hawking say he has to bring his Skype conversation with Sheldon and Leonard to an end?

29 In Sheldon's three-step business plan for opening up a comic book store, step one is "open comic book store." What rumor does he plan to start as step two?

30 *What is step three?*

31 When Penny and Amy complain that they always have to do what the guys want to do, who suggests they should all go dress shopping?

32 Who bought the toy helicopter that Sheldon and Howard try to fix?

33 Before the prom do-over, Penny asks Sheldon if he is planning on engaging in any post-prom __________ __________ with Amy.

34 How many Mississippis did the girl in the pet store touch Dr. Lorvis's arm for so he bought a $2,000 iguana habitat?

35 What piece of furniture does Raj break while he's snooping around Emily's apartment?

36 What does Penny buy for Leonard after he wasn't mentioned in the article about his and Sheldon's paper?

37 Before Sheldon and Penny take the falling-in-love test, he asks her that if it works, would she drive him to which convention in Lake Geneva, Wisconsin?

38 What happens to Leonard when he goes to the petting zoo?

39 What's the name of the Barry Manilow cover band that Amy wants to see in Vegas?

40 Who invents the game Emily or Cinnamon?

Penny: If I do well in sales, I could end up making a lot more money than you.

Leonard: Not a problem. I grew up with a mother who emasculated my father financially and in every other aspect of his life. So really, it's what I think love looks like.

41 What is on the pen Leonard, Howard and Raj find in Professor Abbott's office?

42 ***Why do Sheldon and Raj want to re-create the conditions of a salt mine to see if they can handle it?*** PhD

43 How did Dr. Lorvis manage to get an actual phaser from the original *Star Trek* TV show?

44 When Howard used to eat out with his mother, what did she tell him to fill his pockets with while nobody was looking?

45 During the love experiment, who does Sheldon say he'd have dinner with if he had the choice of anyone in the world?

46 *Who does Penny say she wants to have dinner with?* Master's

47 What does Sheldon do to get around the fact that, according to the Relationship Agreement, he's not allowed to be moody on date night?

48 After the Ping-Pong battle to decide its fate, what happens to Howard's TARDIS?

49 Even though they have agreed not to exchange Christmas gifts, why does Sheldon want to get one for Amy?

50 *What does he get for her?* Master's

51 Why did Howard's mother go to his prom?

> **Howard:** Which Archimedean solid has twenty regular triangular faces, thirty square faces, twelve pentagonal faces, sixty vertices and one hundred twenty edges?
>
> **Leonard, Sheldon and Raj:** *(in unison)* The Rhombicosidodecahedron!

52 How does Penny think her new job in pharmaceutical sales changes the balance of her relationship with Leonard?

53 When the power goes out in Mrs. Wolowitz's house, what does Howard decide to do with the last of her food that's defrosting in the freezer?

54 What is the first name of Dr. Lorvis, the doctor who brings flowers to Penny after she made a sales call at his office?

55 Who did Howard once go to couples therapy with?

56 While waiting at the airport lost luggage office, what regret does Howard share with Bernadette?

57 Who are Dr. Angus McDougal of the University of Edinburgh and Dr. Dimitri Plancovik of Moscow University?

58 How many episodes of *Fun with Flags* has Sheldon made?

59 *Why was one episode of* Fun with Flags *lost?* **Master's**

60 When Sheldon talks about going down a salt mine, why is Penny skeptical?

Sheldon: Everything is quantifiable. That French fry? A seven. Spider-Man? A nine. The number nine—oddly only a four.

61 What does Howard want to take a picture of him and Bernadette holding and post on Instagram?

62 Where is Leonard invited to give a commencement speech?

63 Who gives Stuart money to help him reopen the comic book store?

64 When the guys are having a science retreat weekend in order to focus on coming up with new science ideas, what two movies do they get distracted by and end up watching?

65 What is the title of the final episode of Sheldon's online show *Fun with Flags*?

66 How long do Sheldon and Raj stay underground when they are seeing if they can handle conditions in a mine?

67 What username does Stephen Hawking use to leave negative comments on the preprint server where Leonard and Sheldon post their joint paper on Leonard's theory?

68 During her sales call, how long had Penny touched Dr. Lorvis's arm for?

69 Sheldon likes visiting the ER at Huntington Hospital: "Even if it turns out you don't have Dengue fever, they still let you take a ____________."

70 What score out of ten did Sheldon and Amy get when they took the Relationship Closeness Inventory developed by Berscheid, Snyder and Omoto?

71 What application does Sheldon submit without telling Amy about it first?

72 According to Sheldon: "A good joke not only entertains, it ____________."

73 Why is Amy bad at Ping-Pong but good at serving?

74 Why does Sheldon decide to continue making *Fun with Flags* after he has filmed the last one?

75 Why is the article about the fifty sexiest female scientists in California, which Bernadette was going to appear in, canceled?

76 What is Bernadette's nickname for Sheldon?

77 At Penny's job interview at Bernadette's company, what do she and her interviewer bond over?

78 Why does Sheldon think Leonard and Penny are jealous of his relationship with Amy?

79 What kind of cap and gown does Penny buy for Leonard for his commencement speech?

80 What was the first name of the late Professor Abbott, whose office Leonard, Howard and Raj have to clean out?

81 Why is Penny picking up a bad vibe from Raj's girlfriend, Emily, when she first meets her?

82 How does Howard decide to throw the first pitch at the baseball game "by science"?

83 *How does the crowd react when the ball is pitched this way?* Master's

84 During the fifth anniversary of their first date, what TV program does Sheldon ask Amy if he should start watching?

85 ***When Leonard and Raj are in a restaurant picking up food for Stuart's reopening party, they see a man resembling Nathan Fillion. What line from* Firefly *does Raj ask him to recite to prove his identity?*** PhD

86 How many proms did Penny go to?

87 Sheldon is "a bit of an ___________ seal buff."

88 What does Leonard tell Sheldon is the one reason why he doesn't live with Penny?

Bernadette: Oh my God, I thought everybody liked me, but I'm just a monster.

Dan: But a cute one, like that eyeball guy in *Monsters, Inc.*

89 When Raj is chosen to work on a message to be sent into space for aliens to encounter, who does he ask to work with him?

90 How does a pigeon manage to fly into the CalTech clean room when Leonard and Howard are working there?

91 *Why does Howard give it CPR?* Master's

92 When Howard, Raj and Stuart are cleaning the kitchen, what song do they sing?

93 Before he goes to the hospital to have surgery on his deviated septum, where has Leonard told Sheldon he's going?

94 Raj can't believe Howard isn't curious about his father: "What if he's in prison? What if he's a spy?" What's his third suggestion?

95 How does Sheldon celebrate the return of *Fun with Flags*?

96 When Sheldon is upset that Amy is helping Kripke with his research, what is Penny's advice for him?

97 Why hasn't Sheldon told Leonard that Amy has taught him to drive?

98 What is Howard's favorite fruit?

99 Why does Howard sign up for Sheldon's class at the university?

100 Why does Sheldon run to his room when Amy says he looks handsome for their prom do-over?

101 What is Bernadette's middle name?

102 Who had given Professor Abbott the bottle of champagne with the instruction "to be opened upon your first great discovery"?

103 *How long ago were the bottle of champagne and note given to Professor Abbott?* **Master's**

104 Why is Amy appalled that Bernadette has been asked to be a part of a magazine article about the fifty sexiest female scientists in California?

105 Sheldon is trying to optimize his work environment—what does he ask Leonard and Penny to help him test?

106 *To round off his optimizing efforts, Sheldon has an "inspirational cat poster improved with the reassuring face" of which "physics renegade"?* **Master's**

107 Why do Howard and Bernadette have to go to the airport lost luggage office upon returning to Los Angeles from Florida?

108 Practicing for his first baseball pitch in the university gym, what does Howard say to Bernadette when he sees just how long the 60-foot pitch is?

109 Who does Stuart bring to the prom do-over?

110 Why does Raj get the windows of his car untinted?

111 What does it say on the frame that Penny puts the picture of her and Leonard in front of the car he bought her in?

112 *What color is the frame?* **Master's**

113 Why does Sheldon report Howard to Human Resources?

114 Despite having agreed not to exchange presents, what does Amy give Sheldon for Christmas?

115 According to Howard, who was the only girl Raj ever broke up with?

116 What has Mrs. Wolowitz given Stuart to put in his refurbished comic book store?

117 *Who helps Stuart put it there?* **Master's**

118 When Sheldon isn't invited to a symposium at the former home of Richard Feynman, what does he say it reminds him of from his childhood?

119 What analogy does Penny use to trick Sheldon into giving her advice about her Kevin Smith audition?

120 Six weeks after Sheldon ran away on his "railroad journey of healing" across the country, where does he call Leonard from to say he's been robbed on a train? $E=mc^2$

Raj: Look, the problem with commencement speeches is that they're boring. Ooh, do you own a T-shirt cannon?

Howard: Why would he own a T-shirt cannon?

Raj: I don't know, why do I own one?

121 When Leonard shares his idea that "our universe may be the surface of a multidimensional supercooled liquid," what is on the reward sticker Sheldon gives him?

122 *What does Sheldon do with Leonard's idea?*

123 What was Professor Abbott recording in the books the guys find in his office?

124 After Amy essentially breaks up with him, whose statue does Sheldon turn to for advice?

125 *What does Sheldon ask the statue?* Master's

126 What reason do Sheldon and Amy give Leonard and Penny for deciding to buy a turtle together?

127 In her *Little House on the Prairie* fan fiction, what names does Amy use instead of Amy and Sheldon?

128 Why does Dr. Lorvis lock the guys in his basement?

129 When Howard meets his half brother, he wants him to leave the house. What makes him change his mind?

130 What did Sheldon have engraved on the urn he bought for Leonard in case he died having surgery on his deviated septum?

131 *What did Sheldon have engraved on the urn he bought for himself?* Master's

Howard: There's two kinds of people in this world: those who call tech support, and those who make fun of the people who call tech support.

Bernadette: I call tech support all the time.

Sheldon, Howard and Raj: Ha-ha! You call tech support! What a baby!

132 What advice does Mike Massimino give Howard when he is invited to throw the first pitch at a baseball game?

133 What is Stuart's middle name?

134 During the experiment to see if he and Penny can fall in love, what does Sheldon say he'll regret not sharing if he dies that evening?

135 During Wil Wheaton's podcast, what movie does Kevin Smith say that Penny should come over and read a part for?

136 Where does Bernadette come from?

137 When Sheldon realizes just how much Leonard wants to live with Penny, what does he propose?

138 Why does Sheldon think Guiseppe is a good name for the turtle he and Amy see in the pet store?

139 *What had been Sheldon's first idea for the turtle's name?* **Master's**

140 What do Leonard and Penny wind up doing with the money she gets when she sells the car Leonard bought for her?

Beverly: You've been on and off with this woman for seven years and engaged for one year. One has to wonder if there's a problem. Are you having satisfactory intercourse?

Leonard: Yes, Mother.

Beverly: Only satisfactory, I see.

141 What animal do Mrs. Wolowitz and Stuart like so much they have it on their matching pajamas?

142 How does Stuart know that a lot more women are reading comic books now?

143 When Penny practices her pharmaceutical sales technique with Raj's girlfriend, Emily, what drug does she try to pitch?

144 *What side effect does Penny say the drug has?* Master's

145 What TV show "almost wrecked" Sheldon?

146 Which baseball team asks Howard to throw out the first pitch at a game?

147 *Why do they ask Howard?* Master's

148 ***Sheldon thinks that "Play that Funky Music" by White Cherry is the musical equivalent of whose paradox?*** PhD

149 Who had a bad prom date and so has the idea to have a prom do-over?

150 After Bernadette makes fun of Penny's boss and his grandson at the company picnic for losing the three-legged race, what does the grandson call her?

151 What beauty pagent does Penny discover online that Bernadette took part in?

152 Why does Penny have to arrange for Leonard to give his commencement speech via Skype?

153 After Amy admits that she always does what Penny wants to do, Penny tells her to name an activity and they'll do it. What does Amy suggest?

154 What's the name of Howard's half brother, who turns up at his house?

155 *What does he study, and where is he studying it?* **Master's**

156 What's the name of the man who interviews Penny for a pharmaceutical sales job at Bernadette's company?

157 Why does Penny take her engagement ring off at work?

158 In the Ping-Pong battle to determine the fate of Howard's TARDIS, who are the final two players?

159 *How long does the final, deciding match last?* **Master's**

160 Why can't Penny hang out with Bernadette and Amy all the time in Las Vegas?

161 When Amy secretly conducts an experiment on Penny to test her intelligence against chimpanzees, what is the name of the chimp who solves the puzzle faster than Penny?

162 *What drug has the chimp been given?* Master's

163 What is Raj's girlfriend, Emily's, last name?

164 ***Which four forts are Sheldon's contenders for the "first annual best fort ever contest"?*** PhD

165 Sheldon says he can't help Penny decide whether to audition for Kevin Smith's movie because he is turning over a new leaf. What personality trait has Raj pointed out to him that he wants to change?

166 What two-person costume did Leonard and Sheldon wear one year to Comic-Con?

167 Penny's client Dr. Lorvis has a close relationship with many famous people: "I don't like to brag, but I'm kind of the doctor to the stars' ____________ ____________."

168 Leonard and Sheldon meet another guy in the detaining room at Skywalker Ranch. What has he been caught doing in the sculpture gallery?

169 According to Howard, dinners at his mother's house have always involved good food, good friends and, after midnight, what?

Sheldon: Nice to meet you, Mr. Insightful.
Leonard: The pleasure is mine, Mr. Innovative.

170 What's the answer to Sheldon's science joke: "How many Edisons does it take to screw in a lightbulb?"

171 When Raj's father cuts off his allowance, how does Raj manage to persuade his mother to give him money instead?

172 ***When Sheldon rewrites popular children's songs to get children interested in the hard sciences, which scientist does he sing about in his rendition of "Bingo"?***

PhD

173 When a young Sheldon told his mother he was getting "yellowcake from Chad," she thought he was talking about Twinkies from one of his friends. What did he actually try to buy?

174 What does Leonard want to do with the money Penny gets when she sells the car he bought her?

175 When Sheldon has been robbed and needs picking up from the train station, why doesn't he want to call Amy?

176 According to Sheldon, what's the correct animal to cross with a human to make an interspecies supersoldier?

177 What do Leonard, Howard and Raj decide to do with the bottle of champagne they find in Professor Abbott's office?

178 What kind of diamond does Leonard get for Penny's engagement ring?

179 What two couples' nicknames does Raj come up with for him and Emily?

180 What is the last thing Howard says to his mother before she goes to Florida?

181 What is the name of the first game Amy wants to play during her Christmas dinner?

182 *What is the second game Amy wants to play?*

183 What is Amy referring to when she asks Bernadette: "How big are those Hadron Colliders"?

184 Where does Emily suggest having sex that makes Raj think she has a bit of a dark side?

185 ***What is the subject of the paper that Amy helps Kripke with?*** PhD

186 Which university invites Sheldon and Leonard to give a talk about their paper?

187 What happened to Howard on the day of tryouts that meant he never played Little League baseball as a kid?

188 When Leonard and Sheldon finally Skype with Stephen Hawking, what does he say about their paper?

189 *Why had he posted negative comments about it online?* Master's

190 During their science retreat, what punishment do the guys devise for when someone takes them off topic?

191 Why didn't Sheldon go to his prom?

192 When Howard and Bernadette are on the verge of asking Stuart to move out of the house, what does his father call to say?

193 When the university insists that Sheldon teach a class, why does no one sign up for it?

194 What did Amy do on her prom night?

195 When the doctor shoved a camera up into Leonard's sinuses, what does Penny say it looked like?

196 ***What does Raj think of when he's scared?*** PhD

197 When he is struggling with his new field of work, why does Sheldon ask Leonard, Howard and Raj to make his life miserable?

198 In what sport was Raj a three-time champion at school?

199 *What was the name of Raj's school?* Master's

200 What character does Emily have a tattoo of?

> **Sheldon:** Irony's not really my strong suit. But I have been getting better with sarcasm if you want to give that a try.
>
> **Amy:** Oh, I would love to.
>
> **Sheldon:** Whenever you're ready.

The Emily or Cinnamon Conjecture

Wolowitz created a game where he said a line and the contestant had to determine if Koothrappali said it to Emily or Cinammon.

Season 8, Episode 13: The Anxiety Optimization

1. I want you to know, the bed feels so lonely when you're not in it.
2. Check it out, I got us matching sweaters!
3. You're so lucky, you have the shiniest hair.
4. It's just so perfect that we're both Libras.
5. How can such a little girl eat such a big steak?

The following questions were posted on the official *The Big Bang Theory* web page on cbs.com:

6. Don't be scared, baby, it's only thunder.
7. Looks like I found your tickle spot.
8. I had the craziest dream about you last night.
9. I'd give you a bite, but you know you're not supposed to have chocolate.
10. Of course I want your kisses, but let me brush my teeth first.

ANSWERS

1 Cinnamon
2 Cinnamon
3 Both of them
4 Cinnamon
5 The scene ended on the line, so the answer was never revealed. But if I had to guess, I'd say Cinnamon.
6 Cinnamon
7 Emily
8 Cinnamon
9 Cinnamon
10 Emily

The Exposition Verification

Season 1

1 the Stevenson Award (Episode 12: The Jerusalem Duality)

2 aerospace (Episode 12: The Jerusalem Duality)

3 cornhusker (Episode 11: The Pancake Batter Anomaly)

4 "Um, I don't know, a psychiatrist" (Episode 5: The Hamburger Postulate)

5 autographed copy of the Feynman Lectures (Episode 16: The Peanut Reaction)

6 "None shall pass." (Episode 14: The Nerdvana Annihilation)

7 the third-floor janitor, the lady from the lunchroom, and "my Spanish is not good—either her son or her butcher" (Episode 13: The Bat Jar Conjecture)

8 rocket scientist (Episode 15: The Pork Chop Indeterminacy)

9 gynecologist (Episode 8: The Grasshopper Experiment)

10 his parents don't believe in it—"My parents focused on celebrating accomplishments, and being expelled from a birth canal was not considered one of them." (Episode 16: The Peanut Reaction)

11 peanuts (Episode 2: The Big Bran Hypothesis)

12 Kyle Bernstein's Bar Mitzvah party (Episode 6: The Middle Earth Paradigm)

13 Howard (Episode 9: The Cooper-Hofstadter Polarization)

14 *Physicists Gone Wild*! (Episode 9: The Cooper-Hofstadter Polarization)

15 he eats a granola bar with peanuts in it (Episode 16: The Peanut Reaction)

16 a syphilitic donkey (Episode 17: The Tangerine Factor)

17 "Math" (Episode 15: The Pork Chop Indeterminacy)

18 the third-floor janitor—he was a physicist in the Soviet Union (Episode 13: The Bat Jar Conjecture)

19 he tries to find a suitable place to sit that fulfills all his criteria (Episode 17: The Tangerine Factor)

20 Tequila Sunrise (Episode 8: The Grasshopper Experiment)

21 go straight (Episode 11: The Pancake Batter Anomaly)

22 Grasshopper (Episode 8: The Grasshopper Experiment)

23 fifteen (Episode 11: The Pancake Batter Anomaly)

24 360 (Episode 1: Pilot)

25 Sheldon's mother (Episode 4: The Luminous Fish Effect)

26 they have formed a barbershop quartet and got a gig playing Knott's Berry Farm (Episode 13: The Bat Jar Conjecture)

27 selective mutism (Episode 8: The Grasshopper Experiment)

28 he believes the Szechuan Palace has been passing off orange chicken as tangerine chicken and he intends to confront them (Episode 17: The Tangerine Factor)

29 counterclockwise—or his chest hair mats (Episode 11: The Pancake Batter Anomaly)

30 "you can't grow soup" (Episode 5: The Hamburger Postulate)

31 "fish night-lights" (Episode 4: The Luminous Fish Effect)

32 they've turned it on via the internet using Howard's laptop (Episode 9: The Cooper-Hofstadter Polarization)

33 "Because we can." (Episode 9: The Cooper-Hofstadter Polarization)

Raj: Tonight, I spice my mead with goblin blood!

Sheldon: What computer do you have? And please don't say a white one.

34 Larry at the comic book store (Episode 14: The Nerdvana Annihilation)

35 he wrote about their sex life on his blog (Episode 17: The Tangerine Factor)

36 Robin Hood (Episode 6: The Middle Earth Paradigm)

37 10½ hours (Episode 11: The Pancake Batter Anomaly)

38 Lalita Gupta (Episode 8: The Grasshopper Experiment)

39 four dozen (Episode 4: The Luminous Fish Effect)

40 the Doppler Effect (Episode 6: The Middle Earth Paradigm)

41 2,600 (Episode 2: The Big Bran Hypothesis)

42 bartending shift (Episode 8: The Grasshopper Experiment)

43 Louie/Louise—a 200-pound transvestite with a skin condition (Episode 1: Pilot)

44 cello (Episode 5: The Hamburger Postulate)

45 Schrödinger's Cat (Episode 17: The Tangerine Factor)

46 Penny (Episode 5: The Hamburger Postulate)

47 "masturbating" (Episode 1: Pilot)

48 the Bottle City of Kandor (Episode 9: The Cooper-Hofstadter Polarization)

49 Professor Gablehauser—"In my defense, I prefaced that by saying 'with all due respect.' " (Episode 4: The Luminous Fish Effect)

50 twice, and he washes his hands as often as he can (Episode 8: The Grasshopper Experiment)

51 lifts him up (Episode 6: The Middle Earth Paradigm)

52 Howard (Episode 2: The Big Bran Hypothesis)

53 "when people are upset, the cultural convention is to bring them hot beverages" (Episode 6: The Middle Earth Paradigm)

54 shows her some magic tricks (Episode 15: The Pork Chop Indeterminacy)

55 motorized dirt bike (Episode 16: The Peanut Reaction)

56 6:15 a.m. (Episode 7: The Dumpling Paradox)

57 original series *Battlestar Gallactica* flight suit (Episode 9: The Cooper-Hofstadter Polarization)

58 "It's not a costume, it's a flight suit." (Episode 9: The Cooper-Hofstadter Polarization)

59 he doesn't have enough slots in his wallet to hold all his membership cards (Episode 8: The Grasshopper Experiment)

60 lard (Episode 4: The Luminous Fish Effect)

61 7:05 p.m. (Episode 6: The Middle Earth Paradigm)

62 Molecular Positronium / Long Beach (Episode 10: The Loobenfeld Decay)

63 Dr. Emil Farman-Farmaian (Episode 10: The Loobenfeld Decay)

64 she defected to North Korea (Episode 1: Pilot)

65 Princess Panchali from "The Monkey and the Princess," an Indian folk tale his mother used to read to him when he was a child (Episode 8: The Grasshopper Experiment)

66 to clean it (Episode 2: The Big Bran Hypothesis)

67 Leopold—aka Leo and Lee (Episode 10: The Loobenfeld Decay)

68 a titanium centrifuge (Episode 16: The Peanut Reaction)

69 C-O-N . . . frontation (Episode 6: The Middle Earth Paradigm)

70 "Woodstock" (Episode 9: The Cooper-Hofstadter Polarization)

71 a "generic cat" (Episode 6: The Middle Earth Paradigm)

72 a workshop production of *Rent* (Episode 10: The Loobenfeld Decay)

73 Mimi (Episode 10: The Loobenfeld Decay)

74 Leonard (Episode 11: The Pancake Batter Anomaly)

75 4B (Episode 1: Pilot)

76 the Army Ants (Episode 13: The Bat Jar Conjecture)

77 Raj (Episode 11: The Pancake Batter Anomaly)

78 "fiber content" (Episode 2: The Big Bran Hypothesis)

79 Penny (Episode 16: The Peanut Reaction)

80 that Leonard has used the word "nauseous" when he meant "nauseated" (Episode 17: The Tangerine Factor)

81 it is missing its visor (Episode 14: The Nerdvana Annihilation)

82 a Cup O Noodles (Episode 3: The Fuzzyboots Corollary)

83 chicken (Episode 9: The Cooper-Hofstadter Polarization)

84 "True Colors" by Cyndi Lauper (Episode 16: The Peanut Reaction)

85 a virgin Cuba Libre (Episode 8: The Grasshopper Experiment)

86 3 feet (Episode 14: The Nerdvana Annihilation)

87 "by building an cxact replica of Jerusalem in the middle of the Mexican desert" (Episode 12: The Jerusalem Duality)

88 Raj (Episode 4: The Luminous Fish Effect)

89 165 pounds (Episode 15: The Pork Chop Indeterminacy)

90 he is going to the mall with a girl named Emma (Episode 12: The Jerusalem Duality)

91 Perpetual Motion Squad (Episode 13: The Bat Jar Conjecture)

92 she's a "carbohydrate delivery system" (Episode 2: The Big Bran Hypothesis)

Mary: Honey, why did you get a loom?
Sheldon: Well, I was working with luminous fish and I thought, hey, loom.

93 The Flash (Episode 1: Pilot)

94 Howard (Episode 13: The Bat Jar Conjecture)

95 "To Life! (*L'Chaim!*)" (Episode 8: The Grasshopper Experiment)

96 "the girl who played TV's Blossom" (Episode 13: The Bat Jar Conjecture)

97 DVD burner (Episode 16: The Peanut Reaction)

98 Leslie Winkle (Episode 13: The Bat Jar Conjecture)

99 Frodo (Episode 6: The Middle Earth Paradigm)

100 he can't stop waving it (Episode 15: The Pork Chop Indeterminacy)

101 they see Girl Scouts press all the buttons on the call box, the door buzzes and they follow them in (Episode 1: Pilot)

102 Slippery Nipple (Episode 8: The Grasshopper Experiment)

103 he has asked for turkey and roast beef with lettuce and Swiss on whole wheat, but they have given him turkey and roast beef with Swiss and lettuce on whole wheat—"It's the right ingredients but in the wrong order. In a proper sandwich, the cheese is adjacent to the bread to create a moisture barrier against the lettuce. They might as well have dragged this thing through a car wash." (Episode 14: The Nerdvana Annihilation)

104 Pasadena Marriott (Episode 9: The Cooper-Hofstadter Polarization)

105 a Batman cookie jar (Episode 13: The Bat Jar Conjecture)

106 *The Time Machine* (Episode 14: The Nerdvana Annihilation)

107 "Soft Kitty" (Episode 11: The Pancake Batter Anomaly)

108 "flying carpets" (Episode 9: The Cooper-Hofstadter Polarization)

109 violin (Episode 5: The Hamburger Postulate)

110 their pants (Episode 1: Pilot)

111 eight (Episode 15: The Pork Chop Indeterminacy)

112 gherkins and onion dip (Episode 15: The Pork Chop Indeterminacy)

113 Leonard (Episode 14: The Nerdvana Annihilation)

114 Leonard—he's lactose intolerant (Episode 15: The Pork Chop Indeterminacy)

115 "We are the Champions" by Queen (Episode 13: The Bat Jar Conjecture)

116 Toby Loobenfeld (Episode 10: The Loobenfeld Decay)

117 Wii Boxing (Episode 15: The Pork Chop Indeterminacy)

118 she's going to be at work when some furniture is being delivered (Episode 2: The Big Bran Hypothesis)

119 shower (Episode 1: Pilot)

120 Jacuzzi Bob (Episode 14: The Nerdvana Annihilation)

121 a game where you must play Tetris with one hand while arm-wrestling your opponent with the other (Episode 16: The Peanut Reaction)

122 a Dark Knight sculpture based on the work of Alex Ross (Episode 16: The Peanut Reaction)

123 Halo (Episode 5: The Dumpling Paradox)

124 tell him it's a "nonoptional social convention" (Episode 16: The Peanut Reaction)

125 Howard (Episode 17: The Tangerine Factor)

126 he tells Leonard he accidentally ate a granola bar with peanuts in it and needs to go to the ER (Episode 16: The Peanut Reaction)

127 Morlocks (Episode 14: The Nerdvana Annihilation)

128 Starving Morlocks (Episode 14: The Nerdvana Annihilation)

129 Raj—but the experimental drug wears off and he can't talk to her (Episode 15: The Pork Chop Indeterminacy)

130 Thor (Episode 6: The Middle Earth Paradigm)

131 he's gotten Leonard out of the apartment so they can come in and prepare for the surprise party (Episode 16: The Peanut Reaction)

132 his place on the couch (Episode 1: Pilot)

133 periodic table of elements (Episode 1: Pilot)

134 "All right, the cat's alive. Let's go to dinner." (Episode 17: The Tangerine Factor)

135 centripetal force (Episode 3: The Fuzzyboots Corollary)

136 chocolate milk and Eggos (Episode 11: The Pancake Batter Anomaly)

137 Carol (Episode 16: The Peanut Reaction)

138 move around as if in fast-forward (Episode 14: The Nerdvana Annihilation)

139 4A (Episode 1: Pilot)

140 he takes a picture of her on his phone and posts it on his Facebook page with the caption "Me and my girlfriend" (Episode 9: The Cooper-Hofstadter Polarization)

141 television (Episode 1: Pilot)

142 "Elton John" (Episode 14: The Nerdvana Annihilation)

143 colleagues (Episode 15: The Pork Chop Indeterminacy)

144 Raj (Episode 17: The Tangerine Factor)

Sheldon: *(to Leonard)* Eat this slice of cheese without farting and you can sleep with my sister.

145 Leakey (Episode 6: The Middle Earth Paradigm)

146 there are four dumplings in an order of dumplings—if one of the guys isn't there, what do they do with the fourth dumpling? (Episode 7: The Dumpling Paradox)

147 "a fun sweater with a geometric print" (Episode 16: The Peanut Reaction)

148 they have his name label in them (Episode 15: The Pork Chop Indeterminacy)

149 on his balcony (Episode 14: The Nerdvana Annihilation)

150 a crossword puzzle (Episode 1: Pilot)

151 Gettysburg (Episode 5: The Hamburger Postulate)

152 Wednesday (Episode 7: The Dumpling Paradox)

153 "Where did my life go, Penny?" (Episode 8: The Grasshopper Experiment)

154 "We can go all night." (Episode 13: The Bat Jar Conjecture)

155 eleven (Episode 9: The Cooper-Hofstadter Polarization)

156 he drops his glasses and Howard stands on them (Episode 11: The Pancake Batter Anomaly)

157 "*Doogie Howser*" (Episode 8: The Grasshopper Experiment)

158 by pulling off his shirt (Episode 13: The Bat Jar Conjecture)

Leonard: Can I go back and prevent you from explaining that to me?

Sheldon: Same paradox. If you were to travel back in time and, say, knock me unconscious, you would not then have the conversation that irritated you, motivating you to go back and knock me unconscious.

Leonard: What if I knock you unconscious now?

Sheldon: It won't change the past.

Leonard: But it'd make the present so much nicer.

159 "Sergeant Fuzzyboots" (Episode 3: The Fuzzyboots Corollary)

160 "K-Mart" (Episode 4: The Luminous Fish Effect)

161 milky green (Episode 11: The Pancake Batter Anomaly)

162 a media center (Episode 2: The Big Bran Hypothesis)

163 his twin sister, Missy (Episode 15: The Pork Chop Indeterminacy)

164 he makes it sound like all the guys will be there (Episode 3: The Fuzzyboots Corollary)

165 he wants to answer all the questions—"He's annoying and no one wants to play wih him." (Episode 13: The Bat Jar Conjecture)

166 the Born Oppenheimer Approximation (Episode 1: Pilot)

167 Dr. Finkleday (Episode 4: The Luminous Fish Effect)

168 his arms would have sliced through her—"Lois Lane is falling, accelerating at an initial rate of 32 feet per second. Superman swoops down to save her by reaching out two arms of steel. Miss Lane, who is now traveling at approximately 120 miles per hour, hits them and is immediately sliced into three equal pieces." (Episode 2: The Big Bran Hypothesis)

169 the Sword of Azeroth (Episode 3: The Fuzzy Boots Corollary)

170 a karaoke bar (Episode 1: Pilot)

171 Leslie Winkle (Episode 5: The Hamburger Postulate)

172 Honey Puffs—but upon hearing Penny's yell, he opts for Big Bran (Episode 2: The Big Bran Hypothesis)

173 he "accidentally acquires" her mail and goes to return it to her (Episode 3: The Fuzzyboots Corollary)

174 he refuses to give a speech to unappreciative people (Episode 9: The Cooper-Hofstadter Polarization)

Sheldon: Oh, what fresh hell is this?

175 he tells her she has overreacted a little—which causes her to give Mike another shot (Episode 17: The Tangerine Factor)

176 Mrs. Wolowitz tells her as long as she's around, Howard is out of her will (Episode 7: The Dumpling Paradox)

177 Howard (Episode 15: The Pork Chop Indeterminacy)

178 Leslie Winkle (Episode 3: The Fuzzyboots Corollary)

179 in his apartment during her Halloween party (Episode 6: The Middle Earth Paradigm)

180 he was using Sheldon's urine cup to measure his pancake batter (Episode 11: The Pancake Batter Anomaly)

181 "damsel in distress"—Sheldon: "Twelfth century code of chivalry, not exactly current. You'd also have to be knighted for that to apply." (Episode 17: The Tangerine Factor)

182 Green Lantern and his power ring (Episode 2: The Big Bran Hypothesis)

183 a salsa dancing class (Episode 3: The Fuzzyboots Corollary)

184 "no longer want a time machine" and "need $800" (Episode 14: The Nerdvana Annihilation)

185 he was trying to build a defense robot designed to keep Missy out of his room (Episode 15: The Pork Chop Indeterminacy)

186 "flawless Russian" (Episode 2: The Big Bran Hypothesis)

187 that they're shelved with vegetables even though they're technically a fruit (Episode 4: The Luminous Fish Effect)

188 Peter Pan (Episode 6: The Middle-Earth Paradigm)

189 "We'll see . . ." (Episode 4: The Luminous Fish Effect)

190 he thinks he's committing "genetic fraud"—"There's no guarantee that our DNA is going to produce high-IQ offspring." (Episode 1: Pilot)

191 California Institute of Technology (Caltech) in Pasadena, California (Episode 1: Pilot)

192 the *A* key sticks (Episode 13: The Bat Jar Conjecture)

193 The Flash (Episode 6: The Middle-Earth Paradigm)

194 Sagittarius (Episode 1: The Pilot)

195 she demands her key back (Episode 2: The Big Bran Hypothesis)

196 snoring (Episode 2: The Big Bran Hypothesis)

197 Big Boy (Episode 5: The Hamburger Postulate)

198 because he's a good listener (Episode 6: The Middle-earth Paradigm)

199 eighth grade (Episode 9: The Cooper-Hofstadter Polarization)

200 Lime Jello-O (Episode 11: The Pancake Batter Anomaly)

Penny: Oh, anyways I'm also writing a screenplay. It's about this sensitive girl who comes to LA from Lincoln, Nebraska, to be an actress and who ends up a waitress at the Cheesecake Factory.

Leonard: So it's based on your life?

Penny: No, I'm from Omaha!

The Stephen Hawking Approach

It was such an incredible thrill the day Stephen Hawking came to the set of the show. Over the years, he's been on multiple times. And just about every time, he found a way to poke fun at Sheldon in the most delightful way.

When Sheldon was six years old, he dressed up as Stephen Hawking for Halloween.

Sheldon: I took my dad's desk chair, attached a Speak and Spell to it and made my sister push me up and down the block to trick or treat. Granted, most people thought I was R2-D2, but still, I got a lot of candy.

Season 5, Episode 21: The Hawking Excitation

Howard was asked to work on Stephen Hawking's chair. Afterward, Wolowitz gave Leonard and Raj gears and springs from Hawking's wheelchair.

Howard: I made some adjustmenls on the motor drive, and when I was putting it back together I could not for the life of me figure out where they went.

Season 5, Episode 21: The Hawking Excitation

Wolowitz gave Sheldon's paper to Hawking. Hawking found the thesis to be fascinating, but noted an arithmetic mistake on page two.

Stephen Hawking: It was quite the boner.

Season 5, Episode 21: The Hawking Excitation

Sheldon and Hawking played *Words With Friends* online and then spoke on the phone.

Sheldon: Professor Hawking, how nice of you to call.

Stephen Hawking: Hello. I really enjoyed our game, Dr. Cooper.

Sheldon: Oh, me, too.

Stephen Hawking: Or should I say Dr. Loser? Ha ha ha.

Sheldon: Yes, congratulations. You won fair and square. Very impressive, sir.

Stephen Hawking: Do you like brain teasers?

Sheldon: Oh, I love brain teasers.

Stephen Hawking: What do Sheldon Cooper and a black hole have in common? They both suck.

Leonard starts laughing.

Stephen Hawking: Neener neener!

Season 6, Episode 6: The Extract Obliteration

Sheldon wrestled with the idea of whether or not to continue work in string theory. After a couple of drinks, he prank-called Stephen Hawking.

Voice Mail Message: *(voiceover)* Next message.

Sheldon: *(voiceover)* It's me again! I gave up string theory! You should give up black holes, and we can totally solve crimes together!

Voice Mail Message: *(voiceover)* Next message.

Sheldon: *(voiceover)* Y'know what's great?! Geology. Ooh, look at this geode! That's fun to say! Geeeeode! Geeeeode!

Voice Mail Message: *(voiceover)* Next message.

Sheldon: *(voiceover)* Geeeeode! Geeeeode! *(then, blurting)* I kiss girls now.

Voice Mail Message: *(voiceover)* Next message.

Sheldon: *(voiceover)* Hey, guess who I am?! *(robot voice)* Beep-boop-bop-boop! *(then)* I'm you! Get it?!

Voice Mail Message: *(voiceover)* Next message.

Sheldon: *(voiceover)* Are you mad at me? Oh no, you're mad at me. I'm so sorry! *(then, quickly)* Beep-boop-bop-boop.

Voice Mail Message: *(voiceover)* Next message.

Sheldon: *(voiceover)* Thiospinel sulfide. Thiospinel sulfide. That's even more fun than "geeeeode"—hey, did you see *The Lego Movie*?!

Stephen Hawking: *(offscreen)* What a jackass.

Season 7, Episode 20: The Relationship Diremption

Season 2

1 toaster oven (Episode 12: The Killer Robot Instability)

2 a griffin (Episode 4: The Griffin Equivalency)

3 Scotty (Episode 9: The White Asparagus Triangulation)

4 a security camera (Episode 1: The Bad Fish Paradigm)

5 "It means I wish you weren't going." (Episode 23: The Monopolar Expedition)

6 the children's section of a bookstore (Episode 13: The Friendship Algorithm)

7 *Stu the Cockatoo Is New at the Zoo* (Episode 13: The Friendship Algorithm)

8 flower barrettes that Penny makes (Episode 18: The Work Song Nanocluster)

9 Howard got a friend to fly a spy drone over (Episode 7: The Panty Piñata Polarization)

10 "Mom smokes in the car. Jesus is okay with it but we can't tell Dad." (Episode 1: The Bad Fish Paradigm)

11 Queen Penelope (Episode 3: The Barbarian Sublimation)

12 his mother's meatloaf (Episode 22: The Classified Materials Turbulence)

13 it sticks to the ceiling (Episode 22: The Classified Materials Turbulence)

14 to look for evidence of slow-moving monopoles (Episode 23: The Monopolar Expedition)

15 Barry (Episode 12: The Killer Robot Instability)

16 mitosis—"I believe one day Sheldon will eat an enormous amount of Thai food and split into two Sheldons." (Episode 6: The Cooper-Nowitzki Theorem)

17 a week (Episode 16: The Cushion Saturation)

18 she was a guy dressed as a green Orion slave girl (Episode 2: The Codpiece Topology)

19 tapioca (Episode 13: The Friendship Algorithm)

20 "chocolate" (Episode 13: The Friendship Algorithm)

21 she's frazzled after a bad audition—"It took me two hours to get there, I waited an hour for my turn and before I could even start, they told me I was 'too Midwest' for the part." (Episode 3: The Barbarian Sublimation)

22 he folds them with a purpose-built flip-fold folding board (Episode 1: The Bad Fish Paradigm)

23 The Flash (Episode 18: The Work Song Nanocluster)

24 he doesn't believe in the ancient pagan festival of Saturnalia (Episode 11: The Bath Item Gift Hypothesis)

25 he never met them (Episode 19: The Dead Hooker Juxtaposition)

26 Szechuan Palace (Episode 16: The Cushion Saturation)

27 Golden Dragon—before Szechuan Palace closed, Leonard bought 4,000 containers and keeps them in his car (Episode 16: The Cushion Saturation)

28 the first season of *Battlestar Galactica* (Episode 17: The Terminator Decoupling)

29 Trevor (Episode 4: The Griffin Equivalency)

30 211 (Episodc 13: The Friendship Algorithm)

31 a banana slug (Episode 22: The Classified Materials Turbulence)

32 Arkansas (Episode 23: The Monopolar Expedition)

33 Klingon Boggle (Episode 7: The Panty Piñata Polarization)

34 Sea World (Episode 21: The Vegas Renormalization)

35 "for taking a whiz on a cop car" (Episode 14: The Financial Permeability)

36 watches (Episode 1: The Bad Fish Paradigm)

Sheldon: That's preposterous. I do not resemble C-3PO. Don't get me wrong, I'm flattered. I just don't see it.

37 "residual radium from the luminous dials" (Episode 1: The Bad Fish Paradigm)

38 Penny (Episode 4: The Griffin Equivalency)

39 a brochure for Pasadena City College (Episode 1: The Bad Fish Paradigm)

40 an eye patch (Episode 8: The Lizard-Spock Expansion)

41 she's an actress (Episode 19: The Dead Hooker Juxtaposition)

42 Sheldor the Conqueror (Episode 3: The Barbarian Sublimation)

43 he puts it up on the telephone wire (Episode 7: The Panty Piñata Polarization)

44 "Scissors cuts paper, paper covers rock, rock crushes lizard, lizard poisons Spock, Spock smashes scissors, scissors decapitates lizard, lizard eats paper, paper disproves Spock, Spock vaporizes rock and, as it always has, rock crushes scissors." (Episode 8: The Lizard-Spock Expansion)

45 "I think Sheldon might be the larval form of his species, and someday he'll spin a cocoon and emerge two months later with moth wings and an exoskeleton." (Episode 6: The Cooper-Nowitzki Theorem)

46 "A: 10 consecutive nights, or B: more than 9 nights in a 3 week period, or C: all the weekends of a given month plus three weeknights." (Episode 10: The Vartabedian Conundrum)

47 she dreams that Howard's character visits her in the game and she agrees to spend the afternoon with him questing, followed by a flagon of ale at yon virtual tavern (Episode 3: The Barbarian Sublimation)

48 *People* magazine (Episode 4: The Griffin Equivalency)

49 Mrs. Vartabedian (Episode 10: The Vartabedian Conundrum)

50 visits her in the game (Episode 3: The Barbarian Sublimation)

51 built a hugging machine—"I got a dressmaker's mannequin. I stuffed it with an electric blanket so it was warm, and I built two radio-controlled arms that would hug me and pat my back." (Episode 15: The Maternal Capacitance)

52 hugs her—he's overcome by the magnitude of the gift because the napkin must have Spock's DNA on it (Episode 11: The Bath Item Gift Hypothesis)

53 M.O.N.T.E.—Mobile Omnidirectional Neutralization and Termination Eradicator (Episode 12: The Killer Robot Instability)

54 "It's hot in here. Must be Summer." (Episode 17: The Terminator Decoupling)

55 they kiss in the car (Episode 8: The Lizard-Spock Expansion)

56 in their apartment (Episode 21: The Vegas Renormalization)

57 she forgot it when she made coffee and ran out of milk—"You're the milk thief!" (Episode 21: The Vegas Renormalization)

58 he pretends he's filling in a game registration for her while she plays the game—"I used trickery and deceit." (Episode 3: The Barbarian Sublimation)

59 Chinese food (Episode 20: The Hofstadter Isotope)

60 Planet Bollywood (Episode 4: The Griffin Equivalency)

61 Jimmy Mullins—"He still punched me in the face with my own fists." (Episode 12: The Killer Robot Instability)

62 all the bath products he's bought (Episode 11: The Bath Item Gift Hypothesis)

63 it's the hospital where he was born (Episode 9: The White Asparagus Triangulation)

64 by text (Episode 10: The Vartabedian Conundrum)

65 Indian food (Episode 21: The Vegas Renormalization)

66 his mother's phone number (Episode 7: The Panty Piñata Polarization)

67 Kripke controls the new open science grid computer that Sheldon needs to use to run some simulations of structure formation in the early universe (Episode 13: The Friendship Algorithm)

68 the "check engine" light (Episode 5: The Euclid Alternative)

69 a sheldonectomy (Episode 10: The Vartabedian Conundrum)

70 wealthybigpenis (Episode 4: The Griffin Equivalency)

71 singing Journey's "Any Way You Want It" on Rock Band (Episode 15: The Maternal Capacitance)

72 Vespa (Episode 5: The Euclid Alternative)

73 he goes online and tries out the movements on the floor (Episode 13: The Friendship Algorithm)

74 Morse code (Episode 6: The Cooper-Nowitzki Theorem)

75 if he chokes on his popcorn, no one will administer the Heimlich maneuver (Episode 2: The Codpiece Topology)

Penny: Um, you know it's kinda early. Do you wanna maybe come in for some coffee or something?

Stuart: Oh, gee, it's a little late for coffee isn't it?

Penny: Aw, you think coffee means coffee. That is so sweet.

76 the Big Curry Pot (Episode 17: The Terminator Decoupling)

77 Raj—"Your responses to the questionnaire were truly disturbing." (Episode 13: The Friendship Algorithm)

78 "waitress for six months and then become a movie star" (Episode 14: The Financial Permeability)

79 TV star (Episode 14: The Financial Permeability)

80 she lied when she told Leonard she graduated from community college (Episode 1: The Bad Fish Paradigm)

81 Leonard's pillowcase (Episode 2: The Codpiece Topology)

82 his bat signal (Episode 10: The Vartabedian Conundrum)

83 when she wants to share credit with him on his theorem (Episode 6: The Cooper-Nowitzki Theorem)

84 George Smoot—"a Nobel Prize–winning physicist, one of the great minds of our time. His work in black body form and anisotropy of the cosmic microwave background radiation cemented our understanding of the origin of the universe." (Episode 17: The Terminator Decoupling)

85 by attaching RFID tags to his clothing—"It will enable my laptop to read and identify the items with this wand." (Episode 17: The Terminator Decoupling)

86 three hours eleven minutes (Episode 17: The Terminator Decoupling)

87 Michael (Episode 15: The Maternal Capacitance)

88 It's the factor Howard's made up to measure the likelihood of having sex—"Neediness times dress size

> **Leonard:** Sheldon, we've been on this train ninety seconds and you've already said a thousand words. Just tell us where to sit and shut up.

squared." His formula is based on the Drake Equation, which, as Sheldon points out, "estimates the odds of making contact with extraterrestrials by calculating the product of an increasingly restrictive series of fractional values such as those stars with planets and those planets likely to develop life. N equals R times FP times NE times FL times FI times FC times L." Howard: "Yeah, that one. You can modify it to calculate our chances of having sex by changing the formula to use the number of single women in Los Angeles, the number of those who might find us attractive, and what I call the Wolowitz Coefficient." (Episode 20: The Hofstadter Isotope)

89 "That thing on Phyllis's neck opened up again." (Episode 16: The Cushion Saturation)

90 "a raccoon with what appears to be a distended scrotum" (Episode 13: The Friendship Algorithm)

91 a napkin signed by Leonard Nimoy—"To Sheldon, live long and prosper. Leonard Nimoy." (Episode 11: The Bath Item Gift Hypothesis)

92 he tells him he could go dressed as a *Star Trek* science officer exploring a planet similar to Earth in the 1500s—"Fascinating . . ." (Episode 2: The Codpiece Topology)

93 an ice cream parlor (Episode 19: The Dead Hooker Juxtaposition)

94 he makes a big deal of not being able to open a jar of white asparagus and asks Leonard to open it for him (Episode 9: The White Asparagus Triangulation)

95 no, the jar cracks and Leonard cuts his hand (Episode 9: The White Asparagus Triangulation)

96 a *Spider-Man* comic book (Episode 20: The Hofstadter Isotope)

97 Euclid has speed bumps (Episode 5: The Euclid Alternative)

> **Sheldon:** I have to say I thought the toilet humor would get less funny with repetition. Apparently there is no law of diminishing comedic returns with space poop.

98 *Anne Frank* (Episode 17: The Terminator Decoupling)

99 use them as Nazi artillery (Episode 17: The Terminator Decoupling)

100 Saturday night at 8:15 p.m. (Episode 7: The Panty Piñata Polarization)

101 Lisa (Episode 8: The Lizard-Spock Expansion)

102 a joke peanut brittle can and the hollowed-out buttocks of a superhero action figure—"who shall remain nameless for his own protection. Or her own protection." (Episode 14: The Financial Permeability)

103 it would delay his morning bowel movement until he was at work (Episode 14: The Financial Permeability)

104 Raj (Episode 20: The Hofstadter Isotope)

105 playing his Sony PSP (Episode 6: The Cooper-Nowitzki Theorem)

106 slices his head off (Episode 3: The Barbarian Sublimation)

107 a children's science kit—"101 Totally Cool Science Experiments for Kids" (Episode 11: The Bath Item Gift Hypothesis)

108 his Mee-Maw (Episode 17: The Terminator Decoupling)

109 Moon Pie (Episode 17: The Terminator Decoupling)

110 Kal-El (Episode 9: The White Asparagus Triangulation)

111 "cootie" (Episode 10: The Vartabedian Conundrum)

112 Sheldon tells him "obviously you're not that familiar with Indian cinema" (Episode 1: The Bad Fish Paradigm)

113 she touches his onion rings (Episode 7: The Panty Piñata Polarization)

114 Lucky (Episode 4: The Griffin Equivalency)

115 pet store (Episode 5: The Euclid Alternative)

116 The Wolowitz Zero-Gravity Waste Disposal System (Episode 22: The Classified Materials Turbulence)

117 "crack" (Episode 17: The Terminator Decoupling)

118 set up her sound system (Episode 19: The Dead Hooker Juxtaposition)

119 Secret Agent Laser Obstacle Chess (Episode 18: The Work Song Nanocluster)

120 sausage, mushroom and light olive (Episode 6: The Cooper-Nowitzki Theorem)

121 Sheldon put a flyer on the bulletin board at the university that said, "Roommate wanted. Whistlers need not apply." (Episode 13: The Friendship Algorithm)

122 he's trying to find "the acoustic sweet spot" (Episode 9: The White Asparagus Triangulation)

123 the diverter valve—"It's gonna fail after about ten flushes." (Episode 22: The Classified Materials Turbulence)

124 vintage games (Episode 2: The Codpiece Topology)

125 the Fifth Annual East Rutherford, New Jersey Gay, Lesbian, Bisexual and Transgender Alliance Luau (Episode 18: The Work Song Nanocluster)

126 four—"and two of them were children" (Episode 18: The Work Song Nanocluster)

127 "a bar with women" (Episode 20: The Hofstadter Isotope)

128 he wants to make sure he has something commensurate in value—once he's seen her gift to him, he'll excuse himself from the room and come back with an appropriate item from his stock (Episode 11: The Bath Item Gift Hypothesis)

129 gets it stuck in a ditch (Episode 8: The Lizard-Spock Expansion)

130 Kirk (Episode 9: The White Asparagus Triangulation)

131 Hillary 2008 (Episode 19: The Dead Hooker Juxtaposition)

132 Ramona Nowitzki (Episode 6: The Cooper-Nowitzki Theorem)

133 by moving out of the apartment (Episode 1: The Bad Fish Paradigm)

134 Schroeder, from the Charlie Brown cartoon (Episode 2: The Codpiece Topology)

135 *CSI* (Episode 19: The Dead Hooker Juxtaposition)

136 2311 North Los Robles Avenue, Pasadena, California (Episode 14: The Financial Permeability)

137 a cat who wants to "haz cheezburger" (Episode 7: The Panty Piñata Polarization)

138 a bird (Episode 10: The Vartabedian Conundrum)

139 Sheldon (Episode 18: The Work Song Nanocluster)

140 Anything Can Happen Thursday (Episode 20: The Hofstadter Isotope)

141 lysine (Episode 13: The Friendship Algorithm)

142 he points out that Raj is drinking nonalcoholic beer (Episode 17: The Terminator Decoupling)

143 the Rhode Island School of Design (Episode 20: The Hofstadter Isotope)

144 he gives it a flamethrower (Episode 12: The Killer Robot Instability)

145 David Underhill (Episode 11: The Bath Item Gift Hypothesis)

146 she finds out he's married when she sees nude photos of his wife on his cell phone (Episode 11: The Bath Item Gift Hypothesis)

147 a glass of warm milk with a handful of his mom's Valium in it (Episode 1: The Bad Fish Paradigm)

$E=mc^2$

Leonard: I don't think I can go to the North Pole.

Sheldon: Okay, Leonard, I know you're concerned about disappointing me, but I want you to take comfort from the knowledge that my expectations of you are very low.

148 Captain Sweatpants (Episode 20: The Hofstadter Isotope)

149 Kathy O'Brien (Episode 6: The Cooper-Nowitzki Theorem)

150 fart goblin (Episode 17: The Terminator Decoupling)

151 his flash drive—"My flash drive contains my paper on astrophysical probes of M-theory effects in the early universe that I was going to give to George Smoot at the conference." (Episode 17: The Terminator Decoupling)

152 Mikayla (Episode 21: The Vegas Renormalization)

153 Esther Rosenblatt (Episode 21: The Vegas Renormalization)

154 add Bluetooth (Episode 18: The Work Song Nanocluster)

155 a flow chart (Episode 13: The Friendship Algorithm)

156 Howard (Episode 13: The Friendship Algorithm)

157 at the end of Leonard and Penny's date that they agreed to go on at the end of Season 1 (Episode 1: The Bad Fish Paradigm)

158 clipping his toenails (Episode 6: The Cooper-Nowitzki Theorem)

159 eats it (Episode 3: The Barbarian Sublimation)

160 in the event of Bruce Wayne's death, which Robin will replace him—Sheldon thinks it will be Dick Grayson, Stuart thinks it will be Jason Todd (Episode 20: The Hofstadter Isotope)

161 Altadena (Episode 19: The Dead Hooker Juxtaposition)

162 he wants to acclimatize himself to the conditions at the North Pole (Episode 23: The Monopolar Expedition)

163 a gift certificate for motorcycle lessons (Episode 11: The Bath Item Gift Hypothesis)

164 an indoor recreation center to go rock climbing (Episode 13: The Friendship Algorithm)

165 he passes out and dangles from a rope in midair (Episode 13: The Friendship Algorithm)

166 Marcy Grossman (Episode 12: The Killer Robot Instability)

167 she sits in his spot—"I'm taking a stand . . . metaphorically." (Episode 7: The Panty Piñata Polarization)

168 a Snuggie (Episode 23: The Monopolar Expedition)

169 the guy who always gets killed (Episode 9: The White Asparagus Triangulation)

170 "Raj Mahal" (Episode 4: The Griffin Equivalency)

171 trains (Episode 1: The Bad Fish Paradigm)

172 "Danger! Danger!" (Episode 3: The Barbarian Sublimation)

173 he spilled grape juice on them (Episode 3: The Barbarian Sublimation)

174 puts it on the floor and stamps on it (Episode 17: The Terminator Decoupling)

175 Sheldon (Episode 14: The Financial Permeability)

176 The Kripke Krippler (Episode 12: The Killer Robot Instability)

177 his Aunt Marian (Episode 10: The Vartabedian Conundrum)

178 Spock (Episode 9: The White Asparagus Triangulation)

179 cable company uniforms (Episode 7: The Panty Piñata Polarization)

180 Halle Berry—Sheldon's fifth-favorite Catwoman (Episode 1: The Bad Fish Paradigm)

181 *Star Wars* sheets (Episode 5: The Euclid Alternative)

182 "neuroscience" (Episode 15: The Maternal Capacitance)

183 the Southern California Robot Fighting League Round Robin Invitational, aka the S.C.R.F.L.R.R.I (Episode 12: The Killer Robot Instability)

184 "It's a Saturnalia miracle." (Episode 11: The Bath Item Gift Hypothesis)

185 "Hi. I'm the small package good things come in." (Episode 17: The Terminator Decoupling)

186 green (Episode 16: The Cushion Saturation)

187 an art show he has a piece in (Episode 20: The Hofstadter Isotope)

188 "Blow the Man Down" (Episode 18: The Work Song Nanocluster)

189 Professor X (Episode 1: The Bad Fish Paradigm)

190 Operation (Episode 23: The Monopolar Expedition)

191 makes her cry (Episode 15: The Maternal Capacitance)

192 he writes "I owe Penny $1,800—Kurt" on Leonard's forehead (Episode 14: The Financial Permeability)

193 yes (Episode 14: The Financial Permeability)

194 Roxanne (Episode 13: The Friendship Algorithm)

195 Sheldon hacks Leonard's computer and does it for him (Episode 9: The White Asparagus Triangulation)

Howard: Penny, let me take this opportunity to point out that you are looking particularly ravishing today.

Penny: Not with a thousand condoms, Howard.

Howard: So there is a number.

Sheldon: Worst Renaissance Fair ever!

Leonard: Please let it go, Sheldon.

Sheldon: It was rife with historical inaccuracies. For example, the tavern girl, serving flagons of mead, now her costume was obviously Germanic, but in 1487, the Bavarian purity laws, or Reinheitsgebot, severely limited the availability of mead. At best, they would've had some spiced wine.

Leonard: You're nitpicking!

Sheldon: Oh, really? Well, here's another nit for you. The flagons would not have been made of polypropylene.

196 he tries to kiss her (Episode 12: The Killer Robot Instability)

197 he slipped and fell in the tub—"Now he knows what bathtubs are capable of." (Episode 12: The Killer Robot Instability)

198 McCoy—"Now we've got our medical officer." (Episode 9: The White Asparagus Triangulation)

199 shoes (Episode 16: The Cushion Saturation)

200 it increases to three, from two (Episode 10: The Vartabedian Conundrum)

Season 3

1 Abby and Martha (Episode 12: The Psychic Vortex)

2 sweater (Episode 10: The Gorilla Experiment)

3 a neatly trimmed mustache and beard combo (Episode 1: The Electric Can Opener Fluctuation)

4 difficult mothers (Episode 5: The Creepy Candy Coating Corollary)

5 she dislocates her shoulder (Episode 8: The Adhesive Duck Deficiency)

6 a football cocktail dress (Episode 6: The Cornhusker Vortex)

7 on Leonard and Sheldon's couch (Episode 7: The Guitarist Amplification)

8 out for gelato (Episode 16: The Excelsior Acquisition)

9 tattoo sleeves (Episode 3: The Gothowitz Deviation)

10 Megan Fox from *Transformers* or Katee Sackhoff from *Battlestar Galactica* (Episode 9: The Vengeance Formulation)

11 he gets chased by a dog (Episode 20: The Spaghetti Catalyst)

12 "a hoot and a half" (Episode 1: The Electric Can Opener Fluctuation)

13 they find it in a box of assorted stuff they buy at a garage sale (Episode 17: The Precious Fragmentation)

14 Toby (Episode 2: The Jiminy Conjecture)

15 Jiminy (Episode 2: The Jiminy Conjecture)

16 *Gremlins*—"The instructions are very clear. Don't feed the Gremlins after midnight. Don't get the Gremlins wet. How hard is that?" (Episode 4: The Pirate Solution)

Leonard: I hate my name. It has nerd in it. Len-nerd.

17 he ran a red light while driving Penny to the hospital (Episode 16: The Excelsior Acquisition)

18 his limited-edition Green Lantern lantern—which Sheldon takes to the mixer (Episode 12: The Psychic Vortex)

19 "electricity" (Episode 6: The Cornhusker Vortex)

20 "a spider-infested fire hazard" (Episode 11: The Maternal Congruence)

21 Don Johnson in *Miami Vice* (Episode 22: The Staircase Implementation)

22 Eddie Crispo (Episode 17: The Precious Fragmentation)

23 a commemorative snow cone (Episode 7: The Guitarist Amplification)

24 the children's ball pit (Episode 14: The Einstein Approximation)

25 he has an eidetic memory (Episode 5: The Creepy Candy Coating Corollary)

26 the Department of Defense (Episode 13: The Bozeman Reaction)

27 "preevning" (Episode 23: The Lunar Excitation)

28 his C-men—because his name begins with C (Episode 18: The Pants Alternative)

29 he cheated on her with "some waitress from the university cafeteria" (Episode 11: The Maternal Congruence)

30 he had a soul patch and a perm (Episode 22: The Staircase Implementation)

31 a psychic (Episode 12: The Psychic Vortex)

32 Mickey Mouse ears (Episode 20: The Spaghetti Catalyst)

33 Stuart's uncle is Stan's dermatologist (Episode 16: The Excelsior Acquisition)

34 Higgs boson particle (Episode 13: The Bozeman Reaction)

35 Venkatesh Koothrappali (Episode 17: The Precious Fragmentation)

36 Jackson, Mississippi (Episode 5: The Creepy Candy Coating Corollary)

37 he wanted Wil Wheaton to autograph his one-sixty-fourth scale mint-in-package Wesley Crusher action figure (Episode 5: The Creepy Candy Coating Corollary)

38 beer (Episode 19: The Wheaton Recurrence)

39 his company designs the menus for the Cheesecake Factory (Episode 23: The Lunar Excitation)

40 because there's no gravity on the moon (Episode 23: The Lunar Excitation)

41 Raj (Episode 15: The Large Hadron Collision)

42 he'd be "on the roof skeet-shooting her Franklin Mint collectible plates" (Episode 7: The Guitarist Amplification)

43 have an interview (Episode 4: The Pirate Solution)

44 a patang (Episode 6: The Cornhusker Vortex)

45 two Kawasaki jet skis (Episode 17: The Precious Fragmentation)

46 Leonard put the wrong amount of fuel into Howard's rocket. When it started to smoke, Sheldon put the rocket in the elevator and it blew up (Episode 22: The Staircase Implementation)

Sheldon: I didn't want to upset you. Howard made it very clear that my allegiance should be to male comrades before women who sell their bodies for money.

Leonard: Is it possible he said, "Bros before hos"?

Sheldon: Yes, but I rephrased it to avoid offending the hos.

47 takes him shopping and helps him pick out a suit to wear at the ceremony (Episode 18: The Pants Alternative)

48 it drops an electrified net on him (Episode 13: The Bozeman Reaction)

49 Sheldon's attempt to teach Penny about physics (Episode 10: The Gorilla Experiment)

50 P. F. Chang's—for the $39.95 lovers' special (Episode 15: The Large Hadron Collision)

51 marijuana cookies (Episode 8: The Adhesive Duck Deficiency)

52 Kripke (Episode 9: The Vengeance Formulation)

53 *Science Friday* with Ira Flatow (Episode 9: The Vengeance Formulation)

54 a homunculus (Episode 3: The Gothowitz Deviation)

55 because Leonard sent him a picture of a cat playing the piano entitled "this is funny" (Episode 22: The Staircase Implementation)

56 he's got 3 percent body fat (Episode 5: The Creepy Candy Coating Corollary)

57 "It's true. I've seen him at the beach. He's like a human chicken wing." (Episode 5: The Creepy Candy Coating Corollary)

58 ditches him to talk to a girl jogging by (Episode 6: The Cornhusker Vortex)

Howard: So, Sheldon. How's it feel to get beaten up by a girl?

Sheldon: It's not the first time. I have a twin sister whose assaults began in utero. If only I'd had the presence of mind to reabsorb her. Then I'd have a mole with hair in it instead of a tedious yearly Christmas letter.

59 he pumps helium gas into Sheldon's office (Episode 9: The Vengeance Formulation)

60 it unhooks in the front (Episode 10: The Gorilla Experiment)

61 they kept turning the electric can opener on and off (Episode 1: The Electric Can Opener Fluctuation)

62 Bethany and Sarah (Episode 3: The Gothowitz Deviation)

63 Hello Kitty: Deluxe—"It comes with a little coin purse." (Episode 6: The Cornhusker Vortex)

64 the president of the university and the Board of Directors (Episode 9: The Vengeance Formulation)

65 his *Flash* #123—the classic "Flash of Two Worlds" issue (Episode 2: The Jiminy Conjecture)

66 Leonard (Episode 17: The Precious Fragmentation)

67 a snowflake preserved in a 1 percent solution of polyvinyl acetal resin (Episode 1: The Electric Can Opener Fluctuation)

68 he was working on it and kind of wanted to show it to his girlfriend Joyce Kim (Episode 22: The Staircase Implementation)

69 "It's a wave!" (Episode 14: The Einstein Approximation)

70 applaud (Episode 14: The Einstein Approximation)

71 holidays (Episode 11: The Maternal Congruence)

72 loud noises, clowns and nuns (Episode 10: The Gorilla Experiment)

73 the two-dimensional world described in Edwin Abbott's mathematical fantasy, *Flatland* (Episode 12: The Psychic Vortex)

74 he drinks sherry and hits on her (Episode 4: The Pirate Solution)

Sheldon: *(to Penny)* Which panties do you wear on Mondays?

75 because Wil Wheaton tells him that the reason he didn't attend the sci-fi convention in 1995 was because his grandmother had died—"I came here to defeat Wil Wheaton, the man who destroyed my dreams. But I can't defeat Wil Wheaton, the man who loved his Mee-Maw." (Episode 5: The Creepy Candy Coating Corollary)

76 magic beans (Episode 17: The Precious Fragmentation)

77 "squat" (Episode 4: The Pirate Solution)

78 "diddly squat" (Episode 4: The Pirate Solution)

79 something colorful, or a full set of prom-style white tie and tails (Episode 18: The Pants Alternative)

80 Professor Crawley from the entomology department at CalTech (Episode 2: The Jiminy Conjecture)

81 Leonard and Penny having sex (Episode 23: The Lunar Excitation)

82 windows that don't open, multiuser linens, keys shaped like credit cards (Episode 21: The Plimpton Stimulation)

83 he gives her chocolates (Episode 3: The Gothowitz Deviation)

84 thcy all have long hair and full beards (Episode 1: The Electric Can Opener Fluctuation)

85 broke off into focus groups and critiqued each other (Episode 11: The Maternal Congruence)

86 Ubuntu (Episode 22: The Staircase Implementation)

87 he's found in contempt (Episode 16: The Excelsior Acquisition)

88 Monday (Episode 3: The Gothowitz Deviation)

89 she's a world-renowned cosmological physicist from Princeton (Episode 21: The Plimpton Stimulation)

90 Sheldon (Episode 11: The Maternal Congruence)

91 “the physics is theoretical, but the fun is real” (Episode 7: The Guitarist Amplification)

92 “shrimp in mobster sauce”—“For all we know, the mobster sauce contains actual chunks of deceased mobsters.” (Episode 13: The Bozeman Reaction)

93 in the elevator shaft (Episode 2: The Jiminy Conjecture)

94 if either of them got a hot girlfriend, that person would have his girlfriend hook the other guy up with one of her girlfriends (Episode 5: The Creepy Candy Coating Corollary)

95 soup (Episode 8: The Adhesive Duck Deficiency)

96 helping Penny get dressed after she slipped in the shower, he sneaked a peek—“the hero always peeks” (Episode 8: The Adhesive Duck Deficiency)

97 a toy saber-toothed cat (Episode 6: The Cornhusker Vortex)

98 Howard (Episode 13: The Bozeman Reaction)

99 he’s put a lot of effort in to the friendship and wouldn’t want it wasted (Episode 20: The Spaghetti Catalyst)

100 a solution of hydrogen peroxide and a solution of saturated potassium iodide (Episode 9: The Vengeance Formulation)

101 “Die, Sheldon, Die!” (Episode 22: The Staircase Implementation)

102 a feminine hygiene product or a bowel-regulating yogurt (Episode 21: The Plimpton Stimulation)

103 Leonard Hofstadter (Episode 15: The Large Hadron Collision)

104 Leonard Hofstadter, Darth Vader and Rupert Murdoch—because he owns Fox and they canceled *Firefly* (Episode 15: The Large Hadron Collision)

105 he thinks that a menial job will free the important part of his brain to concentrate on his physics problem (Episode 14: The Einstein Approximation)

106 "Hello, old friend. Daddy's home." (Episode 1: The Electric Can Opener Fluctuation)

107 he's destroyed her ability to tolerate idiots (Episode 23: The Lunar Excitation)

108 his Incredible Hulk hands signed by Stan Lee (Episode 12: The Psychic Vortex)

109 Bochco (Episode 13: The Bozeman Reaction)

110 *Oshikuru: Demon Samurai* (Episode 3: The Gothowitz Deviation)

111 through a napkin (Episode 21: The Plimpton Stimulation)

112 Sheldon drives her (Episode 8: The Adhesive Duck Deficiency)

113 beefaroni (Episode 4: The Pirate Solution)

114 "Dickensian" (Episode 1: The Electric Can Opener Fluctuation)

115 a dirty sock (Episode 23: The Lunar Excitation)

116 he wants Stan to sign a Batman comic—Batman is a DC Comics property, not Marvel (Episode 16: The Excelsior Acquisition)

117 he plays the guitar and is looking for some session work (Episode 7: The Guitarist Amplification)

118 his butt (Episode 3: The Gothowitz Deviation)

119 Judge Kirby (Episode 16: The Excelsior Acquisition)

120 because he asks her to marry him—after only three dates and before they've even had sex (Episode 9: The Vengeance Formulation)

Leonard: You guys wanna do something tonight?

Howard: I can't. I gotta pick my mom up from her water aerobics class—eighteen overweight women flapping their arm fat in a swimming pool. Looks like the manatee tank at Sea World.

121 At the Cheesecake Factory he sits at a keyboard and sings the Four Tops song "Bernadette" with new lyrics dedicated to her (Episode 9: The Vengeance Formulation)

122 lion / azure (Episode 22: The Staircase Implementation)

123 through meditation (Episode 18: The Pants Alternative)

124 go to his cousin's wedding with him. Stuart agrees that Leonard can come too as long as he pretends to be Penny's cousin (Episode 16: The Excelsior Acquisition)

125 he's the muscle (Episode 17: The Precious Fragmentation)

126 Bozeman, Montana (Episode 13: The Bozeman Reaction)

127 Dr. Slutbunny (Episode 21: The Plimpton Stimulation)

128 whether he was born with bone claws (Episode 2: The Jiminy Conjecture)

129 a mean little skull—she says she'll see if she can make him smile (Episode 3: The Gothowitz Deviation)

130 hepatitis (Episode 3: The Gothowitz Deviation)

131 little pieces of cut-up hot dogs (Episode 20: The Spaghetti Catalyst)

132 ALF (Episode 17: The Precious Fragmentation)

133 his mother's house in Texas (Episode 1: The Electric Can Opener Fluctuation)

134 Corolla (Episode 5: The Creepy Candy Coating Corollary)

135 his *Fantastic Four* #48—first appearance of Silver Surfer (Episode 2: The Jiminy Conjecture)

136 service animals (Episode 20: The Spaghetti Catalyst)

137 Fed-Ex'd it back to Peter Jackson (Episode 17: The Precious Fragmentation)

138 secretly keeps it (Episode 17: The Precious Fragmentation)

139 stand over the sink and eat it out of the package with his bare hands like an animal (Episode 15: The Large Hadron Collision)

140 The Cheesecake Factory (Episode 11: The Maternal Congruence)

141 a turkey stuffed with a brisket stuffed with gefilte fish—"It's not as good as it sounds." (Episode 4: The Pirate Solution)

142 a restraining order (Episode 16: The Excelsior Acquisition)

143 next to the restraining order he got from Leonard Nimoy (Episode 16: The Excelsior Acquisition)

144 he grew up in Texas—"Football is ubiquitous in Texas." (Episode 6: The Cornhusker Vortex)

145 the Carrot of Power (Episode 5: The Creepy Candy Coating Corollary)

146 because he gives speeches all the time—what he can't do is shut up (Episode 18: The Pants Alternative)

147 that they will just be friends (Episode 2: The Jiminy Conjecture)

148 go into Penny's apartment and have sex again (Episode 2: The Jiminy Conjecture)

149 Raj tells him he hid the dirty sock Sheldon had spotted on the roof somewhere in the apartment and unless he meets her, it will remain there forever (Episode 23: The Lunar Excitation)

150 because in the Roommate Agreement friendship rider it stipulates that if one friend is invited to CERN (under construction at the time), he shall take the other one (Episode 15: The Large Hadron Collision)

151 a man steals his bags (Episode 13: The Bozeman Reaction)

152 takes off his pants and shows his butt (Episode 18: The Pants Alternative)

153 he says it was "just fine" (Episode 2: The Jiminy Conjecture)

154 "It was . . . okay." (Episode 2: The Jiminy Conjecture)

155 "Um, blackened salmon?" (Episode 3: The Gothowitz Deviation)

156 his favorite fictional characters—including Frodo (Episode 15: The Large Hadron Collision)

157 she quotes Yoda from *The Empire Strikes Back*—"Do. Or do not. There is no try." (Episode 19: The Wheaton Recurrence)

158 "Oh. Oh. Thank you." (Episode 19: The Wheaton Recurrence)

159 she had carpal tunnel surgery (Episode 11: The Maternal Congruence)

160 they slept together naked to keep their core body temperature from plummeting (Episode 1: The Electric Can Opener Fluctuation)

161 microbiology (Episode 5: The Creepy Candy Coating Corollary)

162 Albino Bob (Episode 19: The Wheaton Recurrence)

163 go to the comic book store dressed as female comic book characters—Leonard as Supergirl, Sheldon as Wonder Woman, Howard as Batgirl and Raj as Catwoman (Episode 19: The Wheaton Recurrence)

164 empowered (Episode 19: The Wheaton Recurrence)

165 why all his characters have first and last names that start with the same letter (Episode 16: The Excelsior Acquisition)

166 heartburn (Episode 20: The Spaghetti Catalyst)

167 Howard (Episode 2: The Jiminy Conjecture)

168 she tells him she wrote it naked (Episode 21: The Plimpton Stimulation)

169 she comes into his room and sleeps with him (Episode 21: The Plimpton Stimulation)

170 Billy Sparks (Episode 5: The Creepy Candy Coating Corollary)

171 courage (Episode 8: The Adhesive Duck Deficiency)

172 2003 (Episode 22: The Staircase Implementation)

173 "Lost boys, children of the night." (Episode 3: The Gothowitz Deviation)

174 a bust of Sir Isaac Newton (Episode 11: The Maternal Congruence)

175 the people on the first floor who were moving out (Episode 22: The Staircase Implementation)

176 $100 (Episode 22: The Staircase Implementation)

177 he doesn't want to use the toilet in the cell (Episode 16: The Excelsior Acquisition)

178 Howard and Raj make an online dating profile for him (Episode 23: The Lunar Excitation)

179 lack of adhesive ducks (Episode 8: The Adhesive Duck Deficiency)

180 French toast (Episode 3: The Gothowitz Deviation)

181 he's transformed into Gollum (Episode 17: The Precious Fragmentation)

182 Sheldon (Episode 6: The Cornhusker Vortex)

183 by watching movies written by Chris Columbus—Penny: "Okay. So, what do you watch on Thanksgiving?" Sheldon: "The parade." (Episode 4: The Pirate Solution)

184 movers (Episode 21: The Plimpton Stimulation)

185 a landlord to whom she owes money (Episode 21: The Plimpton Stimulation)

186 Comic-Con and the new *Star Trek* movie (Episode 1: The Electric Can Opener Fluctuation)

187 Camry (Episode 5: The Creepy Candy Coating Corollary)

188 "Run fast, run far." (Episode 22: The Staircase Implementation)

189 Mitzy (Episode 11: The Maternal Congruence)

190 they're too busy devouring Howard's mother's "I love you" brisket and a Tupperware of roasted potatoes and carrots (Episode 8: The Adhesive Duck Deficiency)

191 his fingerprint records so he can be ruled out as a suspect (Episode 13: The Bozeman Reaction)

192 "Any group big enough to trample me to death. The general rule of thumb is 36 adults or 70 children." (Episode 18: The Pants Alternative)

193 Adam West (Episode 17: The Precious Fragmentation)

194 The Gap (Episode 3: The Gothowitz Deviation)

195 "What is the sixth noble gas?" (Episode 22: The Staircase Implementation)

196 The Wesley Crushers (Episode 19: The Wheaton Recurrence)

197 his neighbor's chicken got loose and chased him up the big elm tree in front of Sheldon's house (Episode 2: The Jiminy Conjecture)

198 in the tub (Episode 9: The Vengeance Formulation)

199 why he's alone in a tub instead of spending time with a wonderful girl like Bernadette (Episode 9: The Vengeance Formulation)

200 put them in order of the size of their contributions to their respective fields (Episode 7: The Guitarist Amplification)

Sheldon: Incidentally, one can get beaten up in school simply by referring to oneself as "one."

The Food Order Complexity

Sheldon: Did you remember to ask for the chicken with broccoli to be diced, not shredded?

Leonard: Yes.

Sheldon: Even though the menu description specifies shredded?

Leonard: Yes.

Sheldon: Brown rice, not white?

Leonard: Yes.

Sheldon: Did you stop at the Korean grocery and get the good hot mustard?

Leonard: Yes.

Sheldon: Did you pick up the low-sodium soy sauce from the market?

Leonard: Yes.

Sheldon: Thank you.

Leonard: You're welcome.

Sheldon: What took you so long?

Season 2, Episode 4: The Griffin Equivalency

Sheldon: Is my hamburger medium well?
Leonard: Yes.
Sheldon: Dill slices, not sweet?
Leonard: Yes.
Sheldon: Individual relish packets?
Leonard: Yes.
Sheldon: Onion rings?
Leonard: Yes.
Sheldon: Extra breading?
Leonard: I asked.
Sheldon: What did they say?
Leonard: No.
Sheldon: Did you protest?
Leonard: Yes.
Sheldon: Vociferously?
Leonard: No.
Sheldon: Well, then what took you so long?
Leonard: Just eat.

Season 2, Episode 7: The Panty Piñata Polarization

Leonard: Here's your tea, Mother.
Beverly: Oolong?
Leonard: Yes.
Beverly: Loose, not bagged?
Leonard: Yes.
Beverly: Steeped three minutes?
Leonard: Yes.
Beverly: Two-percent milk?
Leonard: Yes.
Beverly: Warmed separately?
Leonard: Yes.
Beverly: One teaspoon sugar?
Leonard: Yes.
Beverly: Raw sugar?
Leonard: Yes.
Beverly: *(sips, then)* It's cold.
Leonard: I'll start again.

Season 2, Episode 15: The Maternal Capacitance

Sheldon: Did you remember to ask for the chicken with broccoli to be diced not shredded?

Penny: Yes.

Sheldon: Even though the menu description specifies shredded?

Penny: Yes.

Sheldon: Brown rice, not white?

Penny: Yes.

Sheldon: Did you stop at the Korean grocery and get the good hot mustard?

Penny: Yes.

Sheldon: Did you pick up the low-sodium soy sauce from the market?

Penny: Yes.

Sheldon: Good. *(then)* See how it's done, Leonard?

Season 2, Episode 19: The Dead Hooker Juxtaposition

Leonard: Great timing, food just got here.

Sheldon: Siam Palace?

Leonard: Yes.

Sheldon: Mee krob and chicken satay?

Leonard: Yes.

Sheldon: Extra peanut sauce?

Leonard: No. But you can have mine.

Sheldon: Very well. Oh, and on the topic of sharing things that are yours, there is a gentleman caller bringing flowers to your fiancée as we speak.

Leonard: What? *(crossing out)* Why didn't you say that first?

Sheldon: Why didn't you get extra peanut sauce? We can both play this game.

Season 8, Episode 7: The Misinterpretation Agitation

Season 4

1. jogging (Episode 2: The Cruciferous Vegetable Amplification)
2. he's afraid he'll get deported—"I'm brown and I talk funny." (Episode 7: The Apology Insufficiency)
3. The Flash (Episode 11: The Justice League Recombination)
4. Shamy (Episode 1: The Robotic Manipulation)
5. Sheldon (Episode 23: The Engagement Reaction)
6. sharing a bed in the Big Sur hotel (Episode 13: The Love Car Displacement)
7. Katee Sackhoff, Bernadette and George Takei (Episode 4: The Hot Troll Deviation)
8. Zack (Episode 10: The Alien Parasite Hypothesis)
9. the Serpent and the Old Woman (Episode 22: The Wildebeest Implementation)
10. "Every time he moves, there's a one in five chance he'll kill himself." (Episode 22: The Wildebeest Implementation)
11. two film reels of the movie (Episode 8: The 21-Second Excitation)
12. a dogopus—"A hybrid dog and octopus. Man's underwater best friend." (Episode 2: The Cruciferous Vegetable Amplification)
13. a theremin (Episode 12: The Bus Pants Utilization)
14. *The Taming of the Shrew* (Episode 16: The Cohabitation Formulation)
15. when she was in the hospital—"Well, there was the time I had my tonsils out, and I shared a room with a little Vietnamese girl. She didn't make it through the night, but up until then it was kind of fun." (Episode 8: The 21-Second Excitation)

16 a shot of tequila—"that's not how it looks in the picture" (Episode 7: The Apology Insufficiency)

17 over his mother's garage (Episode 12: The Bus Pants Utilization)

18 his battle ostrich—"The only bird I ever loved." (Episode 19: The Zarnecki Incursion)

19 Howard (Episode 19: The Zarnecki Incursion)

20 Tex-Mex (Episode 17: The Toast Derivation)

21 travel supervisor (Episode 13: The Love Car Displacement)

22 "KBB"—killed by badger (Episode 2: The Cruciferous Vegetable Amplification)

23 she'd told her father that they'd gotten back together (Episode 9: The Boyfriend Complexity)

24 from an orangutan in the primate lab (Episode 6: The Irish Pub Formulation)

25 Denny's, near Bakersfield (Episode 13: The Love Car Displacement)

26 a bottle of wine (Episode 8: The 21-Second Excitation)

27 Leonard—trying out his new persona of confident lady-killer (Episode 7: The Apology Insufficiency)

28 Counterfactuals (Episode 3: The Zazzy Substitution)

29 Johnson (Episode 10: The Alien Parasite Hypothesis)

30 Glenn (Episode 13: The Love Car Displacement)

31 a Gatorade (Episode 8: The 21-Second Excitation)

Leonard: I can't believe you've never seen *Raiders of the Lost Ark*.

Penny: And I can't believe you've never read *Eat, Pray, Love*.

Leonard: When she comes out with *Eat, Pray, Run Away From a Giant Boulder*, I'll read it.

32 "he sucks" (Episode 11: The Justice League Recombination)

33 Leonard and Priya are having "astronomically inaccurate" *Star Trek* sex in Raj's bedroom (Episode 24: The Roommate Transmogrification)

34 "Don't Go Breaking My Heart" by Elton John and Kiki Dee (Episode 17: The Toast Derivation)

35 "Walking on Sunshine" by Katrina and the Waves (Episode 17: The Toast Derivation)

36 the Surprisingly Helpful Equation Linked Differential Optimized Numerator: S.H.E.L.D.O.N.—he also suggested Project Nodlehs, "Sheldon" backwards (Episode 12: The Bus Pants Utilization)

37 Glissinda (Episode 4: The Hot Troll Deviation)

38 Steve Patterson, "the greasy old fat guy in Facilities Management" (Episode 4: The Hot Troll Deviation)

39 Gerard (Episode 17: The Toast Derivation)

40 Steve from Wichita (Episode 12: The Bus Pants Utilization)

41 finches—"When two groups of finches competed over the same food source, eventually one of them would evolve a different beak shape so they could feed on something else." (Episode 18: The Prestidigitation Approximation)

42 yelled at him and sounded like Mrs. Wolowitz (Episode 23: The Engagement Reaction)

43 Apple Genius Bar (Episode 5: The Desperation Emanation)

Leonard: Okay, fine. I'm a horrible human being. I'm the Darth Vader of Pasadena.

Sheldon: You're far too short to be Darth Vader. At best you might be a turncoat Ewok.

44 Lee (Episode 8: The 21-Second Excitation)

45 she's going back to Todd's house to confront him herself (Episode 19: The Zarnecki Incursion)

46 shoemaker (Episode 6: The Irish Pub Formulation)

47 when you see somebody wearing shoes you like, you just snap a picture of them and the app goes on the internet to find out where you can buy them (Episode 12: The Bus Pants Utilization)

48 60 (Episode 2: The Cruciferous Vegetable Amplification)

49 Mouth-to-Mouth Mona (Episode 24: The Roommate Transmogrification)

50 in a urinal (Episode 6: The Irish Pub Formulation)

51 "bodyguard" (Episode 11: The Justice League Recombination)

52 Wyatt (Episode 9: The Boyfriend Complexity)

53 Penny (Episode 21: The Agreement Dissection)

54 "Are you insane? I'm not going to prostitute myself just so we can get some new equipment." (Episode 15: The Benefactor Factor)

55 Joy (Episode 5: The Desperation Emanation)

56 they go to see physicist Dr. Brian Greene talk about his new book, *The Hidden Reality* (Episode 20: The Herb Garden Germination)

57 Howard leans in and he kisses him (Episode 9: The Boyfriend Complexity)

58 Special Agent Angela Page (Episode 7: The Apology Insufficiency)

59 microbiology (Episode 24: The Roommate Transmogrification)

Leonard: No, seriously, I think I've finally figured out my problem with women.

Sheldon: The capybara is the largest member of the rodent family.

Leonard: What does that have to do with me and women?

Sheldon: Nothing. It was a desperate attempt to introduce an alternate topic of conversation.

60 Steve Wozniak offers to autograph his vintage 1977 Apple II computer (Episode 2: The Cruciferous Vegetable Amplification)

61 "The Miller's Tale" by Chaucer—"It would have been hidden in sock drawers if people in the fourteenth century had worn socks." (Episode 8: The 21-Second Excitation)

62 28 minutes (Episode 1: The Robotic Manipulation)

63 the Wolowitz Programmable Hand (Episode 1: The Robotic Manipulation)

64 "hippy" (Episode 5: The Desperation Emanation)

65 Smeldor (Episode 7: The Apology Insufficiency)

66 Steve Wozniak (Episode 2: The Cruciferous Vegetable Amplification)

67 he was on *Dancing with the Stars* (Episode 2: The Cruciferous Vegetable Amplification)

68 October 6 (Episode 18: The Prestidigitation Approximation)

69 he was told there would be a raffle (Episode 17: The Toast Derivation)

70 she passes out (Episode 23: The Engagement Reaction)

71 "cervix" (Episode 8: The 21-Second Excitation)

72 Craigslist (Episode 18: The Prestidigitation Approximation)

73 "Winnie-the-Pooh" (Episode 1: The Robotic Manipulation)

74 reverse psychology—she tells him they aren't suited for each other, and if he hadn't ended it, she would've done it for him (Episode 3: The Zazzy Substitution)

75 his cushion from the couch—"I'm giving you my spot on the couch." (Episode 7: The Apology Insufficiency)

76 travel makes her constipated (Episode 13: The Love Car Displacement)

77 "Brown Eyed Girl" by Van Morrison (Episode 5: The Desperation Emanation)

78 in a woman's basement in Alhambra—"I think it's a front for human trafficking, but they do a really good job." (Episode 8: The 21-Second Excitation)

79 128 (Episode 1: The Robotic Manipulation)

80 "a little over $1,400" (Episode 2: The Cruciferous Vegetable Amplification)

81 "She never even got to see my penis." (Episode 22: The Wildebeest Implementation)

82 "They are pants one wears over one's regular pants when one sits on bus seats that other people have previously sat on." (Episode 12: The Bus Pants Utilization)

83 the "dirt people" (Episode 15: The Benefactor Factor)

84 Wil Wheaton (Episode 8: The 21-Second Excitation)

85 "Well, if it isn't Wil Wheaton, the Jar Jar Binks of the *Star Trek* universe." (Episode 8: The 21-Second Excitation)

86 Leonard was once on the verge of giving away rocket secrets to a North Korean spy (Episode 7: The Apology Insufficiency)

87 Carlsbad, California (Episode 19: The Zarnecki Incursion)

88 he sets up a table at the park with a sign that reads "Cats: $20"—every person who takes a cat gets $20 (Episode 3: The Zazzy Substitution)

89 Brussels sprouts (Episode 2: The Cruciferous Vegetable Amplification)

90 he's got cholera (Episode 2: The Cruciferous Vegetable Amplification)

91 they compare notes on Leonard in the sack (Episode 23: The Engagement Reaction)

92 "triumphant" (Episode 14: The Thespian Catalyst)

93 Penny (Episode 1: The Robotic Manipulation)

94 overuse of the phrase "oh my God" (Episode 9: The Boyfriend Complexity)

95 because he knows they made a pact not to—"April 12, 2005. Bob's Big Boy, Toluca Lake. Raj had just introduced us to Priya for the first time, and she was enjoying the sweet taste of Hindu rebellion in the form of a Bob's Super Big Boy hamburger. In order to preserve your friendship, you and Howard made a pinky swear that neither of you would attempt to woo her. I had a patty melt." (Episode 6: The Irish Pub Formulation)

96 Donnie (Episode 9: The Boyfriend Complexity)

97 beer pong (Episode 9: The Boyfriend Complexity)

98 Bernadette is thinking of breaking up with Howard (Episode 20: The Herb Garden Germination)

99 a girls' night (Episode 21: The Agreement Dissection)

100 she's driving while wearing flip-flops (Episode 1: The Robotic Manipulation)

101 two—"everyday and dress" (Episode 18: The Prestidigitation Approximation)

102 Dr. Robert Oppenheimer (Episode 3: The Zazzy Substitution)

Raj: Please don't send me back to India! It's so crowded! It's like the whole country is one endless Comic-Con, except everybody's wearing the same costume—"Indian Guy."

103 "she may be a slave to her baser urges, like you" (Episode 10: The Alien Parasite Hypothesis)

104 lead attorney for the biggest car company in India (Episode 6: The Irish Pub Formulation)

105 "Sheldon Cooper's a smelly pooper." (Episode 20: The Herb Garden Germination)

106 pharmaceutical (Episode 24: The Roommate Transmogrification)

107 she went to Saudi Arabia and met a prince who had an interest in neurobiology—"Technically, Faisal is my fiancé, but I do have a state-of-the-art two-photon microscope and a place to stay in Riyadh in the winter." (Episode 15: The Benefactor Factor)

108 Green Lantern (Episode 11: The Justice League Recombination)

109 Lieutenant Uhura (Episode 18: The Prestidigitation Approximation)

110 Nancy (Episode 3: The Zazzy Substitution)

111 one "without wheels" (Episode 9: The Boyfriend Complexity)

112 one that uses handwriting recognition to solve differential equations (Episode 12: The Bus Pants Utilization)

113 her mother (Episode 5: The Desperation Emanation)

114 hits her in the face with a pillow (Episode 8: The 21-Second Excitation)

115 Wii Archery (Episode 20: The Herb Garden Germination)

116 "oddly titillating" (Episode 3: The Zazzy Substitution)

117 Wonder Woman (Episode 11: The Justice League Recombination)

118 Penny (Episode 13: The Love Car Displacement)

119 mango caterpillar (Episode 6: The Irish Pub Formulation)

120 "approximately 171" (Episode 1: The Robotic Manipulation)

121 fourteen (Episode 1: The Robotic Manipulation)

122 Raj (Episode 24: The Roommate Transmogrification)

123 Ricky (Episode 21: The Agreement Dissection)

124 she thinks neurobiology has more real-world applications and importance than theoretical physics (Episode 3: The Zazzy Substitution)

125 a Bat'leth (Episode 19: The Zarnecki Incursion)

126 Todd asked to see Sheldon's Bat'leth, Sheldon gave it to him and then Todd took it and closed the door (Episode 19: The Zarnecki Incursion)

127 Leonard is driving at 120 mph (Episode 13: The Love Car Displacement)

128 he accidentally drank from Leonard's glass of water and is worrying he'll get sick and die (Episode 23: The Engagement Reaction)

129 *Where No Sheldon Has Gone Before* (Episode 14: The Thespian Catalyst)

130 Johnson Elementary School (Episode 20: The Herb Garden Germination)

131 rum cake (Episode 7: The Apology Insufficiency)

132 he throws up the rum cake on her shoes (Episode 7: The Apology Insufficiency)

133 mixing in ground-up insects for a month—"Excuse me, that was not a betrayal, that was an experiment to determine at what concentration food starts tasting 'mothy.'" (Episode 6: The Irish Pub Formulation)

134 Liberal arts (Episode 15: The Benefactor Factor)

135 the Lenwoloppali Differential Equation Scanner (Episode 12: The Bus Pants Utilization)

136 "it was hell" (Episode 1: The Robotic Manipulation)

137 Bengal tiger (Episode 16: The Cohabitation Formulation)

138 his bedroom (Episode 2: The Cruciferous Vegetable Amplification)

139 "R2-D-Bag" (Episode 2: The Cruciferous Vegetable Amplification)

140 she kisses him—"She stuck her tongue down my throat" (Episode 15: The Benefactor Factor)

141 his "stadium pal" (Episode 8: The 21-Second Excitation)

142 having a baby—"Between the two of us our genetic material has the potential of producing the first in a line of intellectually superior benign overlords" (Episode 1: The Robotic Manipulation)

143 he's tweeted him (Episode 17: The Toast Derivation)

144 "samples from a bag of excrement that had been lit on fire on my front porch" (Episode 7: The Apology Insufficiency)

145 Hermann von Helmholtz (Episode 3: The Zazzy Substitution)

146 Bernadette has texted her saying she's with Priya (Episode 22: The Wildebeest Implementation)

147 30.96 (Episode 1: The Robotic Manipulation)

Penny: Sheldon, you can't reprogram people.
Sheldon: No, *you* can't reprogram people.

148 he tells her that Howard crashed the Mars Rover in order to impress a woman (Episode 7: The Apology Insufficiency)

149 they each put a hand in a jar that has a spider in it, and the first one to withdraw his hand is the sidekick (Episode 10: The Alien Parasite Hypothesis)

150 wrestling (Episode 10: The Alien Parasite Hypothesis)

151 Batman (Episode 11: The Justice League Recombination)

152 Howard's card trick (Episode 18: The Prestidigitation Approximation)

153 "a Brobdingnagian monstrosity" (Episode 4: The Hot Troll Deviation)

154 a talking Thomas the Tank Engine—"with real puffing smoke" (Episode 6: The Irish Pub Formulation)

155 his executive assistant (Episode 12: The Bus Pants Utilization)

156 a plastic cup taped to his eye (Episode 18: The Prestidigitation Approximation)

157 "pontoon plane" (Episode 8: The 21-Second Excitation)

158 when man fuses with robot—"The earliest estimate of the singularity—when man will be able to transfer his consciousness into machines and achieve immortality." (Episode 2: The Cruciferous Vegetable Amplification)

159 they light the candles and watch *Wheel of Fortune* on TV. (Episode 19: The Zarnecki Incursion)

160 karaoke—"get plastered and blow the roof off this place" (Episode 17: The Toast Derivation)

Amy: Are you familiar with the recent study of Tanzanian chimpanzees by Nishida and Hosaka out of Kyoto University?

Penny: No, but I can name all the Kardashians.

161 "The fun-loving and morally loose Miss Maggie McGarry." (Episode 6: The Irish Pub Formulation)

162 Lucky Baldwin's—"Pasadena's favorite Irish watering hole." (Episode 6: The Irish Pub Formulation)

163 Operation "Priya Wouldn't Wanna Be-Ya" (Episode 22: The Wildebeest Implementation)

164 "I need an orderly with a wheelchair. I've got a robot hand grasping a man's penis out here." (Episode 1: The Robotic Manipulation)

165 she turns it off and back on again (Episode 1: The Robotic Manipulation)

166 he removes the "2" from the front of the building (Episode 5: The Desperation Emanation)

167 using his toothbrush (Episode 6: The Irish Pub Formulation)

168 73—"Seventy-three is the twenty-first prime number. Its mirror, thirty-seven, is the twelfth, and its mirror, twenty-one, is the product of multiplying—hang on to your hats—seven and three." (Episode 10: The Alien Parasite Hypothesis)

169 Glenn (Episode 13: The Love Car Displacement)

170 he was one of her professors in college (Episode 13: The Love Car Displacement)

171 "What is the circumference of your areolae?" (Episode 8: The 21-Second Excitation)

172 the "check engine" light is on (Episode 1: The Robotic Manipulation)

173 he has a big crush on Bernadette—"I found poems he wrote about her. One particular phrase that both stands out and disturbs is, 'Oh, Bernadette, please play my clarinet.' " (Episode 20: The Herb Garden Germination)

174 she's passed on the gossip that Sheldon and Amy have had sex (Episode 20: The Herb Garden Germination)

175 Leonard, Sheldon, Penny and Amy (Episode 13: The Love Car Displacement)

176 it features 21 extra seconds of previously unseen footage (Episode 8: The 21-Second Excitation)

177 that foreigners give presents to Americans on Thanksgiving (Episode 6: The Irish Pub Formulation)

178 that foreigners wash Americans' clothes on the Fourth of July (Episode 6: The Irish Pub Formulation)

179 his mother—she'd read Mr. Spock (Episode 14: The Thespian Catalyst)

180 goes into the bathroom to throw up (Episode 21: The Agreement Dissection)

181 she thinks Priya is testing Bernadette's loyalty to Penny and the group (Episode 22: The Wildebeest Implementation)

182 sitar music—it's also his ringtone for Raj (Episode 19: The Zarnecki Incursion)

183 "Oh, I don't think so." (Episode 17: The Toast Derivation)

184 "I am so done with Twitter." (Episode 17: The Toast Derivation)

185 breaking in new high-heeled shoes (Episode 22: The Wildebeest Implementation)

186 Sheldon and Amy are engaged in sexual intercourse; Amy's thinking about starting a herb garden (Episode 20: The Herb Garden Germination)

187 Captain Arrogance (Episode 4: The Hot Troll Deviation)

188 Dr. Arroganto (Episode 4: The Hot Troll Deviation)

189 bouillon (Episode 22: The Wildebeest Implementation)

190 he tells Raj that he offered his heart to Priya, and she stomped on it—very hard (Episode 6: The Irish Pub Formulation)

191 why is she still hanging out with Leonard so much even though she broke up with him (Episode 8: The 21-Second Excitation)

192 "Labradoodle" (Episode 14: The Thespian Catalyst)

193 two (Episode 1: The Robotic Manipulation)

194 "in the South preadolescent children are forced through a process called cotillion" (Episode 21: The Agreement Dissection)

195 he tries to reverse engineer it—measuring residual heat levels to determine which card's been touched, and hacking into the Oak Ridge National Laboratory to use the Cray Supercomputer to analyze shuffling patterns (Episode 18: The Prestidigitation Approximation)

196 "black helicopters" (Episode 18: The Prestidigitation Approximation)

197 the new Sandra Bullock movie—"You know, Sandy B always brings it." (Episode 8: The 21-Second Excitation)

198 while looking for the bathroom, he backs away from a coughing man and winds up in an isolation room (Episode 23: The Engagement Reaction)

199 Penny (Episode 8: The 21-Second Excitation)

200 Imatote. Alba. Twad. "I'm a total buttwad." (Episode 8: The 21-Second Excitation)

Raj: Oh, Leonard. You remind me of the funny old story about a man who walks into a women's correctional institution with a stack of paperwork that would allow the female convicts to go free.

Leonard: You're saying I couldn't get laid in a women's prison with a handful of pardons.

Raj: Are you going to let me tell the story or not?

The Schrödinger Speculation

Sheldon: Well, let's see. We might consider Schrödinger's cat.

Penny: Schrödinger . . . is that the woman in 2A?

Sheldon: No, that's Mrs. Grossinger. And she doesn't have a cat, she has a Mexican hairless. Annoying little animal. Yip, yip, yip, yip.

Penny: Sheldon.

Sheldon: Sorry, you diverted me. Anyway, in 1935, Erwin Schrödinger, in an attempt to explain the Copenhagen interpretation of quantum physics, proposed an experiment where a cat is placed in a box with a sealed vial of poison that will break open at a random time. Since no one knows when or if the poison has been released, until the box is opened, the cat can be thought of as both alive and dead.

Penny: I'm sorry. I don't get the point.

Sheldon: Of course you don't get it. I haven't made it yet. You'd have to be psychic to get it and there's no such thing as "psychic."

Penny: Sheldon, what's the point?!

Sheldon: Just like Schrödinger's cat, your potential relationship with Leonard right now can be thought of as both good and bad. It is only by opening the box that you'll find out which it is.

Penny: So you're saying I should go out with him?

Sheldon: No, no, no. Let me start again. In 1935, Erwin Schrödinger, in an attempt to explain the Copenhagen interpretation of quantum physics . . .

Defeated, Penny listens as Sheldon drones on.

Season 1, Episode 17: The Tangerine Factor

Leonard: Oh. Um, okay, but before you say anything, have you ever heard of Schrödinger's cat?

Penny: Actually, I've heard far too much about Schrödinger's cat.

Leonard: Good.

Leonard kisses her. It's a good kiss.

Penny: All right, the cat's alive. Let's go get some dinner.

Season 1, Episode 17: The Tangerine Factor

Penny's walking up the stairs with her date, Eric.

Penny: . . . no, it wasn't my cat. It was an experiment designed by some guy named Schrödinger.

Eric: From the Charlie Brown cartoons?

Penny: No, he was some kind of scientist.

Season 2, Episode 2: The Codpiece Topology*

When a select group of scientists was invited to attend a weekend symposium at the former home of Richard Feynman, Sheldon wasn't included:

Sheldon: I can just picture 'em all in Feynman's house right now—probably discussing Schrödinger and at the same time not discussing Schrödinger. See, they're missing out on hilarious jokes like that.

Amy: And at the same time, not.

Season 8, Episode 20: The Fortification Implementation

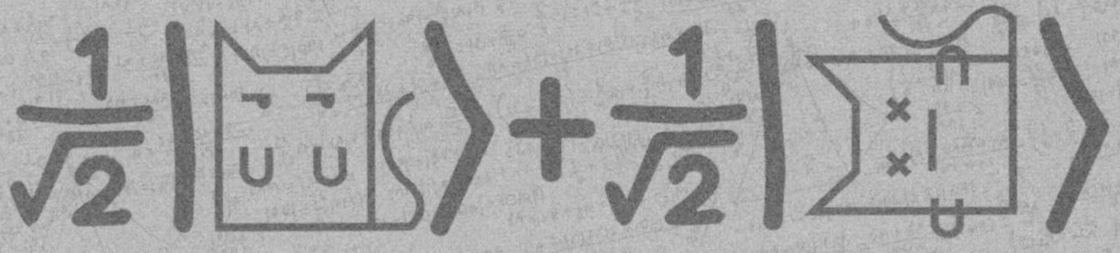

** This was one of the first moments, for me, that showed the effect Sheldon was having on Penny.*

Season 5

1 Longclaw from *Game of Thrones* (Episode 5: The Russian Rocket Reaction)

2 her old bathing suit (Episode 12: The Shiny Trinket Maneuver)

3 he picked up a girl in the store (Episode 7: The Good Guy Fluctuation)

4 Frankie Goes to Bollywood (Episode 4: The Wiggly Finger Catalyst)

5 Ferdinand T. Flag (Episode 14: The Beta Test Initiation)

6 "the vampires of the flower world" (Episode 9: The Ornithophobia Diffusion)

7 a measuring cup—"That's good—wineglasses should have handles." (Episode 1: The Skank Reflex Analysis)

8 the Super Mario Bros. theme (Episode 23: The Launch Acceleration)

9 switches it with Leonard's—it's "only logical" (Episode 20: The Transporter Malfunction)

10 from the street—it had been discarded (Episode 2: The Infestation Hypothesis)

11 Howard pranks Sheldon back by pretending to have a heart attack (Episode 7: The Good Guy Fluctuation)

12 Froot Loops (Episode 15: The Friendship Contraction)

13 while Howard is talking to Mike on the phone, Mrs. Wolowitz yells to Howard, "Howard, your Froot Loops are getting soggy!" (Episode 15: The Friendship Contraction)

14 cook paninis (Episode 2: The Infestation Hypothesis)

15 "I'm gonna have to move." (Episode 18: The Werewolf Transformation)

Leonard: Raj, you're our group historian. Has Sheldon ever begged before?

Raj: Three times. He begged the Fox network not to cancel *Firefly*. He begged the TNT network to cancel *Babylon Five*. And when he got food poisoning at the Rose Bowl Parade, he begged a deity he doesn't believe in to end his life quickly.

16 the pretend boyfriend Amy invented to get her family off her back (Episode 19: The Weekend Vortex)

17 one who can play guitar and is considerably taller than Leonard (Episode 3: The Pulled Groin Extrapolation)

18 Kazakhstan (Episode 24: The Countdown Reflection)

19 his new office is beneath the geology lab where they are running their sieve shakers (Episode 17: The Rothman Disintegration)

20 lichen (Episode 22: The Stag Convergence)

21 he spent the money on drugs (Episode 3: The Pulled Groin Extrapolation)

22 "I'm not gonna die in space! I'm gonna die the way God intended, in my late fifties, with a heart full of pastrami." (Episode 23: The Launch Acceleration)

23 a side of corn succotash, a pitcher of margaritas and a hot fudge sundae (Episode 4: The Wiggly Finger Catalyst)

24 calling her on the telephone—"The telephone. Leonard, in your own simple way, you may be the wisest of us all." (Episode 8: The Isolation Permutation)

25 he says they're not magic tricks, they're illusions (Episode 3: The Pulled Groin Extrapolation)

26 one of Howard's young cousins who is having a birthday party (Episode 12: The Shiny Trinket Maneuver)

27 Amy (Episode 14: The Beta Test Initiation)

28 he thinks Leonard has no intention of going—"You accept an invitation to a party at the home of my sworn enemy, he tells everyone we're going to be there, and when we don't show, he looks the fool." (Episode 5: The Russian Rocket Reaction)

29 because it's worth at least $100, and the gravy boat Sheldon bought them cost only $88 and that means Sheldon will be in Howard's debt—he might ask Sheldon to kill a man . . . (Episode 24: The Countdown Reflection)

30 "Will you marry me?" (Episode 23: The Launch Acceleration)

31 a pitcher Howard is using (Episode 12: The Shiny Trinket Maneuver)

32 the Born Again Boat Ride (Episode 6: The Rhinitis Revelation)

33 five thorny crowns (Episode 6: The Rhinitis Revelation)

34 a seagull stole it—"I got the message." (Episode 16: The Vacation Solution)

35 Lion-O from *Thundercats* drawn by Jim Lee (Episode 7: The Good Guy Fluctuation)

36 they're both brilliant scientists (Episode 17: The Rothman Disintegration)

37 "I couldn't give the furry crack of a rat's behind." (Episode 17: The Rothman Disintegration)

38 Raj's embarrassing toast at Howard's bachelor party (Episode 22: The Stag Convergence)

39 he's "dating" Siri (Episode 14: The Beta Test Initiation)

40 on Sheldon's spot (Episode 9: The Ornithophobia Diffusion)

41 "They do men's and women's hair in the same room at the same time." (Episode 18: The Werewolf Transformation)

42 a necklace with a five-pointed star pendant (Episode 24: The Countdown Reflection)

43 it makes their voices very low—Penny: “Leonard, I am your father.” Leonard: “I have never been more attracted to a woman who sounds like a man in my life.” (Episode 23: The Launch Acceleration)

44 a unicorn (Episode 16: The Vacation Solution)

45 “Like shooting nerds in a barrel.” (Episode 10: The Flaming Spittoon Acquisition)

46 Wild West and Witches (Episode 10: The Flaming Spittoon Acquisition)

47 Oreos (Episode 6: The Rhinitis Revelation)

48 she puts Leonard into checkmate (Episode 18: The Werewolf Transformation)

49 snapped (Episode 17: The Rothman Disintegration)

50 so he can take it to space and then she'll have something that has been in space (Episode 24: The Countdown Reflection)

51 go on a hunger strike—“It might take years before she's in any kind of danger, but still.” (Episode 6: The Rhinitis Revelation)

52 Penny and Leonard 2.0—“We can test it internally, shake out the bugs and if we both feel it's solid, then we roll it out to the public.” (Episode 13: The Recombination Hypothesis)

53 Tammy Bodnick (Episode 11: The Speckerman Recurrence)

Bernadette: I don't think I can meet the girl who was always mean to me. Tammy Bodnick. One time, while I was in gym class, she stole all my clothes and left an elf costume in my locker.

Penny: Oh, that's awful.

Bernadette: Worst part was, it was too big.

54 a tubby girl in a Sailor Moon costume—"There was about 200 pounds of Sailor Moon between us." (Episode 22: The Stag Convergence)

55 Physics Mad-libs (Episode 16: The Vacation Solution)

56 a deep field telescope (Episode 5: The Russian Rocket Reaction)

57 Shelly (Episode 6: The Rhinitis Revelation)

58 Dimitri Rezinov (Episode 24: The Countdown Reflection)

59 grabs a sweater and a pair of jeans (Episode 11: The Speckerman Recurrence)

60 in the middle of grabbing more clothes, she's suddenly conscience-stricken, and puts them back (Episode 11: The Speckerman Recurrence)

61 "Bazinga, punk. Now we're even." (Episode 7: The Good Guy Fluctuation)

62 Cookie Monster (Episode 23: The Launch Acceleration)

63 Irene (Episode 8: The Isolation Permutation)

64 she sees the video of Raj's speech and learns that Howard hasn't told her about sleeping with his second cousin, the prostitute or having a threesome with Raj (Episode 22: The Stag Convergence)

65 taking her dress shopping—"Get in here, grab a handful and start stuffing." (Episode 21: The Hawking Excitation)

66 "Hogwarts Express" (Episode 12: The Shiny Trinket Maneuver)

67 "Nice hat, Bob Tahecin." (Episode 12: The Shiny Trinket Maneuver)

68 one that will get him to transfer his childhood emotional attachments to her (Episode 23: The Launch Acceleration)

Howard: Whoa, you just bit my tongue!
Raj: I nibbled. I was being playful.

69 he's kind of outgrown *Star Trek*—"stock characters, ludicrous plots, beam me up. What a load of hooey." (Episode 5: The Russian Rocket Reaction)

70 she slept with a guy (Episode 7: The Good Guy Fluctuation)

71 a conver-sensation (Episode 8: The Isolation Permutation)

72 on the roof of Leonard, Sheldon and Penny's apartment building (Episode 24: The Countdown Reflection)

73 because on the day of their wedding, the Google satellite passes over Pasadena, and they can have a wedding photograph from space (Episode 24: The Countdown Reflection)

74 at a health club (Episode 4: The Wiggly Finger Catalyst)

75 *Needy Baby Greedy Baby* (Episode 13: The Recombination Hypothesis)

76 she severed the webbing between her toes (Episode 10: The Flaming Spittoon Acquisition)

77 leaves him (Episode 4: The Wiggly Finger Catalyst)

78 he has her sign his Relationship Agreement—all 31 pages of it (Episode 10: The Flaming Spittoon Acquisition)

79 a din-fast date (Episode 2: The Infestation Hypothesis)

80 honey (Episode 3: The Pulled Groin Extrapolation)

81 Captain (Episode 1: The Skank Reflex Analysis)

82 Bernadette has just suggested a girl who is married to a patient in one of her drug trials and he's in the placebo group . . . (Episode 4: The Wiggly Finger Catalyst)

83 Karen Berberick—"To this day, she doesn't know we were going out. It made it easier on her when I broke things off." (Episode 14: The Beta Test Initiation)

84 bacon grease (Episode 6: The Rhinitis Revelation)

Kripke: When you invite a man to a bachelor party, the implication is there will be strippers. Maybe not completely nude, but at least panties and G-strings. That's not unreasonable.

85 "awesome or nothing" (Episode 23: The Launch Acceleration)

86 in the movie theater, while she's on a date with Stuart (Episode 10: The Flaming Spittoon Acquisition)

87 peeling the plastic film off the phone (Episode 14: The Beta Test Initiation)

88 she asks Amy to be her maid of honor (Episode 8: The Isolation Permutation)

89 Brown Dynamite (Episode 15: The Friendship Contraction)

90 "To Sheldon, sorry this took so long. Your friend, Wil Wheaton." (Episode 5: The Russian Rocket Reaction)

91 Penny (Episode 4: The Wiggly Finger Catalyst)

92 he knows sign language (Episode 4: The Wiggly Finger Catalyst)

93 make "Rocket Man" by Elton John Howard's ringtone and the next time he's talking to them, Raj calls so they hear the song (Episode 15: The Friendship Contraction)

94 he commits paintball suicide by storming the field and exposing himself to the splats of the opposing side so the guys are motivated to avenge him (Episode 1: The Skank Reflex Analysis)

95 when you're in bed with him (Episode 16: The Vacation Solution)

96 he keeps demanding she make him fried chicken (Episode 6: The Rhinitis Revelation)

97 Leonard, Sheldon, Penny and Amy—they all got ordained online so they could perform the ceremony together (Episode 24: The Countdown Reflection)

98 "pickle jar" (Episode 16: The Vacation Solution)

99 be an Amtrak junior conductor for the day—"They let me blow the whistle, Leonard." (Episode 23: The Launch Acceleration)

100 "promiscuity" (Episode 6: The Rhinitis Revelation)

101 he's scared of horses (Episode 8: The Isolation Permutation)

102 Sandra Bullock—"because she's great in everything" (Episode 13: The Recombination Hypothesis)

103 take out a prenup (Episode 16: The Vacation Solution)

104 a necklace with a ruby pendant—"It was a little expensive, but no one can put a price on love. Although the people at Cartier took a pretty good shot at it." (Episode 4: The Wiggly Finger Catalyst)

105 Animal Control, to report a "dangerous wild animal" (Episode 9: The Ornithophobia Diffusion)

106 a pretzel (Episode 14: The Beta Test Initiation)

107 keeping tabs on his Twitter followers (Episode 12: The Shiny Trinket Maneuver)

108 he called first dibs—at the Christmas party, when Professor Rothman was trying to have intercourse with the Toys for Tots collection box (Episode 17: The Rothman Disintegration)

109 she is jealous of the affection and attention he gives it—"I guess you gotta have hollow bones to get some sugar around here." (Episode 9: The Ornithophobia Diffusion)

110 a huge painting of the two of them (Episode 17: The Rothman Disintegration)

111 see who can bounce a basketball higher (Episode 17: The Rothman Disintegration)

112 “train” (Episode 3: The Pulled Groin Extrapolation)

113 Sheldon is a “condescending jerk” and mean to him all the time (Episode 21: The Hawking Excitation)

114 “Tamagotchi” (Episode 16: The Vacation Solution)

115 “nephew” (Episode 18: The Werewolf Transformation)

116 he doesn’t like them thinking he’s jealous that Amy went out on a date with Stuart (Episode 10: The Flaming Spittoon Acquisition)

117 doing the hokey-pokey—“I put my left leg in, I took my left leg out, I put my left leg in, and something just snapped.” (Episode 3: The Pulled Groin Extrapolation)

118 a kissing machine (Episode 2: The Infestation Hypothesis)

119 Raj—both of them with increasing enthusiasm, much to Leonard’s discomfort (Episode 2: The Infestation Hypothesis)

120 with his hand (Episode 23: The Launch Acceleration)

121 trick shots (Episode 19: The Weekend Vortex)

122 he’s a notary public—“one of my lesser dreams”—and has been notarizing banking documents for Raj (Episode 4: The Wiggly Finger Catalyst)

123 she doesn’t want her parents to find out she’s gay (Episode 20: The Transporter Malfunction)

124 that he’s “comfortable in a sari” (Episode 20: The Transporter Malfunction)

125 a pair of glasses that makes any movie you want into 3D (Episode 11: The Speckerman Recurrence)

126 a Mexican peso (Episode 12: The Shiny Trinket Maneuver)

127 “skank reflex” (Episode 1: The Skank Reflex Analysis)

> **Sheldon:** Can I ask you a question about women?
>
> **Leonard:** We got you that book last year. Wasn't everything in there?
>
> **Sheldon:** No, I'm having a relationship problem with Amy. And by the way, that book gave me nightmares.

128 "I have no interest in model trains, stores that sell them, nor their heartbreaking clientele." (Episode 3: The Pulled Groin Extrapolation)

129 a butterfly—"It was so small and beautiful, but I was so hungry." (Episode 18: The Werewolf Transformation)

130 they give him a Yorkie puppy (Episode 20: The Transporter Malfunction)

131 Stephen Hawking—"I took my dad's desk chair, attached a Speak and Spell to it and made my sister push me up and down the block to trick or treat. Granted, most people thought I was R2-D2, but still, I got a lot of candy." (Episode 21: The Hawking Excitation)

132 cuddling (Episode 8: The Isolation Permutation)

133 "Get your women in line!" (Episode 8: The Isolation Permutation)

134 Nancy (Episode 11: The Speckerman Recurrence)

135 karate chops Leonard on the side of the neck, a la Captain Kirk—"To send a message. She is not for you." (Episode 3: The Pulled Groin Extrapolation)

136 *Next Men* #21—first appearance of Hellboy (Episode 7: The Good Guy Fluctuation)

137 gears and springs from Hawking's wheelchair—"I made some adjustments on the motor drive and when I was putting it back together I could not for the life of me figure out where they went." (Episode 21: The Hawking Excitation)

138 scotch (Episode 22: The Stag Convergence)

139 Dale (Episode 10: The Flaming Spittoon Acquisition)

140 they want a rest from her—"She keeps telling us stories about bridesmaid traditions in other cultures, and they're all about getting naked and washing each other." (Episode 8: The Isolation Permutation)

141 diarrhea and constipation—"We labeled them stop and go." (Episode 22: The Stag Convergence)

142 making an enormous ball of twine (Episode 2: The Infestation Hypothesis)

143 "the best I've ever had" (Episode 4: The Wiggly Finger Catalyst)

144 his mother's fried chicken (Episode 6: The Rhinitis Revelation)

145 the Chicken Dance—although Leonard only kind of manages to do the gestures (Episode 3: The Pulled Groin Extrapolation)

146 he wears long underwear (Episode 23: The Launch Acceleration)

147 "That's mighty white of you." (Episode 6: The Rhinitis Revelation)

148 it's Zachary Quinto and not Leonard Nimoy—"Live long and suck it, Zachary Quinto!" (Episode 13: The Recombination Hypothesis)

149 Lovey Dovey (Episode 9: The Ornithophobia Diffusion)

150 run screaming out of the apartment (Episode 2: The Infestation Hypothesis)

Bernadette: *(on Howard)* I had no choice. I had to tell his mother. He can't go to space. He's like a baby bird. Did you know he once got an asthma attack from reading an old library book?

151 it's back out on the street, and Howard and Raj, all unsuspecting, gleefully carry it back into the apartment building (Episode 2: The Infestation Hypothesis)

152 "It's okay, I serve soup to poor people!" (Episode 11: The Speckerman Recurrence)

153 *Neuron* (Episode 12: The Shiny Trinket Maneuver)

154 if it was cooked . . . and if it was beef (Episode 6: The Rhinitis Revelation)

155 9:00 p.m. (Episode 7: The Good Guy Fluctuation)

156 superheroes (Episode 23: The Launch Acceleration)

157 "multiplication" (Episode 16: The Vacation Solution)

158 hemorrhoid cream—and Penny speaks the punchline: she's "sittin' pretty" (Episode 1: The Skank Reflex Analysis)

159 Penny (Episode 4: The Wiggly Finger Catalyst)

160 61 (Episode 5: The Russian Rocket Reaction)

161 nine (Episode 5: The Russian Rocket Reaction)

162 Stuart (Episode 15: The Friendship Contraction)

163 the weekend of his wedding to Bernadette (Episode 23: The Launch Acceleration)

164 an "empty financial" one (Episode 12: The Shiny Trinket Maneuver)

165 list the ingredients in Pringles—"The uterus quivers, does it not?" (Episode 24: The Countdown Reflection)

166 by stroking it—it's "a sweetie" (Episode 9: The Ornithophobia Diffusion)

167 a missile silo (Episode 6: The Rhinitis Revelation)

168 mint-condition *Fantastic Four* Annual #3 from 1965—the one where Mr. Fantastic and the Invisible Girl get married (Episode 24: The Countdown Reflection)

169 Rogaine hair restorer (Episode 11: The Speckerman Recurrence)

170 Gorilla Fingers Fowler (Episode 11: The Speckerman Recurrence)

171 Howard (Episode 4: The Wiggly Finger Catalyst)

172 Houston (Episode 6: The Rhinitis Revelation)

173 her mother (Episode 3: The Pulled Groin Extrapolation)

174 "Dear Amy, Self-respect and a hymen are better than friends and fun. Love, Mom." (Episode 3: The Pulled Groin Extrapolation)

175 "party planner" (Episode 24: The Countdown Reflection)

176 a pocket watch (Episode 12: The Shiny Trinket Maneuver)

177 a tiara (Episode 12: The Shiny Trinket Maneuver)

178 "Your name on my list. From this moment on, you are my mortal enemy." (Episode 5: The Russian Rocket Reaction)

179 "Here ya go." (Episode 24: The Countdown Reflection)

180 "What am I, a football?" (Episode 24: The Countdown Reflection)

181 in the video game Red Dead Redemption (Episode 12: The Shiny Trinket Maneuver)

182 Penny (Episode 4: The Wiggly Finger Catalyst)

183 coffee (Episode 6: The Rhinitis Revelation)

184 a smile (Episode 6: The Rhinitis Revelation)

185 Howard becoming an astronaut—"You go up to that space station, and you make me proud." (Episode 23: The Launch Acceleration)

186 her gynecologist (Episode 3: The Pulled Groin Extrapolation)

187 Since she makes way more money than he does, she'd go to work while he stayed home with the kids—"You know, you'll watch *Barney* and pull Cheerios out of their noses and go on play dates, and I'll work and have conversations with people my own age and enjoy my life." (Episode 12: The Shiny Trinket Maneuver)

188 he shoots himself in the foot (Episode 14: The Beta Test Initiation)

189 he's a biter (Episode 15: The Friendship Contraction)

190 he cuts his thumb and passes out (Episode 16: The Vacation Solution)

191 to thank them for paying for her takeout food all the time (Episode 20: The Transporter Malfunction)

192 Kathy Geiger (Episode 11: The Speckerman Recurrence)

193 Penny (Episode 7: The Good Guy Fluctuation)

194 "a waterfall of liquid gold" (Episode 1: The Skank Reflex Analysis)

195 the house Howard shares with his mother (Episode 3: The Pulled Groin Extrapolation)

196 he could tie a string to its leg and fly it like a kite (Episode 9: The Ornithophobia Diffusion)

197 Strawberry Quik (Episode 23: The Launch Acceleration)

198 koala bears—"I don't know what it is, but when they start munching on eucalyptus, I just melt inside." (Episode 12: The Shiny Trinket Maneuver)

199 Jesus—"Look where it got him." (Episode 6: The Rhinitis Revelation)

200 Jerry's Junction (Episode 3: The Pulled Groin Extrapolation)

Sheldon: Boldly go, Howard Wolowitz.

Season 6

1 Penny's eyelash curler (Episode 3: The Higgs Boson Observation)

2 he spanks her (Episode 10: The Fish Guts Displacement)

3 Bernadette (Episode 13: The Bakersfield Expedition)

4 they all present him with a possible account of what his father wrote, but only one is true—Howard will never know which one (Episode 19: The Closet Reconfiguration)

5 "I told everyone it was herpes." (Episode 1: The Date Night Variable)

6 she'll die of gout (Episode 11: The Santa Simulation)

7 a *Rockford Files* rerun (Episode 15: The Spoiler Alert Segmentation)

8 cream sherry (Episode 15: The Spoiler Alert Segmentation)

9 a rap star—"like Snoop Dogg but with a healthy respect for the police" (Episode 18: The Contractual Obligation Implementation)

10 he makes her his emergency contact on his CalTech university employee information sheet (Episode 16: The Tangible Affection Proof)

11 Mrs. Wolowitz's underwear—"I had to take another shower. It wasn't enough. Nothing will ever be enough." (Episode 6: The Extract Obliteration)

12 Nicolas Cage, Christopher Walken and Al Pacino (Episode 23: The Love Spell Potential)

13 Amy (Episode 24: The Bon Voyage Reaction)

14 "Buzz Lightyear" (Episode 2: The Decoupling Fluctuation)

15 because she's been an emotional wreck since the dentist she was dating dumped her (Episode 15: The Spoiler Alert Segmentation)

16 a guy she used to date with the girl he dumped Penny for (Episode 16: The Tangible Affection Proof)

17 he stuffed Howard and his briefcase in the locker (Episode 18: The Contractual Obligation Implementation)

18 Sheldon's assistant, Alex, asks him out on a date (Episode 12: The Egg Salad Equivalency)

19 playing outside (Episode 3: The Higgs Boson Observation)

20 "full of eggs and only appealing for a short time" (Episode 12: The Egg Salad Equivalency)

21 explode when the people say something stupid (Episode 20: The Tenure Turbulence)

22 the prayer for eating bread—"We don't have one for falling out of space!" (Episode 4: The Re-Entry Minimization)

23 Brewbacca's (Episode 21: The Closure Alternative)

24 Sleeping Beauty (Episode 18: The Contractual Obligation Implementation)

Sheldon: *(into phone)* President Siebert, listen to reason. Yeah, I understand I don't use the parking spot, but that's not the point . . . Yes, I'm aware you told me not to call you at home, but you didn't answer the door, and I know you were there because I saw you through the mail slot . . . Well, that's some salty language. May I remind you that you're the president of a major university, not the president of the Potty Mouth Club . . . There it is again. Do you kiss your mother with that mouth? . . . Oh, well, I'm sorry for your loss. Good night, sir.

25 Snow White—Amy: "Sheldon, all Snow White needs is one little kiss to wake up." Sheldon: "I heard you the first time." (Episode 18: The Contractual Obligation Implementation)

26 he brings a whiteboard, chair and laptop to the spot and does his work from there (Episode 9: The Parking Spot Escalation)

27 Leonard's car gets stolen (Episode 13: The Bakersfield Expedition)

28 a girl tells him she thought his speech was cool, so they leave together (Episode 16: The Tangible Affection Proof)

29 by email (Episode 24: The Bon Voyage Reaction)

30 a pie-eating contest (Episode 4: The Re-Entry Minimization)

31 it doesn't come with kung fu grip (Episode 14: The Cooper/Kripke Inversion)

32 "To Stuart, your comic book store is 'out of this world,' just like the guy in this picture was." (Episode 5: The Holographic Excitation)

33 Mike (Episode 10: The Fish Guts Displacement)

34 having to live with an insanely jealous roommate— "I might have to sleep with a gun under my pillow. Or a chainsaw." (Episode 20: The Tenure Turbulence)

35 *A Streetcar Named Desire* (Episode 17: The Monster Isolation)

36 Words with Friends (Episode 6: The Extract Obliteration)

37 Albert Einstein (Episode 5: The Holographic Excitation)

38 "stay here, order a pizza and watch one of your beloved *Star War Trek* things" (Episode 16: The Tangible Affection Proof)

Kripke: You gave it to her good, huh?
Sheldon: No, I gave it to her well.

39 he talks to her without alcohol (Episode 24: The Bon Voyage Reaction)

40 *Alphas* (Episode 21: The Closure Alternative)

41 $500 each (Episode 14: The Cooper/Kripke Inversion)

42 Coop and Wheels (Episode 6: The Extract Obliteration)

43 Rolling Thunder (Episode 6: The Extract Obliteration)

44 a sad-tini (Episode 1: The Date Night Variable)

45 sneaks out of the window (Episode 17: The Monster Isolation)

46 bangs (Episode 23: The Love Spell Potential)

47 being a pretty waitress at the Cheesecake Factory (Episode 20: The Tenure Turbulence)

48 Leonard (Episode 11: The Santa Simulation)

49 Wil Wheaton (Episode 7: The Habitation Configuration)

50 Stephen Hawking (Episode 24: The Bon Voyage Reaction)

51 a Valentine's Day gift for Amy (Episode 16: The Tangible Affection Proof)

52 83 (Episode 22: The Proton Resurgence)

53 rubber cement (Episode 10: The Fish Guts Displacement)

54 while she is sleeping, he swabs her cheek and has it cultured in a lab (Episode 10: The Fish Guts Displacement)

55 in the university gym—on an elliptical machine (Episode 20: The Tenure Turbulence)

56 her corduroys make too much noise (Episode 8: The 43 Peculiarity)

57 "dead ogres" (Episode 23: The Love Spell Potential)

Penny: I hate it when you make me sit through all the credits.

Leonard: Well, sometimes there's a secret ending, like in *The Avengers*.

Penny: Yeah, but I don't think that's gonna happen in a documentary about the Holocaust.

58 a mocked-up video where it looks like he's getting sucked into a wormhole and attacked by a weird alien creature, that he makes to fool Howard and Raj (Episode 8: The 43 Peculiarity)

59 one of the lint traps in the laundry room (Episode 19: The Closet Reconfiguration)

60 melted Crayolas and duct tape (Episode 9: The Parking Spot Escalation)

61 his pacemaker (Episode 22: The Proton Resurgence)

62 the serial killer who ate all those prostitutes (Episode 18: The Contractual Obligation Implementation)

63 through the wire fence in the alleyway behind the restaurant after she has climbed out of the window (Episode 23: The Love Spell Potential)

64 "A micro Valentine for a microbiologist." (Episode 16: The Tangible Affection Proof)

65 "From her micro husband." (Episode 16: The Tangible Affection Proof)

66 Vasquez Rocks (Episode 13: The Bakersfield Expedition)

67 hydrodynamic simulations of black holes (Episode 24: The Bon Voyage Reaction)

68 VapoRub—Sheldon: "You may notice some tingling." Amy: "I'm counting on it." (Episode 10: The Fish Guts Displacement)

69 Zeusowitz (Episode 1: The Date Night Variable)

70 Sheldon has a girlfriend, so he's getting laid all the time (Episode 14: The Cooper/Kripke Inversion)

71 Hogwarts (Episode 17: The Monster Isolation)

72 "foreskin" (Episode 5: The Holographic Excitation)

73 Howard's (Episode 18: The Contractual Obligation Implementation)

74 a Long Island Iced Tea (Episode 7: The Habitation Configuration)

75 Wil Wheaton's house—to confront him because he'd been rude to Amy (Episode 7: The Habitation Configuration)

76 "Latin" (Episode 17: The Monster Isolation)

77 Penny (Episode 10: The Fish Guts Displacement)

78 B– (Episode 6: The Extract Obliteration)

79 Cinderella (Episode 18: The Contractual Obligation Implementation)

80 they lose her (Episode 22: The Proton Resurgence)

81 his mother (Episode 1: The Date Night Variable)

82 grape (Episode 11: The Santa Simulation)

83 petroleum (Episode 11: The Santa Simulation)

84 accidentally breaks the TSA agent's nose with her elbow (Episode 23: The Love Spell Potential)

85 takes him off their joint bank account (Episode 14: The Cooper/Kripke Inversion)

86 green apple (Episode 2: The Decoupling Fluctuation)

87 he's missing gravity (Episode 3: The Higgs Boson Observation)

88 Sheldon Cooper's Council of Ladies (Episode 12: The Egg Salad Equivalency)

89 T-shirts with "Sheldon Cooper's Council of Ladies" printed on them (Episode 12: The Egg Salad Equivalency)

90 she scripts a new outgoing voice mail message for both of them (Episode 15: The Spoiler Alert Segmentation)

91 “Magnets: What Do They Stick To?” (Episode 3: The Higgs Boson Observation)

92 because every couple of months he’d have to let his mom’s pants out (Episode 13: The Bakersfield Expedition)

93 “Go Sports” (Episode 1: The Date Night Variable)

94 behaved inappropriately in the workplace—he was giving her a “talking-to” about her own inappropriate behavior towards Leonard and made her uncomfortable (Episode 12: The Egg Salad Equivalency)

95 she wants to spread her scent and mark her territory, because she’s worried Sheldon’s new assistant, Alex, will hit on him (Episode 3: The Higgs Boson Observation)

96 because Mr. Data’s weapon is his mind—Sheldon is wielding it, standing to one side and looking thoughtful (Episode 13: The Bakersfield Expedition)

97 “Uh-oh, is someone a little blue?” (Episode 5: The Holographic Excitation)

98 because he didn’t land on the moon or fly the rocket—“So you just flew around? That’s kinda like my uncle—he’s a flight attendant.” (Episode 18: The Contractual Obligation Implementation)

99 if Thor’s magic hammer bestows power only on one who is worthy, who decides who’s worthy? (Episode 13: The Bakersfield Expedition)

100 “You don’t know his life.” (Episode 13: The Bakersfield Expedition)

101 kisses him on the nose and cheeks (Episode 4: The Re-Entry Minimization)

102 kisses him too (Episode 4: The Re-Entry Minimization)

Sheldon: *(to Leonard)* I'm not saying you don't have attractive qualities. Your choice of friends is impeccable. You're a good sleeper. And last but not least, you buy the grapes I like. You're a real catch compared to some snoring guy with a fridge full of lousy grapes.

103 Willy Wonka (Episode 5: The Holographic Excitation)

104 Raj's is African American and Howard's has a huge nose (Episode 14: The Cooper/Kripke Inversion)

105 Wesley Snipes and Toucan Sam (Episode 14: The Cooper/Kripke Inversion)

106 Bernadette (Episode 23: The Love Spell Potential)

107 Cornell University (Episode 22: The Proton Resurgence)

108 a 90-minute video detailing his past and his love affair with astrophysics (Episode 20: The Tenure Turbulence)

109 a DVD box set of *Roots* (Episode 20: The Tenure Turbulence)

110 the screen had frozen—"Still one of my top three dates of all time" (Episode 24: The Bon Voyage Reaction)

111 Dumbledore dies in the sixth book (Episode 15: The Spoiler Alert Segmentation)

112 Food that Goes Bump in the Night (Episode 5: The Holographic Excitation)

113 takeout from Siam Palace—it's Thai food night (Episode 19: The Closet Reconfiguration)

114 because she's spent all day cooking Thai food from scratch and Sheldon asks her if she feels silly now (Episode 19: The Closet Reconfiguration)

115 "Being mean is lame. What's cool is being nice." (Episode 2: The Decoupling Fluctuation)

116 "Sheldon After Dark" (Episode 12: The Egg Salad Equivalency)

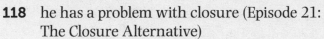

117 so she can lick the plates clean when no one's looking (Episode 7: The Habitation Configuration)

118 he has a problem with closure (Episode 21: The Closure Alternative)

119 "It's the sexiest accent you can have." (Episode 8: The 43 Peculiarity)

120 she tells him that Harry and Ginny get together (Episode 15: The Spoiler Alert Segmentation)

121 "astronaut screams for nine minutes" (Episode 2: The Decoupling Fluctuation)

122 Howard has been playing X-Box instead of doing the laundry (Episode 16: The Tangible Affection Proof)

123 rewrites it (Episode 6: The Extract Obliteration)

124 come on his two-year anniversary date night with Amy (Episode 1: The Date Night Variable)

125 so he can go as Indiana Jones's "mocha-skinned love child," Indian Jones (Episode 5: The Holographic Excitation)

126 he wobbles to the whiteboard, says, "I'm okay" and topples over, taking the board with him (Episode 4: The Re-Entry Minimization)

127 lobster . . . and garlic butter (Episode 17: The Monster Isolation)

128 Janine (Episode 12: The Egg Salad Equivalency)

129 Good King Wenceslas (Episode 11: The Santa Simulation)

130 "It's a possibility." (Episode 14: The Cooper/Kripke Inversion)

131 goes with the girls on their night out to a bar (Episode 11: The Santa Simulation)

132 an Indian casino near Palm Springs (Episode 10: The Fish Guts Displacement)

133 "How do I get twelve-year-old girls excited?"—Leonard and Howard in unison: "No!" (Episode 18: The Contractual Obligation Implementation)

134 sits naked—"I need a nice cool piece of leather to wiggle my naked ass on." (Episode 9: The Parking Spot Escalation)

135 "sea lion" (Episode 4: The Re-Entry Minimization)

136 "boa constrictor" (Episode 14: The Cooper/Kripke Inversion)

137 *Fables* #1 (Episode 13: The Bakersfield Expedition)

138 calling Bernadette and Amy for help (Episode 18: The Contractual Obligation Implementation)

139 holding hands (Episode 2: The Decoupling Fluctuation)

140 he's going to be at the telescope lab (Episode 22: The Proton Resurgence)

141 because Sheldon is a savant at organizing—Howard would only have to show it to him, and "let the goblins in his head take it from there" (Episode 19: The Closet Reconfiguration)

142 a whistle (Episode 14: The Cooper/Kripke Inversion)

143 only three hours (Episode 14: The Cooper/Kripke Inversion)

144 paprika (Episode 8: The 43 Peculiarity)

Amy: I'll tell you what they think. They think our relationship is a joke.

Sheldon: Well, I don't think our relationship is a joke. I think a horse goes into a bar, bartender says, "Why the long face?" That's a joke. It's a good one, too, because a horse has a long face.

145 home fries or an English muffin—"not both, we're watching our weight" (Episode 22: The Proton Resurgence)

146 a veal chop or some scampi (Episode 22: The Proton Resurgence)

147 Gavin (Episode 21: The Closure Alternative)

148 by sitting naked in the driver's seat and wiggling (Episode 9: The Parking Spot Escalation)

149 the university library (Episode 18: The Contractual Obligation Implementation)

150 *Spider-Man* (Episode 10: The Fish Guts Displacement)

151 the Lisatronic 3000 (Episode 5: The Holographic Excitation)

152 *Thor* (Episode 13: The Bakersfield Expedition)

153 "feces" (Episode 17: The Monster Isolation)

154 Bernadette and Amy (Episode 6: The Extract Obliteration)

155 Dr. Peter Higgs—he had to wait fifty years for his discovery to be recognized (Episode 3: The Higgs Boson Observation)

156 the complete works of Jackie Chan (Episode 20: The Tenure Turbulence)

157 the TARDIS from *Doctor Who* (Episode 5: The Holographic Excitation)

158 she has a panic attack and walks away (Episode 18: The Contractual Obligation Implementation)

159 *Buffy the Vampire Slayer*—"It's got action and jokes and hot vampires and romance." (Episode 21: The Closure Alternative)

Sheldon: You know what they say? Revenge is a dish best served nude.

160 TV host Howie Mandel is walking out right behind him (Episode 4: The Re-Entry Minimization)

161 perform a kids' science show for him (Episode 22: The Proton Resurgence)

162 tells him that Penny's boyfriend is a "pretty scary dude" in a crazy gang called the Scientists (Episode 8: The 43 Peculiarity)

163 they set up a webcam to spy on him (Episode 8: The 43 Peculiarity)

164 her bikini wax (Episode 9: The Parking Spot Escalation)

165 somewhere in the desert they crossed into an alternative universe—"where the women in our lives can finally appreciate great literature" (Episode 13: The Bakersfield Expedition)

166 Janine the Machine (Episode 20: The Tenure Turbulence)

167 to determine if it is personal correspondence or memorabilia (Episode 19: The Closet Reconfiguration)

168 hot apple cider with cinnamon sticks (Episode 14: The Cooper/Kripke Inversion)

169 to bring his Pop-Pop back—Pop-Pop was the only person in his family who encouraged Sheldon to pursue science (Episode 11: The Santa Simulation)

170 Gino the Neutrino (Episode 22: The Proton Resurgence)

171 he went into his first anaphylactic shock (Episode 7: The Habitation Configuration)

172 raisinets (Episode 2: The Decoupling Fluctuation)

173 having sex with Howard's dentist, Dr. Schneider (Episode 4: The Re-Entry Minimization)

174 Ricardo Shilly-Shally (Episode 12: The Egg Salad Equivalency)

175 the name Sheldon uses for Alex (Episode 12: The Egg Salad Equivalency.

176 his precious Iron Man helmet—"I wanted it, and you weren't using it. Apparently those are the rules we live by now." (Episode 9: The Parking Spot Escalation)

177 her online blog (Episode 21: The Closure Alternative)

178 by wearing a hockey sweater—"I wanted you to think I was more manly." (Episode 21: The Closure Alternative)

179 to fill in for him at a children's gig in Alhambra (Episode 22: The Proton Resurgence)

180 he hasn't told his mother that they aren't going to live with her (Episode 1: The Date Night Variable)

181 LeVar Burton (Episode 7: The Habitation Configuration)

182 $5,000 (Episode 14: The Cooper/Kripke Inversion)

183 "neck size" (Episode 8: The 43 Peculiarity)

184 it's Sheldon's personal hacky sack record (Episode 8: The 43 Peculiarity)

185 a chess clock (Episode 6: The Extract Obliteration)

186 he says he's had a thing for both Penny and Bernadette, and it's obvious to all that he's never had one for Amy (Episode 11: The Santa Simulation)

187 rolls the dice so they can play out the love spell cast on them in character—she's a half-orc warrior and he's an elven magic user (Episode 23: The Love Spell Potential)

188 Raggedy Ann and Raggedy C-3PO—Sheldon: "It was a compromise. I lost." (Episode 5: The Holographic Excitation)

189 that it's leaps and bounds better that his (Episode 14: The Cooper/Kripke Inversion)

190 it's not at the level he expected—Sheldon has to buckle down and focus (Episode 14: The Cooper/Kripke Inversion)

191 "nonsense and twaddle" (Episode 7: The Habitation Configuration)

192 four months (Episode 24: The Bon Voyage Reaction)

193 "In the event of a divorce, please return to Sheldon Cooper." (Episode 2: The Decoupling Fluctuation)

194 "*There's Waldo*" (Episode 4: The Re-Entry Minimization)

195 sexy cop, *not* slutty cop—"Slutty cop only came with a skirt and two badges." (Episode 5: The Holographic Excitation)

196 sets it on fire and drops it in the sink (Episode 19: The Closet Reconfiguration)

197 Bernadette (Episode 9: The Parking Spot Escalation)

198 he blames Penny—"She doesn't want to live with Leonard, so he has to come live here again. She's the snake in our garden. She's the reason we can't be happy." (Episode 15: The Spoiler Alert Segmentation)

199 Professor Tupperman (Episode 20: The Tenure Turbulence)

200 her wallet, keys and "a coffee can full of change I was meaning to take to the bank" (Episode 9: The Parking Spot Escalation)

Leonard: You want me to make you some tea?

Sheldon: Tea is for when I'm upset. I'm not upset. The university is forcing me to work with Kripke. I am outraged.

Leonard: So . . . cocoa?

Sheldon: Yes, cocoa.

The Vexillology Exposition

The first episode of *Sheldon Cooper Presents: Fun with Flags* was in 2012.

Sheldon: Hello, I'm Dr. Sheldon Cooper, and welcome to the premiere episode of *Sheldon Cooper Presents: Fun with Flags*. Over the next fifty-two weeks, you and I are going to explore the dynamic world of vexillology.

Amy: Hang on, Dr. C. What's vexillology?

Sheldon: Vexillology is the study of flags.

Amy: Cool, I think I just learned something.

Sheldon: Did you have fun doing it?

Amy: I'll say.

Sheldon: Why are you waving a white flag?

Amy: I'm surrendering. To fun.

Season 5, Episode 14: The Beta Test Initiation

Behind the scenes of *Fun with Flags* in The Habitation Configuration (Season 6, Episode 7) was tumultuous when Amy and guest star Wil Wheaton butted heads. A subsequent filming of *Flags* in the same episode featured guest LeVar Burton.

Sheldon has Penny as a guest:

Sheldon: Now, *Fun with Flags* is not just for the flag aficionado, it's also for the flag novice. So, to help me with that, please welcome my friend, neighbor and flag virgin—yeah, not a real virgin, no, she's had coitus many times, sometimes within earshot of this flag enthusiast, once while he was trying to watch *The Incredibles*—Penny.

Season 6, Episode 17: The Monster Isolation

Sheldon filmed what he thought was going to be his final episode:

Sheldon: Welcome back. Our guest today is a returning fan favorite—he puts the reading in your rainbow, the Geordi in your La Forge and the Kunta in your Kinte: Mr. LeVar Burton.

Sheldon: Well, my little Flag-keteers, it looks like our last episode of *Fun with Flags* is at an end. If I could, I would run each and every one of you viewers up a flagpole and salute you. And if you touched the ground, burn you. *(then)* I'd like to take a moment to personally thank Dr. Amy Farrah Fowler, who you may or may not know is the first woman to cohost a flag- or banner-related internet infotainment show.

Amy: Take that, glass ceiling.

Sheldon picks up the white flag from earlier.

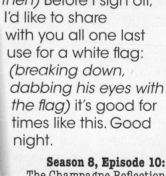

Sheldon: And if I may get serious for a moment, hosting this show has been one crazy ride. *(starting to get emotional)* With all its ups and downs, I wouldn't give it up for the world, except for now, when I'm giving it up. *(then)* Before I sign off, I'd like to share with you all one last use for a white flag: *(breaking down, dabbing his eyes with the flag)* it's good for times like this. Good night.

Season 8, Episode 10:
The Champagne Reflection

But maybe, just maybe, hope isn't lost . . .

Sheldon: *(looking at laptop)* Someone left a comment.

Leonard: Yeah, what'd it say?

Sheldon: *(reading)* "Too bad your show is done. I kinda liked it." *(then)* Leonard, did you hear that? The people are heartbroken! I can't take this away from the world! *Fun with Flags* is back!

Season 7

1 Debbie (Episode 24: The Status Quo Combustion)

2 "my parents' money" (Episode 4: The Raiders Minimization)

3 capuchin (Episode 5: The Workplace Proximity)

4 football (Episode 9: The Thanksgiving Decoupling)

5 the Retractor (Episode 10: The Discovery Dissipation)

6 because she loves it and then he can act cool with her (Episode 21: The Anything Can Happen Recurrence)

7 he's in the middle of a party, having the "best time of my life" (Episode 1: The Hofstadter Insufficiency)

8 Stanford (Episode 18: The Mommy Observation)

9 he wants time alone with Penny (Episode 2: The Deception Verification)

10 a Batman squirt gun (Episode 2: The Deception Verification)

11 $200 (Episode 2: The Deception Verification)

12 bridge-of-nose herpes (Episode 23: The Gorilla Dissolution)

13 fat—"You'd have no girlfriend to see you naked, you'd try to fill the void with food and I'm an enabler who once deep-fried a pancake." (Episode 11: The Cooper Extraction)

14 hugs him (Episode 22: The Proton Transmogrification)

15 not saying yes when she asked him to marry her (Episode 22: The Proton Transmogrification)

Beverly: Leonard, would it make you feel better to hear that your mother approves of your life choices?
Leonard: Yes, it would.
Beverly: You should work on that.

16 tourmalinated (Episode 13: The Occupation Recalibration)

17 flowers and chocolates—“Don’t be surprised if you find five chocolates missing and three gross coconut ones with a bite taken out. It came that way when I bought it.” (Episode 15: The Locomotive Manipulation)

18 hire him to look after Mrs. Wolowitz (Episode 24: The Status Quo Combustion)

19 elephant (Episode 2: The Deception Verification)

20 Jones tweeted he was going to his favorite sushi restaurant for dinner—Sheldon: “I googled an interview from four years ago which was conducted in his favorite sushi restaurant. That’s where he’ll be and that’s where I’m going . . .” Howard: “And that’s where Darth Vader’s gonna pour soy sauce over your head.” (Episode 14: The Convention Conundrum)

21 “I’m hoping to put his love of repetition to good use someday.” (Episode 5: The Workplace Proximity)

22 Sheldon and Penny, Leonard and Bernadette, Howard and Amy (Episode 3: The Scavenger Vortex)

23 *Star Wars* Day, May the Fourth—“May the Fourth be with with you.” (Episode 22: The Proton Transmogrification)

24 a boy (Episode 11: The Cooper Extraction)

25 *The Disappointing Child* (Episode 4: The Raiders Minimization)

26 Raj feels comfortable opening up about his feelings to the girls, and he can’t do that with Howard there (Episode 7: The Proton Displacement)

27 Stuart (Episode 12: The Hesitation Ramification)

28 Wil Wheaton (Episode 19: The Indecision Amalgamation)

Amy: How do you not know how to use glue? Did you ditch preschool?

Penny: Yeah, but only because I was dating a second grader.

29 getting a job at the Cheesecake Factory (Episode 19: The Indecision Amalgamation)

30 Robert Downey Jr.—"I sat through *Iron Man 2*. I believe he owes me two hours of his time." (Episode 14: The Convention Conundrum)

31 a box fell on his head at UPS six years ago (Episode 15: The Locomotive Manipulation)

32 Zack—who spends the rent money on magic beans (Episode 11: The Cooper Extraction)

33 paralyzing fear (Episode 5: The Workplace Proximity)

34 London (Episode 18: The Mommy Observation)

35 an owl (Episode 22: The Proton Transmogrification)

36 Stuart had been cooking in the back room and the hot plate caught fire while he was across the street at the do-it-yourself car wash taking a shower (Episode 24: The Status Quo Combustion)

37 an ugly, itchy sweater that says "Lenny" on it (Episode 8: The Itchy Brain Simulation)

38 he thought she said "Yoda" (Episode 13: The Occupation Recalibration)

39 go for afternoon tea in a nearby hotel (Episode 14: The Convention Conundrum)

40 the hotel is full of mothers with little kids—and the waiter thought Penny was Bernadette's mother (Episode 14: The Convention Conundrum)

41 he's "giving a little talk" (Episode 17: The Friendship Turbulence)

42 Neil Diamond (Episode 3: The Scavenger Vortex)

43 he calls his mother, and she starts guilting him so his blood pressure rises (Episode 16: The Table Polarization)

44 Little Sri Lanka (Episode 5: The Workplace Proximity)

45 he's written a song and wants them to sing backup (Episode 6: The Romance Resonance)

46 the guys turn off the lights until he goes away (Episode 14: The Convention Conundrum)

47 nano vacuum tubes (Episode 7: The Proton Displacement)

48 a bowling ball—in case they go to a bowling alley (Episode 3: The Scavenger Vortex)

49 a Death Star cake—"It combines two of Sheldon's favorite things, chocolate chips and the ability to destroy a planet at the push of a button." (Episode 22: The Proton Transmogrification)

50 he says he'll break up with her—"Amy has made me a more affectionate, open-minded person. And that stops now." (Episode 16: The Table Polarization)

51 Lakers tickets—"Instead of me you can take someone who will actually enjoy it." (Episode 15: The Locomotive Manipulation)

52 it has gone out of business (Episode 8: The Itchy Brain Simulation)

53 a rock and mineral show in Santa Monica (Episode 13: The Occupation Recalibration)

54 Henri Bergson (Episode 12: The Hesitation Ramification)

55 because it will help take Sheldon's mind off his dilemma (Episode 21: The Anything Can Happen Recurrence)

56 Carrie Fisher's—"It's not funny any more, James!" (Episode 14: The Convention Conundrum)

57 "Do you have any single grandmothers?" (Episode 7: The Proton Displacement)

58 asks Amy to reply on his behalf (Episode 17: The Friendship Turbulence)

59 a giant tentacle grabs him and yanks him overboard (Episode 1: The Hofstadter Insufficiency)

60 *Back to the Future Part II* and *Back to the Future Part III* (Episode 1: The Hofstadter Insufficiency)

61 "not applicable" (Episode 4: The Raiders Minimization)

62 an Elvis impersonator (Episode 9: The Thanksgiving Decoupling)

63 "The Wonder Blunder" (Episode 10: The Discovery Dissipation)

64 superheavy (Episode 6: The Romance Resonance)

65 if they see an iceberg, they have a shot (Episode 1: The Hofstadter Insufficiency)

66 $1,200 (Episode 2: The Deception Verification)

67 Café au Leia and Chai Tea-3PO (Episode 22: The Proton Transmogrification)

68 "The Lion Sleeps Tonight" (Episode 14: The Convention Conundrum)

69 *It's a Wonderful Life* (Episode 11: The Cooper Extraction)

70 Bernadette (Episode 11: The Cooper Extraction)

71 posted his online dating profile (Episode 4: The Raiders Minimization)

72 he makes them feel they aren't trying hard enough in their marriage (Episode 10: The Discovery Dissipation)

73 he doesn't want anyone to feel bad at the end of the game (Episode 3: The Scavenger Vortex)

74 a 50-pound sack of rice with one of Sheldon's T-shirts on it that Amy has in her apartment (Episode 11: The Cooper Extraction)

Sheldon: *(to Leonard)* You've spent time with Amy. Can you think of anything she's fond of that has a bunch of flaws she hasn't noticed?

75 just chins and fat and feet (Episode 7: The Proton Displacement)

76 in square meters instead of square centimeters (Episode 6: The Romance Resonance)

77 buys her a car (Episode 17: The Friendship Turbulence)

78 a customer in a diner who flirts with Mark Harmon (Episode 12: The Hesitation Ramification)

79 she's with another guy (Episode 23: The Gorilla Dissolution)

80 he's twelve down in the *TV Guide* crossword puzzle (Episode 19: The Indecision Amalgamation)

81 yodel (Episode 10: The Discovery Dissipation)

82 she burns it with her curling iron (Episode 13: The Occupation Recalibration)

83 Frank Miller's *The Dark Knight Returns* #1 (Episode 13: The Occupation Recalibration)

84 Harvard (Episode 17: The Friendship Turbulence)

85 because she said that when she works at his university she'll be in a different building and won't be bothering him (Episode 5: The Workplace Proximity)

86 Huntington Hospital (Episode 20: The Relationship Diremption)

87 cutting people with knives—"all the other jobs where you get to do that are illegal" (Episode 20: The Relationship Diremption)

88 wear the ugly itchy sweater with "Lenny" on it that Leonard also found in the junk box (Episode 8: The Itchy Brain Simulation)

89 spend the weekend at a bed and breakfast in Napa Valley and have Valentine's Day dinner aboard a fully functioning vintage train (Episode 15: The Locomotive Manipulation)

90 Stephen Hawking (Episode 20: The Relationship Diremption)

91 Howard (Episode 12: The Hesitation Ramification)

92 use his vacation days (Episode 13: The Occupation Recalibration)

93 marijuana (Episode 2: The Deception Verification)

94 Hulk (Episode 14: The Convention Conundrum)

95 "Ferrigno, Bana, Norton and Ruffalo" (Episode 14: The Convention Conundrum)

96 "like you're bathing inside a monster" (Episode 15: The Locomotive Manipulation)

97 he's fired (Episode 23: The Gorilla Dissolution)

98 the feet of a toddler (Episode 8: The Itchy Brain Simulation)

99 *Little House on the Prairie* (Episode 4: The Raiders Minimization)

100 *Garfield* (Episode 4: The Raiders Minimization)

101 she ate somc chocolates (Episode 15: The Locomotive Manipulation)

102 he had paid for it seven years ago—"I was going to mention it at the time, but then I thought, someday this might be a teachable moment." (Episode 8: The Itchy Brain Simulation)

103 C-3P-Wee Herman—he thought he looked like C-3PO and Pee-Wee Herman (Episode 17: The Friendship Turbulence)

104 because it's a "smart decision" (Episode 23: The Gorilla Dissolution)

105 feeling each other's breasts (Episode 2: The Deception Verification)

106 he had an upset stomach, clogged her toilet and snuck out the bathroom window (Episode 20: The Relationship Diremption)

107 Clogzilla (Episode 20: The Relationship Diremption)

108 "He doesn't want to be mistaken for a gang member." (Episode 3: The Scavenger Vortex)

109 "Also, that's the same day he shampoos his beard." (Episode 14: The Convention Conundrum)

110 Fester (Episode 15: The Locomotive Manipulation)

111 "zero" (Episode 19: The Indecision Amalgamation)

112 because "she wants to live in the Stone Age and a cave wasn't available" (Episode 11: The Cooper Extraction)

113 he's been applying strong estrogen cream to his mother's back without wearing gloves (Episode 2: The Deception Verification)

114 Dr. Gunderson (Episode 5: The Workplace Proximity)

115 No-Funderson (Episode 5: The Workplace Proximity)

116 Leonard and Penny—"Penny brought Leonard out of his shell, and it seems like Leonard makes Penny think more deeply about the world." (Episode 18: The Mommy Observation)

117 Bill Nye the Science Guy (Episode 7: The Proton Displacement)

118 an ice cream parlor (Episode 14: The Convention Conundrum)

119 a bear (Episode 14: The Convention Conundrum)

Sheldon: It's been pointed out by my girlfriend that I may have been annoying to you.

Arthur: She sounds like a keeper.

120 maybe the best thing to do is have the courage to end the relationship—"Break it off, shake hands, walk away." (Episode 20: The Relationship Diremption)

121 a magic wand—Raj: "This is so much better than watching TV like a muggle." (Episode 16: The Table Polarization)

122 he downloads annulment papers (Episode 9: The Thanksgiving Decoupling)

123 she wants him to sign the court papers to annul their wedding as soon as possible, as Leonard is annoyed (Episode 9: The Thanksgiving Decoupling)

124 "pyramid" (Episode 11: The Cooper Extraction)

125 they're "both into rock" (Episode 13: The Occupation Recalibration)

126 mutton and coconut milk (Episode 5: The Workplace Proximity)

127 because he's both happy and quiet (Episode 6: The Romance Resonance)

128 "He's afraid the original owners will come back." (Episode 16: The Table Polarization)

129 a lightsaber belt buckle (Episode 7: The Proton Displacement)

130 Penny (Episode 18: The Mommy Observation)

131 the Lightning Sharks (Episode 3: The Scavenger Vortex)

132 a male security guard at closing time (Episode 12: The Hesitation Ramification)

133 Bloom (Episode 18: The Mommy Observation)

Arthur: Where are we?

Sheldon: This is the swampland of Dagobah. It's where Luke was trained in the ways of the Jedi.

Arthur: Too bad, I thought it was Florida.

134 The Los Angeles Bureau of Weights and Measures—Leonard: "I thought the measures were going to be the stars of the show, turns out it was the weights." (Episode 2: The Deception Verification)

135 they faked the results—"someone added simulated signals to the data files" (Episode 10: The Discovery Dissipation)

136 that all the men he's looked up to in his life had gone away—his father, his grandfather and now Arthur (Episode 22: The Proton Transmogrification)

137 it's okay to be sad, just make sure you appreciate those who are still there for you (Episode 22: The Proton Transmogrification)

138 "mo' infections, mo' money" (Episode 6: The Romance Resonance)

139 "Meryl Streep" (Episode 17: The Friendship Turbulence)

140 cobras (Episode 8: The Itchy Brain Simulation)

141 Captain Sweatpants—"Even you, Sweatpants?" (Episode 13: The Occupation Recalibration)

142 "Free popcorn"—with his mouth full (Episode 13: The Occupation Recalibration)

143 turbulence on the plane—they have to hang on to each other (Episode 17: The Friendship Turbulence)

144 a hole—"Kind of like when *Firefly* was canceled. But not as big." (Episode 17: The Friendship Turbulence)

145 the CERN supercollider (Episode 13: The Occupation Recalibration)

146 "shoulder" (Episode 23: The Gorilla Dissolution)

147 they kinda turn her on (Episode 21: The Anything Can Happen Recurrence)

148 "And play." (Episode 21: The Anything Can Happen Recurrence)

Sheldon: *(to Amy)* Do you have any idea what it's like to wait for years and never know if you're finally going to get satisfaction?

149 physiology (Episode 18: The Mommy Observation)

150 "yo' mama" (Episode 12: The Hesitation Ramification)

151 promiscuous (Episode 12: The Hesitation Ramification)

152 "monkey hair" (Episode 23: The Gorilla Dissolution)

153 he's not okay with YouTube changing its user interface from a star-based rating system to a thumbs-up rating system (Episode 1: The Hofstadter Insufficiency)

154 Leonard and Penny have got engaged and are considering living together, and Amy wants to move in with him (Episode 24: The Status Quo Combustion)

155 "I'm just getting on a train and leaving forever." (Episode 24: The Status Quo Combustion)

156 Leonard admits that if his career took off, he might not follow Penny if hers did too (Episode 18: The Mommy Observation)

157 unobjectionable (Episode 4: The Raiders Minimization)

158 whether he should fix his squeaky chair or get a new one (Episode 8: The Itchy Brain Simulation)

159 he drinks some wine—"mmm, grape juice that burns"—gazes into her eyes and then kisses her for the first time (Episode 15: The Locomotive Manipulation)

160 her gout is flaring up (Episode 9: The Thanksgiving Decoupling)

161 Raj—helped by Bernadette and Amy (Episode 9: The Thanksgiving Decoupling)

162 get well—the colleague has been in a horrible accident and is "clinging to life" (Episode 19: The Indecision Amalgamation)

163 "I've had a lot on my plate. We happen to live in a golden age of television." (Episode 20: The Relationship Diremption)

164 a string pragmatist—he applies for grant money to prove something he knows can't be proved, then he spends it on liquor and broads (Episode 20: The Relationship Diremption)

165 Germans—"that's a tough crowd" (Episode 12: The Hesitation Ramification)

166 "butt"—"Once I saw him sit on a bunch of loose change and add it up." (Episode 18: The Mommy Observation)

167 he wandered off at the swap meet and chased a balloon for three miles (Episode 24: The Status Quo Combustion)

168 *Pride and Prejudice* (Episode 4: The Raiders Minimization)

169 he's died (Episode 8: The Itchy Brain Simulation)

170 a sailor's cap (Episode 1: The Hofstadter Insufficiency)

171 extrajumbo mumbo jumbo (Episode 21: The Anything Can Happen Recurrence)

172 that once he commits to the woman in his romantic relationship, all his other pursuits—personally and professionally—will come into focus (Episode 21: The Anything Can Happen Recurrence)

173 Stuart (Episode 18: The Mommy Observation)

174 "Howard found it online the day we met you." (Episode 1: The Hofstadter Insufficiency)

175 anyone can post audition videos online (Episode 12: The Hesitation Ramification)

176 a scientist (Episode 23: The Gorilla Dissolution)

177 because if it was a good movie, she wouldn't be in it (Episode 23: The Gorilla Dissolution)

Bernadette: Howie, I love you. And as your wife, your mother is every bit as much my problem as she is yours. So, I want a divorce.

178 she's fired (Episode 23: The Gorilla Dissolution)

179 Sheldon—"While I've had my misgivings about Penny, Sheldon spoke very fondly of her, and if she is good enough for him, then she's good enough for me." (Episode 24: The Status Quo Combustion)

180 Buzz Aldrin (Episode 18: The Mommy Observation)

181 in a steam room (Episode 14: The Convention Conundrum)

182 in the trash can—if Penny was on her own they'd be on the table or the floor (Episode 2: The Deception Verification)

183 "I was swatting his bottom with your brand new Ping-Pong paddle." (Episode 4: The Raiders Minimization)

184 the Quiet Game—"And he's terrible at it. I always win." (Episode 5: The Workplace Proximity)

185 a treadmill (Episode 23: The Gorilla Dissolution)

186 it slips and crashes into her—"I told you this treadmill would kill me!" (Episode 23: The Gorilla Dissolution)

187 "raccoon" (Episode 6: The Romance Resonance)

188 "Indiana Jones plays no role in the outcome of the story. If he weren't in the film, it would turn out exactly the same."—the Nazis would still find the ark, open it and die (Episode 4: The Raiders Minimization)

189 Raj (Episode 7: The Proton Displacement)

190 he fills up the space with a desk and a load of old stuff (Episode 16: The Table Polarization)

191 he shows her that Sheldon uses her picture as his screensaver on his laptop (Episode 11: The Cooper Extraction)

192 "Um" (Episode 12: The Hesitation Ramification)

193 "What can we do that's free?" (Episode 21: The Anything Can Happen Recurrence)

194 to devote all her time and energy to becoming an actress (Episode 13: The Occupation Recalibration)

195 The Hubei Institute for Nuclear Physics (Episode 6: The Romance Resonance)

196 Sheldon sees his mother having sex with a man (Episode 18: The Mommy Observation)

197 Obi-Wan Kenobi (Episode 22: The Proton Transmogrification)

198 the swamps of Dagobah (Episode 22: The Proton Transmogrification

199 *Serial Ape-ist 2: Monkey See Monkey Kill* (Episode 19: The Indecision Amalgamation)

200 it's dated twenty years in the future (Episode 18: The Mommy Observation)

Sheldon: *(to a psychic)* I don't mean to be rude or discourteous, but before we begin I'd just like to say that there is absolutely no scientific evidence to support clairvoyance of any kind. Which means—again no insult intended—you're a fraud, your profession is a swindle and your livelihood is dependent on the gullibility of stupid people. Again, no offense.

The Convocation Communication

When bad weather canceled Leonard's flight, Penny arranged for him to give the commencement speech to his old high school via Skype from her apartment.

Leonard: Members of the faculty, students, I am excited to speak to you today. I can't help but remember the last time I was in this auditorium and the guys from the lacrosse team played keepaway with my asthma inhaler, but enough about my ten year reunion.

I'd also like to take a moment to thank my beautiful fiancée for helping make this speech possible, even though weather nearly prevented it.

It was L. Frank Baum who said, "No thief, however skillful, can rob one of knowledge, and that is why knowledge is the best and safest treasure . . ." Wow, I'm boring myself. Sorry, I can't see your faces right now, but I bet they look like this . . .

Leonard swings the laptop to a bored Penny, then swings it back.

You know what? I wrote an entire speech to say how high school prepares you and what a wonderful place it is, but I hated it. Maybe high school's great if you look like this . . .

Leonard turns the laptop to face Penny, then back to himself.

But I didn't even feel like I existed in this school. And now that I think about it, I bet a lot of you feel the same way. So, for the remainder of my speech, this is for the invisible kids. Maybe you never fit in, or maybe you're the smallest kid in school, or the heaviest or the weirdest, maybe you're graduating and still haven't had your first kiss—by the way *(re: himself)* nineteen and Geraldine Coco wherever you are, thank you—maybe you don't have any friends, well guess what, that's okay. While all the popular kids are off doing—well I don't know what they were doing, I wasn't there—

Penny: *(interrupting)* I'll tell you later.

Leonard: My point is, while you're spending all the time on your own—building computers or practicing your cello—what you're really doing is becoming interesting. And when people do finally notice you, they're going to find someone a lot cooler than they thought. And for those of you who were popular in high school—it's over—sorry. Thank you and congratulations.

Season 8

1 "a little lady I like to call loneliness" (Episode 8: The Prom Equivalency)

2 he can no longer balance a full-time career, a popular internet show and a girlfriend (Episode 10: The Champagne Reflection)

3 the ability to read people's minds (Episode 16: The Intimacy Acceleration)

4 the steam tunnels below CalTech (Episode 6: The Expedition Approximation)

5 "When I lost my father, I didn't have friends to help me through it. You do." (Episode 15: The Comic Book Store Regeneration)

6 Beverly refers to religion as superstition and Mary thinks Beverly's books are nonsense (Episode 23: The Maternal Combustion)

7 it was the name of the detention block on the first Death Star where Princess Leia was interrogated (Episode 19: The Skywalker Incursion)

8 "That's where all the cool trains are." (Episode 1: The Locomotion Interruption)

9 Armadillo Isaac Newton (Episode 13: The Anxiety Optimization)

10 teach a class (Episode 2: The Junior Professor Solution)

11 Batman (Episode 20: The Fortification Implementation)

12 he is getting divorced from Mrs. Koothrappali (Episode 11: The Clean Room Infiltration)

13 cook Christmas dinner for the gang (Episode 11: The Clean Room Infiltration)

14 Howard's Aunt Gladys (Episode 15: The Comic Book Store Regeneration)

Leonard: Yes, you're a super weaner!

Sheldon: Well, now I have to correct you. As a bit of an elephant seal buff, the more accurate comparison would be when two mother seals actively seek to nourish the same pup. So I believe the term you're looking for is a "double mother suckler."

Leonard: Yeah, you're right—that is the term I'm looking for. You are a dirty double mother suckler.

15 dark matter (Episode 2: The Junior Professor Solution)

16 all the compromises they make for each other (Episode 12: The Space Probe Disintegration)

17 that he kissed a girl on the North Sea expedition (Episode 24: The Commitment Determination)

18 marge (Episode 18: The Leftover Thermalization)

19 his Public Restroom Kit (Episode 19: The Skywalker Incursion)

20 "Me and Amy, Howard and Bernadette, Raj and his girlfriend, Penny and Chardonnay, Penny and you."—Penny: "Actually, I drink Sauvignon Blanc." (Episode 3: The First Pitch Insufficiency)

21 *Scientific American* (Episode 18: The Leftover Thermalization)

22 Flag or Not a Flag (Episode 10: The Champagne Reflection)

23 56 (Episode 9: The Septum Deviation)

24 a traditional Victorian Christmas (Episode 11: The Clean Room Infiltration)

25 Sheldon (Episode 23: The Maternal Combustion)

26 a kind of interactive theater where you are timed at solving puzzles to get out (Episode 16: The Intimacy Acceleration)

27 a zombie (Episode 16: The Intimacy Acceleration)

28 he has to help a neighbor's kid with his homework (Episode 14: The Troll Manifestation)

Penny: *(about Sheldon)* Isn't this when he says "bazooka" or something?

29 that Stuart's rival store, Capitol Comics, gives you genital warts (Episode 4: The Hook-Up Reverberation)

30 "buy a big bag to put the money in" (Episode 4: The Hook-Up Reverberation)

31 Sheldon (Episode 12: The Space Probe Disintegration)

32 Raj (Episode 22: The Graduation Transmission)

33 "mating rituals" (Episode 8: The Prom Equivalency)

34 five (Episode 7: The Misinterpretation Agitation)

35 her nightstand (Episode 17: The Colonization Application)

36 a helicopter you control with an iPad (Episode 18: The Leftover Thermalization)

37 Gary-Con—a convention for Dungeons & Dragons co-creator, Gary Gygax (Episode 16: The Intimacy Acceleration)

38 he got bitten by a baby goat (Episode 24: The Commitment Determination)

39 Fairly Manilow (Episode 5: The Focus Attenuation)

40 Howard (Episode 13: The Anxiety Optimization)

41 an image of a woman in a bathing suit, which slips down when the pen is tilted (Episode 10: The Champagne Reflection)

42 because the government has funded an experiment to detect dark matter and they are planning to send research teams down into abandoned salt mines (Episode 6: The Expedition Approximation)

43 he performed a vasectomy on Gene Roddenberry—Howard: "Wow, he really went where no man has gone before." (Episode 7: The Misinterpretation Agitation

44 ketchup packets (Episode 18: The Leftover Thermalization)

45 himself (Episode 16: The Intimacy Acceleration)

46 Robert Downey Jr. (Episode 16: The Intimacy Acceleration)

47 covers his face with a photo of him smiling (Episode 20: The Fortification Implementation)

48 the front panel of it becomes the door to Amy's bedroom (Episode 19: The Skywalker Incursion)

49 in the hope she'll feel so guilty she'll never make him celebrate Christmas again (Episode 11: The Clean Room Infiltration)

50 a framed photo of him sitting on Santa's lap that plays Christmas harp music when you press a button (Episode 11: The Clean Room Infiltration)

51 she was a chaperone (Episode 8: The Prom Equivalency)

52 "I just think that maybe you're a little hung up on the money because I'm less reliant on you now, and that's a little scary." (Episode 6: The Expedition Approximation)

53 throw a dinner party for the entire gang—"It'll be like Ma's feeding us one last time." (Episode 18: The Leftover Thermalization)

54 Oliver (Episode 7: The Misinterpretation Agitation)

55 Raj (Episode 9: The Septum Deviation)

56 he was too busy to drive his mother to the airport the day she went to Florida and she had to take a cab (Episode 16: The Intimacy Acceleration)

Leonard: *(about Sheldon and Amy)* It's nice to see a busy couple keep the spark of bureaucracy alive.

57 user accounts Raj creates so he can post positive comments about Leonard and Sheldon's paper (Episode 14: The Troll Manifestation)

58 232 (Episode 10: The Champagne Reflection)

59 Amy forgot to press "record" (Episode 10: The Champagne Reflection)

60 "You had a panic attack when we went through the car wash." (Episode 6: The Expedition Approximation)

61 molecular cocktails (Episode 21: The Communication Deterioration)

62 his old high school (Episode 22: The Graduation Transmission)

63 Mrs. Wolowitz (Episode 4: The Hook-Up Reverberation)

64 *Back to the Future II* and *Ghostbusters* (Episode 5: The Focus Attenuation)

65 "The Final Episode Flagtacular" (Episode 10: The Champagne Reflection)

66 eleven minutes (Episode 6: The Expedition Approximation)

67 General Relativity (Episode 14: The Troll Manifestation)

68 two Mississippis (Episode 7: The Misinterpretation Agitation)

69 "lollipop" (Episode 4: The Hook-Up Reverberation)

70 8.2 (Episode 3: The First Pitch Insufficiency)

71 to be one of the first people to establish a colony on Mars (Episode 17: The Colonization Application)

72 "informs" (Episode 15: The Comic Book Store Regeneration)

Mary: Are you ashamed of me?
Sheldon: Of course not, I love you. I'm just embarrassed by the things you believe, do and say.

73 she didn't have any friends to play with (Episode 19: The Skywalker Incursion)

74 he gets one comment, which says, "Too bad your show is done. I kinda liked it." (Episode 10: The Champagne Reflection)

75 Amy sent them "a pretty scathing email" (Episode 7: The Misinterpretation Agitation)

76 the Virgin Piña Colada (Episode 13: The Anxiety Optimization)

77 they're both scared of Bernadette—she's "kind of a bully" (Episode 1: The Locomotion Interruption)

78 because Leonard and Penny will never have a relationship as good as theirs (Episode 3: The First Pitch Insufficiency)

79 sexy graduate (Episode 22: The Graduation Transmission)

80 Roger (Episode 10: The Champagne Reflection)

81 Raj had told Emily that he once hooked up with Penny (Episode 4: The Hook-Up Reverberation)

82 with a working prototype of the Mars Rover (Episode 3: The First Pitch Insufficiency)

83 they boo because it goes so slowly (Episode 3: The First Pitch Insufficiency)

84 *The Flash* (Episode 24: The Commitment Determination)

85 "I swear by my pretty floral bonnet I will end you." (Episode 15: The Comic Book Store Regeneration)

86 seven—"Four 'Under the Seas', two 'Enchanted Evenings' and one 'Night to Remember' that I cannot remember for the life of me." (Episode 8: The Prom Equivalency)

87 elephant (Episode 23: The Maternal Combustion)

Sheldon: When I was doing string theory and hit a dead end, why didn't you try to help me?

Amy: I did! You said the only math biologists know is if you have three frogs and one hops away that leaves two frogs.

88 Sheldon—"The last time I brought it up you had an emotional breakdown, got on a train and ran away." (Episode 12: The Space Probe Disintegration)

89 Leonard (Episode 21: The Communication Deterioration)

90 someone left the loading doors open (Episode 11: The Clean Room Infiltration)

91 he accidentally injured it when he tried to catch it (Episode 11: The Clean Room Infiltration)

92 "It's a Hard Knock Life" from *Annie* (Episode 23: The Maternal Combustion)

93 a public swimming pool (Episode 9: The Septum Deviation)

94 he might be in a Beatles cover band—"If he's got your nose and haircut, he'd make a killer Ringo." (Episode 20: The Fortification Implementation)

95 by opening Professor Abbott's bottle of champagne (Episode 10: The Champagne Reflection)

96 "Let it go." (Episode 15: The Comic Book Store Regeneration)

97 because "driving me to work is one of the things that gives your life purpose" (Episode 12: The Space Probe Disintegration)

98 crunch berries—"from Cap'n Crunch" (Episode 24: The Commitment Determination)

99 he's been thinking about getting his doctorate (Episode 2: The Junior Professor Solution)

100 he's scared he'll have to have sex after the prom (Episode 8: The Prom Equivalency)

101 Maryann (Episode 14: The Troll Manifestation)

102 his mom (Episode 10: The Champagne Reflection)

103 50 years (Episode 10: The Champagne Reflection)

104 because she should be celebrated for her achievements, not her looks (Episode 7: The Misinterpretation Agitation)

105 his noise-canceling headphones (Episode 13: The Anxiety Optimization)

106 Richard Feynman (Episode 13: The Anxiety Optimization)

107 the airline lost Howard's bag containing his mother's ashes (Episode 16: The Intimacy Acceleration)

108 "You realize this isn't one of those times I want you to exaggerate how long something is!" (Episode 3: The First Pitch Insufficiency)

109 Howard's second cousin, Jeanie, who Howard lost his virginity to (Episode 8: The Prom Equivalency)

110 "Got a hot girlfriend now. I want the haters to know." (Episode 1: The Locomotion Interruption)

111 "Best Fiancé Ever" (Episode 6: The Expedition Approximation)

112 pink (Episode 6: The Expedition Approximation)

113 for shooting a spitball at him which "violated the sanctity of my mouth" (Episode 2: The Junior Professor Solution)

114 his Mee-Maw's cookies—she called and got the recipe from her (Episode 11: The Clean Room Infiltration)

115 Jenny Craig (Episode 24: The Commitment Determination)

116 the furniture from her den (Episode 15: The Comic Book Store Regeneration)

117 Raj (Episode 15: The Comic Book Store Regeneration)

118 when his brother and sister would build forts in the living room and wouldn't let him in (Episode 20: The Fortification Implementation)

119 trains—"If I was at a train station and one train would take me to my current job and the other train would take me to an audition for a movie, which train should I get on?" (Episode 21: The Communication Deterioration)

120 Kingman, Arizona (Episode 1: The Locomotion Interruption)

121 a kitty saying, "mee-wow" (Episode 14: The Troll Manifestation)

122 he wrote a paper under both their names (Episode 14: The Troll Manifestation)

123 his food diary (Episode 10: The Champagne Reflection)

124 Gollum (Episode 24: The Commitment Determination)

125 what he should do with an engagement ring—"You're an expert on rings." (Episode 24: The Commitment Determination)

126 it's time to take a step forward in their relationship (Episode 17: The Colonization Application)

127 Amelia and Cooper (Episode 14: The Troll Manifestation)

128 so he can hit on Penny (Episode 7: The Misinterpretation Agitation)

129 his half brother is amazed and impressed that Howard is an astronaut (Episode 20: The Fortification Implementation)

130 "Here lie the ashes of Leonard Hofstadter. He thought he was right, but his roommate knew better." (Episode 9: The Septum Deviation)

131 "I'm with stupid." (Episode 9: The Septum Deviation)

Beverly: Do you suppose you would've flourished more in a reward-based environment?

Sheldon: Perhaps. But my mom made me spaghetti with chopped-up hot dogs whenever I wanted, so who cares?

132 not to do it—"There's no upside. If you do well, no one cares. And if you screw up, you're an idiot on YouTube forever." (Episode 3: The First Pitch Insufficiency)

133 David (Episode 24: The Commitment Determination)

134 it's his birthday (Episode 16: The Intimacy Acceleration)

135 *Clerks 3* (Episode 20: The Fortification Implementation)

136 Yorba Linda, California (Episode 14: The Troll Manifestation)

137 that they do it gradually—they could live together one night a week (Episode 12: The Space Probe Disintegration)

138 "it looked Italian" (Episode 17: The Colonization Application)

139 Seth (Episode 17: The Colonization Application)

140 spreading it out on the bed and having sex on it (Episode 6: The Expedition Approximation)

141 the penguin (Episode 8: The Prom Equivalency)

142 he's had to put a seat on the comic store toilet (Episode 18: The Leftover Thermalization)

143 Femevra, a new birth-control pill (Episode 4: The Hook-Up Reverberation)

144 it can cause acne—"which, if you ask me, kind of increases its effectiveness as a contraceptive" (Episode 4: The Hook-Up Reverberation)

145 *Smallville* (Episode 24: The Commitment Determination)

146 Los Angeles Angels of Anaheim (Episode 3: The First Pitch Insufficiency)

147 because it's Space Day at the stadium and they wanted an astronaut (Episode 3: The First Pitch Insufficiency)

148 Russell's (Episode 19: The Skywalker Incursion)

149 Bernadette (Episode 8: The Prom Equivalency)

150 "that mean kid with the big boobies" (Episode 10: The Champagne Reflection)

151 Miss California Quiznos 1999—"You look like a talking cupcake." (Episode 14: The Troll Manifestation)

152 their flight is canceled (Episode 22: The Graduation Transmission)

153 basket weaving at the craft museum (Episode 12: The Space Probe Disintegration)

154 Josh Wolowitz (Episode 20: The Fortification Implementation)

155 oceanography, in San Diego (Episode 20: The Fortification Implementation)

156 Dan (Episode 1: The Locomotion Interruption)

157 she makes more sales if people think she's single (Episode 7: The Misinterpretation Agitation)

158 Raj and Amy (Episode 19: The Skywalker Incursion)

159 40 seconds (Episode 19: The Skywalker Incursion)

160 her boss moved up her field ride and she hasn't got as much time to study as she thought she had (Episode 5: The Focus Attenuation)

161 Barnabas (Episode 15: The Comic Book Store Regeneration)

162 Adderall (Episode 15: The Comic Book Store Regeneration)

163 Sweeney (Episode 2: The Junior Professor Solution)

164 Fort Knox, Fort Ticonderoga, Fort Sumter and Fort Cozy McBlanket (Episode 20: The Fortification Implementation)

165 a tendency to force his ideas on people (Episode 21: The Communication Deterioration)

166 centaur (Episode 21: The Communication Deterioration)

167 "urinary tracts" (Episode 7: The Misinterpretation Agitation)

168 making out with a Chewbacca statue (Episode 19: The Skywalker Incursion)

169 "heartburn that makes you pray for death" (Episode 18: The Leftover Thermalization)

170 "Who cares? He stole the idea and doesn't deserve his own joke." (Episode 15: The Comic Book Store Regeneration)

171 he tells her his father can't afford to give him money because of his "active social life" (Episode 22: The Graduation Transmission)

172 James Clerk Maxwell (Episode 21: The Communication Deterioration)

173 uranium from an African warlord in Chad (Episode 23: The Maternal Combustion)

174 put it into a joint account (Episode 6: The Expedition Approximation)

175 because he failed and he doesn't want her to think less of him (Episode 1: The Locomotion Interruption)

176 koala—"You would wind up with an army so cute it couldn't be attacked." (Episode 2: The Junior Professor Solution)

Sheldon: If you've got a problem basing a relationship on a contract, I'd like to tell you about thirteen plucky colonies that entered into a relationship agreement called the U.S. Constitution. And it may not be cool to say so, but I think that love affair is still pretty hot today.

Penny: *(after auditioning)* The whole experience reminded me of what I hated about that world: the anxiety, the depression, the negativity. I don't want to feel those things, I want to sell drugs to people who feel those things.

177 when one of them gets their first big breakthrough, they'll celebrate by opening it and toasting Professor Abbott (Episode 10: The Champagne Reflection)

178 a repurposed diamond drill bit (Episode 23: The Maternal Combustion)

179 Emippali and Koothrapemily (Episode 2: The Junior Professor Solution)

180 "Okay, Ma, say hi to Aunt Gladys . . . Yeah, I love you, too. Bye." (Episode 15: The Comic Book Store Regeneration)

181 Ball of Wool (Episode 11: The Clean Room Infiltration)

182 Hot Boiled Beans (Episode 11: The Clean Room Infiltration)

183 Bernadette's breasts (Episode 5: The Focus Attenuation)

184 a graveyard (Episode 24: The Commitment Determination)

185 light-cone quantization (Episode 15: The Comic Book Store Regeneration)

186 Berkeley (Episode 19: The Skywalker Incursion)

187 he found his dad's *Playboy* collection and threw his arm out (Episode 3: The First Pitch Insufficiency)

188 he liked it and thought the premise was intriguing (Episode 14: The Troll Manifestation)

189 "If you were sitting in a chair for forty years, you'd get bored too." (Episode 14: The Troll Manifestation)

190 put duct tape on their arm and rip it off, tearing the hairs out—Raj: "And I really can't let that happen or the girl who does my eyebrows will think I've been cheating on her." (Episode 5: The Focus Attenuation)

191 he "had a date with a proper education" (Episode 8: The Prom Equivalency)

192 happy birthday (Episode 24: The Commitment Determination)

193 "Apparently, I have a reputation for being obnoxious." (Episode 2: The Junior Professor Solution)

194 she was on the cleanup crew (Episode 8: The Prom Equivalency)

195 "the scary boat tunnel in *Willy Wonka*" (Episode 9: The Septum Deviation)

196 Voyager 1, the space probe—"By the time I was born, Voyager 1's mission was supposed to be over. It had seen Jupiter and Saturn and all their moons, but it kept going. When I left India for America I was never more scared in my life. I had no idea what lay ahead. Whenever I feel that way, I think about how Voyager is still out there, somewhere beyond our solar system—going further than anyone ever thought it could." (Episode 6: The Expedition Approximation)

197 he believes he's created too pleasant an environment for himself (Episode 13: The Anxiety Optimization)

198 badminton (Episode 19: The Skywalker Incursion)

199 Sanskriti School for Well-Born Boys (Episode 19: The Skywalker Incursion)

200 Sally from *The Nightmare Before Christmas* (Episode 8: The Prom Equivalency)

Beverly: Sounds like Sheldon was a handful.
Mary: Oh, he was a handful.
Sheldon: *(to Leonard)* I was a handful.
Leonard: You still are.

OUT OF
ORDER
CAUTION

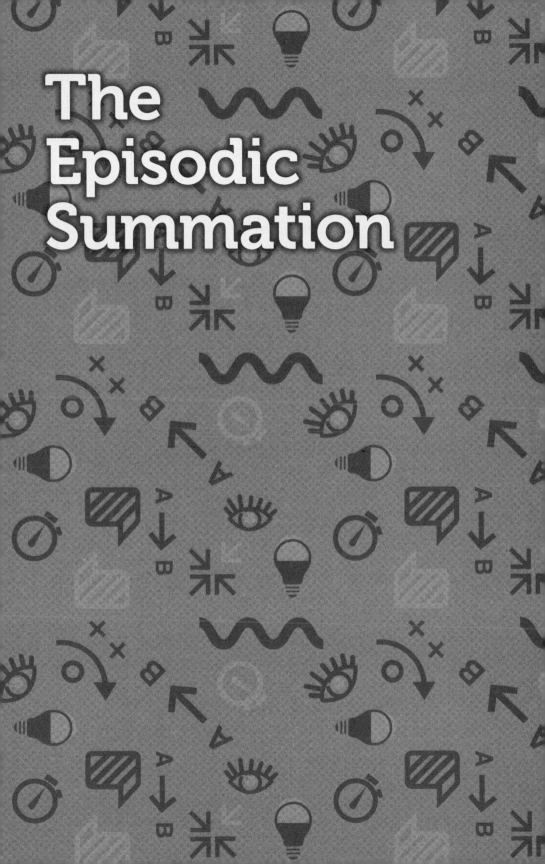

The Episodic Summation

Season 1

Episode 1: **Pilot**

Two brainy best friends, Leonard (series star JOHNNY GALECKI) and Sheldon (series star JIM PARSONS), could tell you anything you want to know about quantum physics—but when it comes to dealing with everyday life here on Earth, they're lost in the cosmos. Leonard and Sheldon are brilliant physicists, the kind of "beautiful minds" that understand how the universe works. But none of that genius helps them interact with people, especially women. All this begins to change when a free-spirited beauty named Penny (series star KALEY CUOCO-SWEETING) moves in next door. Sheldon, Leonard's roommate, is quite content spending his nights playing Klingon Boggle with their socially dysfunctional friends, fellow CalTech scientists Wolowitz (series star SIMON HELBERG) and Koothrappali (series star KUNAL NAYYAR). However, Leonard sees in Penny a whole new universe of possibilities . . . including love.

Written by: Chuck Lorre & Bill Prady
Directed by: James Burrows
U.S. Broadcast Premiere: September 24, 2007

Episode 2: **The Big Bran Hypothesis**

After Leonard tries to do a favor for Penny, Sheldon ruins the plan. Leonard volunteers to sign for a package, hoping to make a good impression on Penny. However, when he involves his obsessive-compulsive roommate, Leonard sees his attempt at chivalry go horribly awry.

Story by: Chuck Lorre & Bill Prady
Teleplay by: Robert Cohen & Dave Goetsch
Directed by: Mark Cendrowski
U.S. Broadcast Premiere: October 1, 2007

Episode 3: **The Fuzzyboots Corollary**

Leonard is depressed to learn that Penny is dating someone. As a result, encouraged by his friends and fellow scientists, Leonard actually summons the nerve to ask a woman out on a date. Recurring guest star SARA GILBERT (*Roseanne*) appears as Leslie.

Story by: Chuck Lorre
Teleplay by: Bill Prady & Steven Molaro
Directed by: Mark Cendrowski
U.S. Broadcast Premiere: October 8, 2007

Howard: Whaddup, science bitches?

Penny: Wow! So in your world, you're like the cool guys.
Howard: Recognize!

Episode 4: **The Luminous Fish Effect**

After being fired from his job, Sheldon attempts to explore the "dreadful" life beyond physics. But his initial thrill of shopping with Penny devolves over time to him weaving ponchos as a shut-in, forcing Leonard to call on Sheldon's mother, Mary (LAURIE METCALF—*Roseanne*).

Story by: Chuck Lorre & Bill Prady
Teleplay by: David Litt & Lee Aronsohn
Directed by: Mark Cendrowski
U.S. Broadcast Premiere: October 15, 2007

Episode 5: **The Hamburger Postulate**

After sensing that his pursuit of Penny isn't going anywhere, Leonard agrees to an unexpected sexual encounter with fellow scientist Leslie Winkle. The one-night stand throws Leonard and Sheldon deep into uncharted social waters.

Story by: Jennifer Glickman
Teleplay by: Dave Goetsch & Steven Molaro
Directed by: Andrew D. Weyman
U.S. Broadcast Premiere: October 22, 2007

Episode 6: **The Middle-Earth Paradigm**

The socially stunted guys are nervous when Penny invites them to a party she's hosting. But they are ecstatic to find out that it's a Halloween party and enthusiastically don their respective nerdy costumes, which unfortunately fail to impress Penny's brutish ex-boyfriend. Afterward, Koothrappali experiences the unexpected with a partygoer, Cheryl.

Story by: Dave Goetsch
Teleplay by: David Litt & Robert Cohen
Directed by: Mark Cendrowski
U.S. Broadcast Premiere: October 29, 2007

Episode 7: **The Dumpling Paradox**

When Wolowitz seduces Penny's friend and ends up having sex with her in Penny's apartment, Penny sleeps on Leonard and Sheldon's couch. Meanwhile, with Wolowitz occupied, the guys discover that they are without a fourth member of their group. In desperation, they ask Penny to join one of their two-person Halo teams.

Story by: Chuck Lorre & Bill Prady
Teleplay by: Lee Aronsohn & Jennifer Glickman
Directed by: Mark Cendrowski
U.S. Broadcast Premiere: November 5, 2007

Episode 8: **The Grasshopper Experiment**

Koothrappali becomes overwhelmed when his parents arrange a blind date for him, but he discovers he actually can talk to a member of the opposite sex after a few drinks. However, complications arise when his beautiful date shows more interest in Sheldon.

Story by: Dave Goetsch & Steven Molaro
Teleplay by: Lee Aronsohn & Robert Cohen
Directed by: Ted Wass
U.S. Broadcast Premiere: November 12, 2007

Episode 9: **The Cooper-Hofstadter Polarization**

Sheldon and Leonard are invited to present their joint findings at a physics conference, but Sheldon refuses. Penny steps in to mediate, but this only deepens the rift between the two best friends.

Story by: Bill Prady & Stephen Engel
Teleplay by: Chuck Lorre & Lee Aronsohn & Dave Goetsch
Directed by: Joel Murray
U.S. Broadcast Premiere: March 17, 2008

Episode 10: **The Loobenfeld Decay**

After hearing Penny sing, Leonard lies to avoid seeing her perform. Sheldon goes one step further with a more elaborate lie, leading to the appearance of his nonexistent cousin. D. J. QUALLS (*Road Trip*) guest stars.

Story by: Chuck Lorre
Teleplay by: Bill Prady & Lee Aronsohn
Directed by: Mark Cendrowski
U.S. Broadcast Premiere: March 24, 2008

Episode 11: **The Pancake Batter Anomaly**

When Sheldon gets sick, Leonard and the boys know what is in store for them and avoid him like the plague; this leaves an unsuspecting Penny to nurse the world's worst patient back to health.

Story by: Chuck Lorre & Lee Aronsohn
Teleplay by: Bill Prady & Stephen Engel
Directed by: Mark Cendrowski
U.S. Broadcast Premiere: March 31, 2008

Episode 12: **The Jerusalem Duality**

When Leonard and Sheldon meet a 15-year-old physics prodigy, Sheldon is distraught that this boy genius is younger and smarter. In an attempt to restore a sense of purpose, the boys come up with a solution to derail the young prodigy's research.

Story by: Jennifer Glickman & Stephen Engel
Teleplay by: Dave Goetsch & Steven Molaro
Directed by: Mark Cendrowski
U.S. Broadcast Premiere: April 14, 2008

Episode 13: **The Bat Jar Conjecture**

The guys decide to compete in the university's Physics Bowl, but since Sheldon's only focus is to prove his mental superiority, the guys kick him off the team. To take his spot, they enlist his nemesis Leslie Winkle.

Story by: Stephen Engel & Jennifer Glickman
Teleplay by: Bill Prady & Robert Cohen
Directed by: Mark Cendrowski
U.S. Broadcast Premiere: April 21, 2008

Episode 14: **The Nerdvana Annihilation**

When Leonard and the guys buy a time machine prop from a classic 1960 movie, its arrival creates problems for Penny, and she tells the boys that their obsession with comics and toys is "pathetic."

Story by: Bill Prady
Teleplay by: Stephen Engel & Steven Molaro
Directed by: Mark Cendrowski
U.S. Broadcast Premiere: April 28, 2008

Episode 15: **The Pork Chop Indeterminacy**

Leonard, Wolowitz and Koothrappali all become smitten with Sheldon's twin sister, Missy (guest star COURTNEY HENGGELER), and Leonard devises a plan to eliminate his rivals. The plan backfires, however, when Sheldon declares he will decide whom his sister dates.

Story by: Chuck Lorre
Teleplay by: Lee Aronsohn & Bill Prady
Directed by: Mark Cendrowski
U.S. Broadcast Premiere: May 5, 2008

> **Missy:** *(about Sheldon)* He was trying to build some sort of armed robot to keep me out of his room.
>
> **Sheldon:** Made necessary by her insistence on going into my room.

Episode 16: **The Peanut Reaction**

When Penny learns that Leonard doesn't celebrate birthdays, she attempts to throw him a surprise party; she is sidetracked by Sheldon, however, who unexpectedly gets to live out one of his greatest fantasies at an electronics store.

Story by: Bill Prady & Lee Aronsohn
Teleplay by: Dave Goetsch & Steven Molaro
Directed by: Mark Cendrowski
U.S. Broadcast Premiere: May 12, 2008

Episode 17: **The Tangerine Factor**

When Penny breaks up with her boyfriend, Leonard finally gets up the courage to ask her out on a real date. When she says yes, each seeks the "wisdom" of a reluctant advisor—Sheldon.

Story by: Chuck Lorre & Bill Prady
Teleplay by: Steven Molaro & Lee Aronsohn
Directed by: Mark Cendrowski
U.S. Broadcast Premiere: May 19, 2008

Season 2

Episode 1: **The Bad Fish Paradigm**

After her first date with Leonard goes awry, Penny finds an unwilling confidant in Leonard's antisocial roommate, Sheldon. An embarrassing secret threatens to derail their budding romance on the second season premiere.

Story by: Bill Prady
Teleplay by: Dave Goetsch & Steven Molaro
Directed by: Mark Cendrowski
U.S. Broadcast Premiere: September 22, 2008

Episode 2: **The Codpiece Topology**

Penny and Leonard compete to see who will be the first to move on after their breakup. When Leonard sees Penny with a handsome new guy (guest star TRAVIS SCHULDT—*Scrubs*), he enters into a rebound relationship with Sheldon's nemesis, Leslie Winkle.

Story by: Chuck Lorre
Teleplay by: Bill Prady & Lee Aronsohn
Directed by: Mark Cendrowski
U.S. Broadcast Premiere: September 29, 2008

Sheldon: *(to Penny)* Your "check engine" light is on.

Episode 3: **The Barbarian Sublimation**

Sheldon creates a monster when he introduces Penny to the world of online gaming. Especially when her addiction wreaks havoc on his life.

Story by: Chuck Lorre
Teleplay by: Steven Molaro & Eric Kaplan
Directed by: Mark Cendrowski
U.S. Broadcast Premiere: October 6, 2008

Episode 4: **The Griffin Equivalency**

Raj's ego puts all of his friendships in jeopardy when he gets an inflated sense of self. Newly famous because of an article in a magazine, Raj makes a disastrous play for Leonard's longtime crush, Penny.

Story by: Bill Prady & Chuck Lorre
Teleplay by: Stephen Engel & Tim Doyle
Directed by: Mark Cendrowski
U.S. Broadcast Premiere: October 13, 2008

Episode 5: **The Euclid Alternative**

Leonard and his friends stage an intervention to make Sheldon confront his longstanding fear of driving.

Story by: Bill Prady & Steven Molaro
Teleplay by: Lee Aronsohn & Dave Goetsch
Directed by: Mark Cendrowski
U.S. Broadcast Premiere: October 20, 2008

Episode 6: **The Cooper-Nowitzki Theorem**

A young grad student's attraction to Sheldon confuses everyone—including Sheldon himself.

Story by: Stephen Engel & Daley Haggar
Teleplay by: Tim Doyle & Richard Rosenstock
Directed by: Mark Cendrowski
U.S. Broadcast Premiere: November 3, 2008

Episode 7: **The Panty Piñata Polarization**

Sheldon and Penny engage in a battle of wills as Penny vows to get revenge on Sheldon when he bans her from the apartment for a series of petty infractions.

Story by: Bill Prady & Tim Doyle
Teleplay by: Jennifer Glickman & Steven Molaro
Directed by: Mark Cendrowski
U.S. Broadcast Premiere: November 10, 2008

Sheldon: I believe the appropriate metaphor here involves a river of excrement and a Native American water vessel without any means of propulsion.

Episode 8: **The Lizard-Spock Expansion**

Wolowitz thinks he's found the love of his life (guest star SARA RUE)—until she meets Leonard.

Story by: Bill Prady
Teleplay by: Dave Goetsch & Jennifer Glickman
Directed by: Mark Cendrowski
U.S. Broadcast Premiere: November 17, 2008

Episode 9: **The White Asparagus Triangulation**

Sheldon can barely contain his joy when Leonard starts dating a woman (SARA RUE) who meets Sheldon's exacting standards.

Story by: Dave Goetsch & Steven Molaro
Teleplay by: Stephen Engel & Richard Rosenstock
Directed by: Mark Cendrowski
U.S. Broadcast Premiere: November 24, 2008

Episode 10: **The Vartabedian Conundrum**

Leonard just can't say no. When his relationship with new girlfriend, Stephanie, starts moving too fast, Leonard turns to Penny for advice.

Story by: Chuck Lorre & Steven Molaro
Teleplay by: Bill Prady & Richard Rosenstock
Directed by: Mark Cendrowski
U.S. Broadcast Premiere: December 8, 2008

Episode 11: **The Bath Item Gift Hypothesis**

Christmas is a source of stress for Leonard—whose handsome colleague (MICHAEL TRUCCO) starts dating Penny—and his friends, who are being tormented by Sheldon's obsession with gift-giving etiquette.

Story by: Bill Prady & Richard Rosenstock
Teleplay by: Stephen Engel & Eric Kaplan
Directed by: Mark Cendrowski
U.S. Broadcast Premiere: December 15, 2009

Episode 12: **The Killer Robot Instability**

When Penny's comment about Wolowitz's love life sends him into a depressed stupor, his friends lose their most important teammate in an upcoming fighting robot competition.

Story by: Bill Prady & Richard Rosenstock
Teleplay by: Steven Molaro & Daley Haggar
Directed by: Mark Cendrowski
U.S. Broadcast Premiere: January 12, 2009

Episode 13: **The Friendship Algorithm**

Socially awkward Sheldon develops a scientific procedure for making friends.

Story by: Bill Prady & Richard Rosenstock
Teleplay by: Chuck Lorre & Steven Molaro
Directed by: Mark Cendrowski
U.S. Broadcast Premiere: January 19, 2009

Episode 14: **The Financial Permeability**

Sheldon's "simple" solution to Penny's financial problem leads to a confrontation between Leonard and Penny's hulking ex-boyfriend Kurt (guest star BRIAN PATRICK WADE).

Story by: Chuck Lorre & Steven Molaro
Teleplay by: Richard Rosenstock & Eric Kaplan
Directed by: Mark Cendrowski
U.S. Broadcast Premiere: February 2, 2009

Episode 15: **The Maternal Capacitance**

A disastrous visit from Mrs. Hofstadter (special guest star CHRISTINE BARANSKI) brings Leonard and Penny closer together.

Story by: Chuck Lorre & Bill Prady
Teleplay by: Richard Rosenstock & Steven Molaro
Directed by: Mark Cendrowski
U.S. Broadcast Premiere: February 9, 2009

Episode 16: **The Cushion Saturation**

A paintball game has surprising consequences for Leonard and his friends when it leads to a fight between Penny and Sheldon—and romance for Wolowitz and Leslie.

Story by: Chuck Lorre
Teleplay by: Bill Prady & Lee Aronsohn
Directed by: Mark Cendrowski
U.S. Broadcast Premiere: March 2, 2009

Episode 17: **The Terminator Decoupling**

A train trip to San Francisco takes a major detour when Leonard, Sheldon, Wolowitz and Raj discover that beautiful sci-fi actress SUMMER GLAU (*Terminator: The Sarah Connor Chronicles*) is onboard. Nobel Laureate for Physics and "Big Bang" theorist Dr. George Smoot also makes a cameo.

Story by: Bill Prady & Dave Goetsch
Teleplay by: Tim Doyle & Stephen Engel
Directed by: Mark Cendrowski
U.S. Broadcast Premiere: March 9, 2009

Episode 18: **The Work Song Nanocluster**

Penny's home hair products business becomes a complete nightmare when a caffeine-addled Sheldon takes over.

Story by: Bill Prady & Lee Aronsohn
Teleplay by: Dave Goetsch & Richard Rosenstock
Directed by: Mark Cendrowski
U.S. Broadcast Premiere: March 16, 2009

Episode 19: **The Dead Hooker Juxtaposition**

There's a new queen bee in the building! Penny develops a rivalry with a sexy female neighbor who moves in to the building and threatens to become the "new Penny."

Written by: Steven Molaro
Directed by: Mark Cendrowski
U.S. Broadcast Premiere: March 30, 2009

Episode 20: **The Hofstadter Isotope**

While Stuart (guest star KEVIN SUSSMAN), a fellow comic book–loving pal of the guys, romances Penny, Leonard and Wolowitz venture out into the world of "Ladies' Night" at a local bar.

Written by: Dave Goetsch
Directed by: Mark Cendrowski
U.S. Broadcast Premiere: April 13, 2009

Episode 21: **The Vegas Renormalization**

Leonard and Koothrappali take a heartbroken Wolowitz to Las Vegas, leaving Sheldon locked out of his apartment and forced to bunk with Penny.

Story by: Jessica Ambrosetti & Nicole Lorre & Andrew Roth
Teleplay by: Steven Molaro
Directed by: Mark Cendrowski
U.S. Broadcast Premiere: April 27, 2009

Sheldon: *(into phone)* Hello, this is Sheldon Cooper. I am leaving a message for Barry Kripke. Barry, it was pleasant seeing you today in the cafeteria. I saw that you purchased the chef's salad. Apparently you did not know that the chef's salad is kitchen trickery to utilize scrap meat. Nevertheless, I hope you enjoyed it. I'm following up on our pending friendship and look forward to hearing from you regarding its status. *(then)* Sheldon Cooper.

Howard: Renaissance fairs aren't about historical accuracy. They're about taking chubby girls who work at Kinko's and lacing them up in corsets so tight their bosom jumps out and says, "Howdy."

Episode 22: **The Classified Materials Turbulence**

Things begin to look up for Leonard when Penny makes a surprising revelation on her second date with Stuart. Meanwhile, Wolowitz enlists his friends' help when he discovers a critical design flaw in his project for NASA.

Story by: Chuck Lorre & Lee Aronsohn
Teleplay by: Bill Prady & Steven Molaro
Directed by: Mark Cendrowski
U.S. Broadcast Premiere: May 4, 2009

Episode 23: **The Monopolar Expedition**

In the second season finale, Leonard and Penny reconsider their feelings for each other. When Leonard and his friends decide to spend the summer working—at the North Pole—Penny is conflicted.

Written by: Eric Kaplan & Richard Rosenstock
Directed by: Mark Cendrowski
U.S. Broadcast Premiere: May 11, 2009

Season 3

Episode 1: **The Electric Can Opener Fluctuation**

In the third season premiere, Sheldon flees back to Texas in disgrace when he learns that the guys tampered with his arctic expedition data—forcing his friends to follow him, and threatening Leonard's hopes for a romantic encounter with Penny.

Written by: Steven Molaro
Directed by: Mark Cendrowski
U.S. Broadcast Premiere: September 21, 2009

Episode 2: **The Jiminy Conjecture**

Leonard and Penny struggle to recover from an awkward first hookup, while Sheldon and Howard stake their best comic books on a bet to determine the species of a cricket. LEWIS BLACK guest stars as an entymologist who settles the high-stakes bet.

Written by: Jim Reynolds
Directed by: Mark Cendrowski
U.S. Broadcast Premiere: September 28, 2009

Episode 3: **The Gothowitz Deviation**

Howard and Raj visit a Goth nightclub to pick up women, while Sheldon attempts to build a better Penny using chocolate-based behavior modification.

Story by: Lee Aronsohn & Richard Rosenstock
Teleplay by: Bill Prady & Maria Ferrari
Directed by: Mark Cendrowski
U.S. Broadcast Premiere: October 5, 2009

Episode 4: **The Pirate Solution**

Raj must find a new job or be sent back to India. Sheldon, however, has a solution—which leaves Leonard and Penny dealing with Howard as third wheel.

Written by: Steve Holland
Directed by: Mark Cendrowski
U.S. Broadcast Premiere: October 12, 2009

Episode 5: **The Creepy Candy Coating Corollary**

While Sheldon settles a score with his nemesis, *Star Trek: The Next Generation*'s WIL WHEATON (guest starring as himself), Wolowitz begs Leonard to get Penny to set him up with one of her friends.

Story by: Chuck Lorre & Bill Prady
Teleplay by: Lee Aronsohn & Steven Molaro
Directed by: Mark Cendrowski
U.S. Broadcast Premiere: October 19, 2009

Episode 6: **The Cornhusker Vortex**

Sheldon teaches Leonard how to understand football, while a kite-fighting incident threatens Howard and Raj's friendship.

Story by: Bill Prady & Steven Molaro
Teleplay by: David Goetsch & Richard Rosenstock
Directed by: Mark Cendrowski
U.S. Broadcast Premiere: November 2, 2009

Episode 7: **The Guitarist Amplification**

Sheldon plays the peacemaker when an argument between Leonard and Penny proves "inconvenient" to him.

Story by: Chuck Lorre & Lee Aronsohn
Teleplay by: Bill Prady & Richard Rosenstock & Jim Reynolds
Directed by: Mark Cendrowski
U.S. Broadcast Premiere: November 9, 2009

Raj: I don't want to go back to India. It's hot and loud and there's so many people. You have no idea, they're everywhere.

Episode 8: **The Adhesive Duck Deficiency**

With Leonard, Howard and Raj away camping in the desert, an injured Penny has only Sheldon to rely on.

Story by: Chuck Lorre & Bill Prady & Dave Goetsch
Teleplay by: Steven Molaro & Eric Kaplan & Maria Ferrari
Directed by: Mark Cendrowski
U.S. Broadcast Premiere: November 16, 2009

Episode 9: **The Vengeance Formulation**

After he's humiliated on National Public Radio, Sheldon vows to destroy Kripke (guest star JOHN ROSS BOWIE), and the guys help Sheldon exact his revenge. Meanwhile, Wolowitz tries not to destroy his new relationship with Bernadette (guest star MELISSA RAUCH). KATEE SACKHOFF (*Battlestar Galactica*) makes a cameo as Wolowitz's dream girl.

Story by: Chuck Lorre & Maria Ferrari
Teleplay by: Richard Rosenstock & Jim Reynolds & Steve Holland
Directed by: Mark Cendrowski
U.S. Broadcast Premiere: November 23, 2009

Episode 10: **The Gorilla Experiment**

Sheldon takes on his greatest challenge when he attempts to help Penny understand Leonard's work, and Wolowitz becomes jealous when Leonard starts hanging out with his new girlfriend.

Story by: Chuck Lorre & Richard Rosenstock & Steve Holland
Teleplay by: Bill Prady & Steven Molaro & Maria Ferrari
Directed by: Mark Cendrowski
U.S. Broadcast Premiere: December 7, 2009

Episode 11: **The Maternal Congruence**

A visit from Leonard's mother delights Sheldon and horrifies Leonard.

Story by: Lee Aronsohn & Steven Molaro & Richard Rosenstock & Maria Ferrari
Teleplay by: Chuck Lorre & Bill Prady & Dave Goetsch
Directed by: Mark Cendrowski
U.S. Broadcast Premiere: December 14, 2009

Episode 12: **The Psychic Vortex**

While Sheldon and Koothrappali attend a university mixer, Leonard is upset to discover that Penny believes in psychics. DANICA McKELLAR (*The Wonder Years*) guest stars as the object of Raj's attraction.

Story by: Lee Aronsohn & Steven Molaro
Teleplay by: Chuck Lorre & Eric Kaplan & Jim Reynolds
Directed by: Mark Cendrowski
U.S. Broadcast Premiere: January 11, 2010

Episode 13: **The Bozeman Reaction**

When their apartment is robbed, Leonard and Sheldon turn to their friends to create a state-of-the-art security system—and Sheldon struggles to cope.

Story by: Bill Prady & Lee Aronsohn & Jim Reynolds
Teleplay by: Chuck Lorre & Steven Molaro & Steve Holland
Directed by: Mark Cendrowski
U.S. Broadcast Premiere: January 18, 2010

Episode 14: **The Einstein Approximation**

Sheldon's case of "physicist's block" while searching for the answer to a physics problem leads him to work at the Cheesecake Factory with Penny.

Story by: Lee Aronsohn & Dave Goetsch & Steve Holland
Teleplay by: Chuck Lorre & Steven Molaro & Eric Kaplan
Directed by: Mark Cendrowski
U.S. Broadcast Premiere: February 1, 2010

Episode 15: **The Large Hadron Collision**

It's Valentine's Day, and Leonard can only bring one guest on a trip to see CERN's Large Hadron Collider (the world's largest and highest energy particle accelerator) in Switzerland. Will it be Sheldon or Penny?

Story by: Chuck Lorre & Steven Molaro & Jim Reynolds
Teleplay by: Lee Aronsohn & Richard Rosenstock & Maria Ferrari
Directed by: Mark Cendrowski
U.S. Broadcast Premiere: February 8, 2010

Episode 16: **The Excelsior Acquisition**

Sheldon misses his chance to meet comic book legend STAN LEE (as himself) when he winds up in traffic court after he gets a ticket because of Penny.

Story by: Chuck Lorre & Lee Aronsohn & Steven Molaro
Teleplay by: Bill Prady & Steve Holland & Maria Ferrari
Directed by: Peter Chakos
U.S. Broadcast Premiere: March 1, 2010

Episode 17: **The Precious Fragmentation**

When the guys find a rare movie prop ring from *The Lord of the Rings* at a garage sale, it threatens to tear them apart—forcing them to choose the ring or their friendship.

Story by: Lee Aronsohn & Eric Kaplan & Maria Ferrari
Teleplay by: Bill Prady & Steven Molaro & Richard Rosenstock
Directed by: Mark Cendrowski
U.S. Broadcast Premiere: March 8, 2010

Episode 18: **The Pants Alternative**

Sheldon's friends come to his aid when his fear of public speaking stands between him and a coveted award.

Story by: Chuck Lorre & Bill Prady & Steve Holland
Teleplay by: Eric Kaplan & Richard Rosenstock & Jim Reynolds
Directed by: Mark Cendrowski
U.S. Broadcast Premiere: March 22, 2010

Episode 19: **The Wheaton Recurrence**

A fight between Leonard and Penny threatens their relationship, while Sheldon battles WIL WHEATON in bowling.

Story by: Chuck Lorre & Steven Molaro & Nicole Lorre & Jessica Ambrosetti
Teleplay by: Bill Prady & Dave Goetsch, & Jim Reynolds & Maria Ferrari
Directed by: Mark Cendrowski
U.S. Broadcast Premiere: April 2, 2010

Episode 20: **The Spaghetti Catalyst**

When Leonard and Penny aren't speaking, Sheldon goes to extremes to keep them both happy and gets caught in a lie.

Written by: Chuck Lorre & Bill Prady & Lee Aronsohn & Steven Molaro
Directed by: Anthony Rich
U.S. Broadcast Premiere: May 3, 2010

Episode 21: **The Plimpton Stimulation**

Leonard and Sheldon compete for the attention of a famous female physicist—Dr. Elizabeth Plimpton (guest star JUDY GREER).

Story by: Chuck Lorre & Bill Prady & Lee Aronsohn
Teleplay by: Steven Molaro & Jim Reynolds & Maria Ferrari
Directed by: Mark Cendrowski
U.S. Broadcast Premiere: May 10, 2010

Penny: Oh, please. We have a little saying in Nebraska: You can call the cow patty chocolate, but I'm still not going to make a s'more with it.

Episode 22: **The Staircase Implementation**

Leonard tells Penny the story of how he met Sheldon for the first time . . . and what happened to the elevator.

Story by: Lee Aronsohn & Steven Molaro & Steve Holland
Teleplay by: Chuck Lorre & Dave Goetsch & Maria Ferrari
Directed by: Mark Cendrowski
U.S. Broadcast Premiere: May 17, 2010

Episode 23: **The Lunar Excitation**

In the third season finale, Wolowitz and Koothrappali search for Sheldon's perfect match online—and find Sheldon's ideal woman (guest star MAYIM BIALIK). Meanwhile, Penny worries that dating Leonard has ruined her for normal guys.

Story by: Chuck Lorre & Bill Prady & Maria Ferrari
Teleplay by: Lee Aronsohn & Steven Molaro & Steve Holland
Directed by: Peter Chakos
U.S. Broadcast Premiere: May 24, 2010

Season 4

Episode 1: **The Robotic Manipulation**

On the fourth season premiere, Penny finds herself along for the ride on Sheldon's first date ever. Meanwhile, Wolowitz finds a new use for a robotic arm.

Story by: Chuck Lorre & Lee Aronsohn & Dave Goetsch
Teleplay by: Steven Molaro & Eric Kaplan & Steve Holland
Directed by: Mark Cendrowski
U.S. Broadcast Premiere: September 23, 2010

Episode 2: **The Cruciferous Vegetable Amplification**

When Sheldon realizes he won't live long enough to download his consciousness into a robot body, he attempts to extend his lifespan. Apple cofounder STEVE WOZNIAK guest stars as himself.

Story by: Bill Prady & Lee Aronsohn & Steve Holland
Teleplay by: Chuck Lorre & Steven Molaro & Jim Reynolds
Directed by: Mark Cendrowski
U.S. Broadcast Premiere: September 30, 2010

> **Howard:** Women, huh? Can't live with 'em, can't successfully refute their hypotheses.

Episode 3: **The Zazzy Substitution**

The guys are concerned as Sheldon searches for an alternative to human companionship after he and Amy break up.

Story by: Chuck Lorre & Bill Prady & Jim Reynolds
Teleplay by: Lee Aronsohn & Steven Molaro & Maria Ferrari
Directed by: Mark Cendrowski
U.S. Broadcast Premiere: October 7, 2010

Episode 4: **The Hot Troll Deviation**

An embarrassing secret of Wolowitz's comes to light, while Sheldon and Raj have a small war at work. *Battlestar Galactica*'s KATEE SACKHOFF and *Star Trek*'s GEORGE TAKEI guest star as themselves as Wolowitz's love gurus. MELISSA RAUCH reprises her role as Howard's girlfriend, Bernadette.

Story by: Chuck Lorre & Steven Molaro & Adam Faberman
Teleplay by: Bill Prady & Lee Aronsohn & Maria Ferrari
Directed by: Mark Cendrowski
U.S. Broadcast Premiere: October 14, 2010

Episode 5: **The Desperation Emanation**

Leonard realizes he's the only one without a girlfriend, while Sheldon wants to get rid of his.

Story by: Bill Prady & Lee Aronsohn & Dave Goetsch
Teleplay by: Chuck Lorre & Steven Molaro & Steve Holland
Directed by: Mark Cendrowski
U.S. Broadcast Premiere: October 21, 2010

Episode 6: **The Irish Pub Formulation**

A visit from Raj's sister (guest star AARTI MANKAD) creates tension among the guys—especially when Leonard keeps an affair secret from Sheldon, Howard and Raj.

Story by: Chuck Lorre & Lee Aronsohn & Steven Molaro
Teleplay by: Bill Prady & Eric Kaplan & Maria Ferrari
Directed by: Mark Cendrowski
U.S. Broadcast Premiere: October 28, 2010

Episode 7: **The Apology Insufficiency**

When an FBI agent (guest star ELIZA DUSHKU) interviews the guys for Wolowitz's security clearance, Sheldon's answers during the screening put Wolowitz's clearance in jeopardy.

Story by: Chuck Lorre & Lee Aronsohn & Maria Ferrari
Teleplay by: Bill Prady & Steven Molaro & Steve Holland
Directed by: Mark Cendrowski
U.S. Broadcast Premiere: November 4, 2010

Sheldon: You know, it just occurred to me: if there are an infinite number of parallel universes, in one of them, there's probably a Sheldon who doesn't believe parallel universes exist.

Leonard: Probably. What's your point?

Sheldon: No point. It's just one of those things that makes one of the 'me's chuckle.

Episode 8: **The 21-Second Excitation**

When the guys camp in line for a screening, their plans are thwarted by Sheldon's greatest nemesis, WIL WHEATON. Meanwhile, Penny and Bernadette invite Amy to her first slumber party.

Story by: Chuck Lorre & Bill Prady & Jim Reynolds
Teleplay by: Lee Aronsohn & Steven Molaro & Steve Holland
Directed by: Mark Cendrowski
U.S. Broadcast Premiere: November 11, 2010

Episode 9: **The Boyfriend Complexity**

Penny asks Leonard to lie to her father, Wyatt (guest star KEITH CARRADINE), while Howard, Raj and Bernadette pull an all-nighter at a telescope.

Story by: Chuck Lorre & Lee Aronsohn & Jim Reynolds
Teleplay by: Bill Prady & Steven Molaro & Dave Goetsch
Directed by: Mark Cendrowski
U.S. Broadcast Premiere: November 18, 2010

Episode 10: **The Alien Parasite Hypothesis**

Amy finds she has sexual feelings for Penny's ex, Zack (guest star BRIAN THOMAS SMITH), while Koothrappali and Wolowitz try to prove who would be the better superhero.

Story by: Chuck Lorre & Steven Molaro & Steve Holland
Teleplay by: Lee Aronsohn & Jim Reynolds & Maria Ferrari
Directed by: Mark Cendrowski
U.S. Broadcast Premiere: December 9, 2010

Episode 11: **The Justice League Recombination**

The guys find a "super" use for Penny's new boyfriend, Zack, when they enter a costume contest as the Justice League.

Story by: Chuck Lorre & Lee Aronsohn & Maria Ferrari
Teleplay by: Bill Prady & Steven Molaro & Steve Holland
Directed by: Mark Cendrowski
U.S. Broadcast Premiere: December 16, 2010

Episode 12: **The Bus Pants Utilization**

Leonard's idea for a smartphone app derails his friendship with Sheldon as they fight for control of the project.

Story by: Chuck Lorre & Lee Aronsohn & Maria Ferrari
Teleplay by: Bill Prady & Steven Molaro & Eric Kaplan
Directed by: Mark Cendrowski
U.S. Broadcast Premiere: January 6, 2011

Episode 13: **The Love Car Displacement**

Tension runs high when everyone is staying at the same hotel for a science event and Bernadette runs into her ex-boyfriend (guest star RICK FOX, three-time NBA champion with the Los Angeles Lakers).

Story by: Chuck Lorre & Bill Prady & Dave Goetsch
Teleplay by: Lee Aronsohn & Steven Molaro & Steve Holland
Directed by: Anthony Rich
U.S. Broadcast Premiere: January 20, 2011

Episode 14: **The Thespian Catalyst**

Sheldon wants Penny to give him acting lessons, hoping that they will help him become a better teacher. Meanwhile, Koothrappali fantasizes about his best friend's girlfriend.

Story by: Chuck Lorre & Lee Aronsohn & Jim Reynolds
Teleplay by: Bill Prady & Steven Molaro & Maria Ferrari
Directed by: Mark Cendrowski
U.S. Broadcast Premiere: February 3, 2011

Episode 15: **The Benefactor Factor**

A wealthy donor to the university makes Leonard consider how far he's willing to go for the sake of science. JESSICA WALTER (*Arrested Development*) guest stars as the widowed benefactress and JOSHUA MALINA (*The West Wing*) guest stars as the university president.

Story by: Bill Prady & Lee Aronsohn & Dave Goetsch
Teleplay by: Chuck Lorre & Eric Kaplan & Steve Holland
Directed by: Mark Cendrowski
U.S. Broadcast Premiere: February 10, 2011

Episode 16: **The Cohabitation Formulation**

As Wolowitz contemplates taking things with Bernadette to the next level, he must choose between his girlfriend and his mother. Meanwhile, Leonard rekindles his relationship with Raj's sister, Priya.

Story by: Chuck Lorre & Lee Aronsohn & Dave Goetsch
Teleplay by: Bill Prady & Steven Molaro & Jim Reynolds
Directed by: Mark Cendrowski
U.S. Broadcast Premiere: February 17, 2011

Episode 17: **The Toast Derivation**

When the gang starts hanging out at Raj's and Sheldon realizes it's actually Leonard who is the center of their social group, Sheldon decides to get a new group of friends.

Story by: Bill Prady & Dave Goetsch & Maria Ferrari
Teleplay by: Chuck Lorre & Steven Molaro & Jim Reynolds
Directed by: Mark Cendrowski
U.S. Broadcast Premiere: February 24, 2011

Episode 18: **The Prestidigitation Approximation**

Leonard must choose between his new girlfriend, Priya, and his friendship with Penny. Meanwhile, Howard drives Sheldon crazy with a magic trick.

Story by: Bill Prady & Steve Holland & Eddie Gorodetsky
Teleplay by: Chuck Lorre & Steven Molaro & Eric Kaplan
Directed by: Mark Cendrowski
U.S. Broadcast Premiere: March 10, 2011

Episode 19: **The Zarnecki Incursion**

When someone hacks Sheldon's online gaming account, the guys go on a quest to find the culprit.

Story by: Chuck Lorre & Steven Molaro & Maria Ferrari
Teleplay by: Bill Prady & Dave Goetsch & Jim Reynolds
Directed by: Peter Chakos
U.S. Broadcast Premiere: March 31, 2011

Episode 20: **The Herb Garden Germination**

Sheldon and Amy experiment on their friends by spreading gossip, while Howard takes a big step in his relationship with Bernadette.

Story by: Chuck Lorre & Eric Kaplan & Eddie Gorodetsky
Teleplay by: Bill Prady & Steven Molaro & Steve Holland
Directed by: Mark Cendrowski
U.S. Broadcast Premiere: April 7, 2011

Episode 21: **The Agreement Dissection**

Priya uses her lawyer skills to pick apart the Roommate Agreement . . . and put Sheldon in his place. Meanwhile, the girls take Sheldon dancing.

Story by: Bill Prady & Dave Goetsch & Eddie Gorodetsky
Teleplay by: Chuck Lorre & Steven Molaro & Eric Kaplan
Directed by: Mark Cendrowski
U.S. Broadcast Premiere: April 28, 2011

Sheldon: For the record, I do have genitals. They're functional and aesthetically pleasing.

Episode 22: **The Wildebeest Implementation**

Raj attempts to cure his social anxiety disorder of talking to women, while Penny uses Bernadette to spy on Leonard and his girlfriend.

Story by: Chuck Lorre & Steven Molaro & Eric Kaplan
Teleplay by: Bill Prady & Eddie Gorodetsky & Maria Ferrari
Directed by: Mark Cendrowski
U.S. Broadcast Premiere: May 5, 2011

Episode 23: **The Engagement Reaction**

When Howard finally breaks the news to his mom that he's engaged to Bernadette, it lands her in the hospital.

Story by: Bill Prady & Eric Kaplan & Jim Reynolds
Teleplay by: Chuck Lorre & Steven Molaro &Steve Holland
Directed by: Howard Murray
U.S. Broadcast Premiere: May 12, 2011

Episode 24: **The Roommate Transmogrification**

When Bernadette receives her PhD, the guys take joy in reminding an emasculated Wolowitz that he is the only one in their group who isn't a doctor. Meanwhile, Koothrappali becomes Sheldon's new roommate after hearing Leonard and Priya engaging in a *Star Trek* bedroom fantasy, in the fourth season finale.

Story by: Chuck Lorre & Steven Molaro & Eddie Gorodetsky
Teleplay by: Bill Prady & Eric Kaplan & Jim Reynolds
Directed by: Mark Cendrowski
U.S. Broadcast Premiere: May 19, 2011

Season 5

Episode 1: **The Skank Reflex Analysis**

The fifth season premiere picks up where the fourth season finale left off as the gang deals with the aftermath of Penny and Raj's night together. While Penny worries that she's screwed things up permanently with her friends, Sheldon takes command of the paintball team. Emmy nominee CHRISTINE BARANSKI (*The Good Wife*) reprises her role as Leonard's emotionally distant mother.

Story by: Eric Kaplan & Maria Ferrari & Anthony Del Broccolo
Teleplay by: Chuck Lorre & Bill Prady & Steven Molaro
Directed by: Mark Cendrowski
U.S. Broadcast Premiere: September 22, 2011

The Zoology Supposition

On birds:

Sheldon came to terms with his fear of birds and came to love the one that hung out on this windowsill, who he named Lovey Dovey.

Season 5, Episode 9: The Ornithophobia Diffusion

On badgers:

Sheldon told them his Uncle Carl was killed by a badger, aka "KBB."

Season 4, Episode 2: The Cruciferous Vegetable Amplification

On griffins:

When Sheldon was a kid, the family cat, Lucky, got run over by a Montgomery Ward delivery van:

Sheldon: While others mourned Lucky, I realized his untimely demise provided me with the opportunity to replace him with something more suited to my pet needs. A faithful companion that I could snuggle with at night and yet would be capable of killing upon telepathic command.

Wolowitz: So, not a puppy.

Sheldon: Please. Nothing so pedestrian. I wanted a griffin.

Leonard: A griffin.

Sheldon: Yes, half eagle, half lion.

Leonard: And mythological.

Sheldon: Irrelevant. I was studying recombinant DNA technology and I was confident I could create one, but my parents were unwilling to secure the necessary eagle eggs and lion semen. Of course, my sister got swimming lessons when she wanted them.

Season 2, Episode 4: The Griffin Equivalency

On guinea pigs:

Stephanie: I'm sorry, you tried to build your own CAT scanner?

Sheldon: I didn't try, I succeeded. In fact, I was briefly able to see the inside of my sister's guinea pig, Snowball, before he caught fire. It led to an interesting expression in our house: "Not a Snowball's chance in a CAT scanner."

Season 2, Episode 9: The White Asparagus Triangulation

On the dogapus:

When Sheldon was worried he'd die too young to witness the singularity—"when man will be able to transfer his consciousness into machines and achieve immortality"—the dogapus was also one of the things he was going to miss.

Sheldon: You don't get it, Leonard. I'm going to miss so much. The unified field theory, cold fusion, the dogapus.

Leonard: What's a dogapus?

Sheldon: A hybrid dog and octopus. Man's underwater best friend.

Leonard: Is somebody working on that?

Sheldon: I was going to. I planned on giving it to myself on my three hundredth birthday.

Leonard: Uh-huh. *(then)* Hang on a second. You hate dogs.

Sheldon: A dogapus can play fetch with eight balls. No one can hate that.

Season 4, Episode 2: The Cruciferous Vegetable Amplification

On koalas:

Sheldon: "I don't know what it is, but when they start munching on eucalyptus, I just melt inside."

Season 5, Episode 12: The Shiny Trinket Maneuver

Sheldon: *(to Penny)* [Amy would] see right through that. We go to the zoo all the time. She knows my koala face. And for future reference, it's this.

Sheldon does his koala face.

Season 5, Episode 12: The Shiny Trinket Maneuver

According to Sheldon, "koala" is the correct animal for interspecies supersoldier.

Season 8, Episode 2: The Junior Professor Solution

On spiders:

Sheldon rewrote songs to get children interested in the hard sciences:

Sheldon: The itsy bitsy spider was not an insect at all because it has eight legs and two body parts.

Season 8, Episode 21: The Communication Deterioration

On bats:

Sheldon: *(singing to the tune of "Eye of the Tiger" by Survivor)* It's the eye of the tiger, it's the ear of the bat/ it's the whiskers of the catfish and the walrus—

Howard: Hang on. Not that your song isn't terrible—it is—but how do you mention bats and leave out sonar?

Sheldon: You didn't let me finish. *(resuming end of chorus)* And also regarding the baaaat, it has sonar.

Season 8, Episode 21: The Communication Deterioration

On dung beetles:

Sheldon: Even the lowly dung beetle chooses to plot its course by using the Milky Way.

Raj: Is that true?

Sheldon: Everything I say is true. Now of course, the dung beetle also enjoys eating feces, living in feces and making little balls out of feces. So, y'know, pick and choose which aspects of its lifestyle you want to embrace.

Season 7, Episode 1: The Hofstadter Insufficiency

Bernadette: I'm too small for Twister. And roller coasters. And sitting with my feet on the floor. Hope you enjoyed the prenatal cigarettes, Mom.

Episode 2: **The Infestation Hypothesis**

A battle of wills between Sheldon and Penny leaves Amy caught in the middle, while Leonard tries to spice up his long-distance relationship with Priya, who has moved back to India.

Story by: Bill Prady & Steven Molaro & Maria Ferrari
Teleplay by: Chuck Lorre & Jim Reynolds & Steve Holland
Directed by: Mark Cendrowski
U.S. Broadcast Premiere: September 22, 2011

Episode 3: **The Pulled Groin Extrapolation**

Leonard attends a coworker's wedding as Amy's date. Meanwhile, Howard tries to convince Bernadette to live with his mom after they get married by suggesting a trial run with the two of them staying with his mom over the weekend.

Story by: Chuck Lorre & Eric Kaplan & Jim Reynolds
Teleplay by: Bill Prady & Steven Molaro & Dave Goetsch
Directed by: Mark Cendrowski
U.S. Broadcast Premiere: September 29, 2011

Episode 4: **The Wiggly Finger Catalyst**

When Raj is upset he's the only one of the four guys who is not in a relationship, Penny sets out to find the perfect date, introducing him to Emily (guest star KATIE LeCLERC—*Switched at Birth*), a girl he can actually talk to!

Story by: Chuck Lorre & David Goetsch & Anthony Del Broccolo
Teleplay by: Bill Prady & Steven Molaro & Steve Holland
Directed by: Mark Cendrowski
U.S. Broadcast Premiere: October 6, 2011

Episode 5: **The Russian Rocket Reaction**

Sheldon's old nemesis, WIL WHEATON, returns and invites everyone to a housewarming party. Sheldon threatens to "defriend" Leonard if he attends. But when he hears that BRENT SPINER (guest starring as himself), the actor who played Commander Data, will be there, Sheldon decides to go to the party after all . . . only to discover new levels of treachery. Meanwhile, Howard gets an out-of-this-world opportunity that Bernadette reacts to strongly.

Story by: Bill Prady & Steven Molaro & Jim Reynolds
Teleplay by: Chuck Lorre & Eric Kaplan & Maria Ferrari
Directed by: Mark Cendrowski
U.S. Broadcast Premiere: October 13, 2011

Episode 6: **The Rhinitis Revelation**

Craving a little motherly love, Sheldon competes with the gang for his mother's attention when she comes to visit.

Story by: Chuck Lorre & Eric Kaplan & Steve Holland
Teleplay by: Bill Prady & Steven Molaro & Jim Reynolds
Directed by: Howard Murray
U.S. Broadcast Premiere: October 20, 2011

Episode 7: **The Good Guy Fluctuation**

A cute comic book artist (guest star COURTNEY FORD) puts Leonard's relationship with Priya to the test; while Sheldon, getting into the spirit of Halloween, tries to scare the guys.

Story by: Chuck Lorre & Dave Goetsch & Maria Ferrari
Teleplay by: Bill Prady & Steven Molaro & Steve Holland
Directed by: Mark Cendrowski
U.S. Broadcast Premiere: October 27, 2011

Episode 8: **The Isolation Permutation**

Amy is heartbroken when Bernadette and Penny go shopping for wedding dresses without her.

Story by: Chuck Lorre & Eric Kaplan & Tara Hernandez
Teleplay by: Bill Prady & Steven Molaro & Steve Holland
Directed by: Mark Cendrowski
U.S. Broadcast Premiere: November 3, 2011

Episode 9: **The Ornithophobia Diffusion**

Can friends with benefits still be friends without? Leonard and Penny try hanging out alone, while Sheldon must overcome his fear of birds.

Story by: Chuck Lorre & Dave Goetsch & Anthony Del Broccolo
Teleplay by: Bill Prady & Steven Molaro & Eric Kaplan
Directed by: Mark Cendrowski
U.S. Broadcast Premiere: November 10, 2011

Episode 10: **The Flaming Spittoon Acquisition**

Sheldon becomes jealous and considers taking his relationship with Amy to the next level when Stuart from the comic book store asks her out on a date.

Story by: Chuck Lorre & Steven Molaro & Dave Goetsch
Teleplay by: Bill Prady & Jim Reynolds & Steve Holland
Directed by: Mark Cendrowski
U.S. Broadcast Premiere: November 17, 2011

Episode 11: **The Speckerman Recurrence**

Leonard must face his fears after being contacted by his high school tormentor (guest star LANCE BARBER), while Penny realizes that she might have been a bully herself.

Story by: Chuck Lorre & Bill Prady & Steve Holland
Teleplay by: Steven Molaro & Eric Kaplan & Anthony Del Broccolo
Directed by: Anthony Rich
U.S. Broadcast Premiere: December 8, 2011

Episode 12: **The Shiny Trinket Maneuver**

Sheldon gets in trouble with Amy when he isn't impressed by her recent accomplishment, and it's up to Penny to teach him how to be a better boyfriend. Howard, meanwhile, must come to grips with Bernadette's dislike of children.

Story by: Chuck Lorre & Steve Holland & Tara Hernandez
Teleplay by: Bill Prady & Steven Molaro & Jim Reynolds
Directed by: Mark Cendrowski
U.S. Broadcast Premiere: January 12, 2012

Episode 13: **The Recombination Hypothesis**

The possibility of Leonard and Penny getting back together could prove disastrous when Leonard offers Penny a spur of the moment invitation to a romantic dinner for two on the 100th episode of the series.

Story by: Chuck Lorre
Teleplay by: Bill Prady & Steven Molaro
Directed by: Mark Cendrowski
U.S. Broadcast Premiere: January 19, 2012

Episode 14: **The Beta Test Initiation**

Leonard and Penny experiment with dating again by "beta testing" their relationship, while Raj develops a peculiar relationship with his phone's virtual assistant.

Story by: Chuck Lorre & Steven Molaro & Eric Kaplan
Teleplay by: Bill Prady & Dave Goetsch & Maria Ferrari
Directed by: Mark Cendrowski
U.S. Broadcast Premiere: January 26, 2012

Episode 15: **The Friendship Contraction**

Sheldon's selfish demands force Leonard to reconsider their friendship. Could this be the end of the Roommate Agreement? Meanwhile, Howard tries to pick his astronaut nickname, but NASA astronaut MIKE MASSIMINO (guest starring as himself) has other ideas.

Story by: Chuck Lorre & Eric Kaplan & Jim Reynolds
Teleplay by: Bill Prady & Steven Molaro & Steve Holland
Directed by: Mark Cendrowski
U.S. Broadcast Premiere: February 2, 2012

Episode 16: **The Vacation Solution**

When Sheldon is forced to take a vacation by the university, he goes to work with Amy in her neurobiology lab. Meanwhile, Bernadette wants Howard to sign a prenuptial agreement.

Story by: Chuck Lorre & Anthony Del Broccolo & Tara Hernandez
Teleplay by: Bill Prady & Steven Molaro & Maria Ferrari
Directed by: Mark Cendrowski
U.S. Broadcast Premiere: February 9, 2012

Episode 17: **The Rothman Disintegration**

When a corner office at the university opens up, Sheldon must compete for it with his office nemesis, Barry Kripke. Meanwhile, Penny receives an unusual gift from Amy.

Story by: Chuck Lorre & Bill Prady & Steve Holland
Teleplay by: Steven Molaro & Eric Kaplan, & Jim Reynolds
Directed by: Mark Cendrowski
U.S. Broadcast Premiere: February 16, 2012

Episode 18: **The Werewolf Transformation**

Sheldon's life is turned upside down after his barber becomes hospitalized. Now that there's been a change in his routine, Sheldon finds himself reevaluating his entire life. Meanwhile, astronaut training causes Howard to rethink his decision to go into space.

Story by: Chuck Lorre & Todd Craig & Gary Torvinen
Teleplay by: Bill Prady & Steven Molaro & Jim Reynolds & Maria Ferrari
Directed by: Mark Cendrowski
U.S. Broadcast Premiere: February 23, 2012

Episode 19: **The Weekend Vortex**

It's on . . . like Alderaan, when the guys plan a weekend *Star Wars* gaming marathon! But when Sheldon chooses the guys-only weekend over a weekend with Amy to visit her aunt, he is destined to feel the Force!

Story by: Chuck Lorre & Bill Prady & Tara Hernandez
Teleplay by: Steven Molaro & Eric Kaplan & Steve Holland
Directed by: Mark Cendrowski
U.S. Broadcast Premiere: March 8, 2012

Amy: You are aware that your ritualistic knocking behavior is symptomatic of obsessive-compulsive disorder?

Sheldon: Is not. Is not. Is not.

Amy: Denial. Denial. Denial.

Stuart: Can I help you find anything?

Amy: A comic that doesn't depict a woman whose bosom can be used as a flotation device.

Episode 20: **The Transporter Malfunction**

It's a dream come true for Sheldon when he has a close encounter with his hero, Mr. Spock. Legendary sci-fi icon LEONARD NIMOY guest stars, lending his voice to a unique reprisal of his three-time Emmy-nominated *Star Trek* role.

Story by: Chuck Lorre & Bill Prady & Maria Ferrari
Teleplay by: Steven Molaro & Jim Reynolds & Steve Holland
Directed by: Mark Cendrowski
U.S. Broadcast Premiere: March 29, 2012

Episode 21: **The Hawking Excitation**

When Wolowitz gets to work with world-renowned scientist STEPHEN HAWKING (guest starring as himself), Sheldon is willing to do anything to meet his hero.

Story by: Bill Prady & Steven Molaro & Steve Holland
Teleplay by: Chuck Lorre & Eric Kaplan & Maria Ferrari
Directed by: Mark Cendrowski
U.S. Broadcast Premiere: April 5, 2012

Episode 22: **The Stag Convergence**

Howard's wedding plans are in jeopardy after the guys (and WIL WHEATON) throw him a bachelor party. After details of his sexual history are leaked online, Bernadette reconsiders marrying Howard.

Story by: Bill Prady & Steve Holland & Eric Kaplan
Teleplay by: Chuck Lorre & Steven Molaro & Jim Reynolds
Directed by: Peter Chakos
U.S. Broadcast Premiere: April 26, 2012

Episode 23: **The Launch Acceleration**

When NASA reschedules Howard's mission and puts his wedding plans in jeopardy, he's forced to face his fears and Bernadette's dad (guest star CASEY SANDER). Meanwhile, Leonard says something surprising to Penny in the bedroom.

Story by: Chuck Lorre & Steven Molaro & Jim Reynolds
Teleplay by: Bill Prady & Steve Holland & Maria Ferrari
Directed by: Mark Cendrowski
U.S. Broadcast Premiere: May 3, 2012

Episode 24: **The Countdown Reflection**

Howard Wolowitz crosses over into the final frontiers of space . . . and marriage in the fifth season finale. When Howard and Bernadette decide they want to be married before his NASA space launch, the gang rushes to put on a wedding. NASA Astronaut MIKE MASSIMINO guest stars as himself.

Story by: Bill Prady & Eric Kaplan & Steve Holland
Teleplay by: Chuck Lorre & Steven Molaro & Jim Reynolds
Directed by: Mark Cendrowski
U.S. Broadcast Premiere: May 10, 2012

Season 6

Episode 1: **The Date Night Variable**

On the sixth season premiere, Howard discovers that he can't escape his mother—even in space! Caught in an argument between Bernadette and his mom, Howard deals with woman trouble from the International Space Station. Back on Earth, meanwhile, Raj faces his loneliness by turning his existence as a third wheel into an art form.

Story by: Chuck Lorre & Eric Kaplan & Steve Holland
Teleplay by: Steven Molaro & Jim Reynolds & Maria Ferrari
Directed by: Mark Cendrowski
U.S. Broadcast Premiere: September 27, 2012

Episode 2: **The Decoupling Fluctuation**

When Sheldon learns that Penny is thinking about breaking up with Leonard, he tries to intervene. But Sheldon is no good at keeping secrets. Meanwhile, Howard is being picked on in space by the other astronauts (guest stars PASHA LYCHNIKOFF and MIKE MASSIMINO).

Story by: Chuck Lorre & Jim Reynolds & Maria Ferrari
Teleplay by: Steven Molaro & Eric Kaplan & Steve Holland
Directed by: Mark Cendrowski
U.S. Broadcast Premiere: October 4, 2012

Episode 3: **The Higgs Boson Observation**

While the pressures of being in space start to take their toll on Howard, Amy feels threatened when Sheldon hires a young female assistant, Alex (guest star MARGO HARSHMAN).

Story by: Steven Molaro & Dave Goetsch & Steve Holland
Teleplay by: Chuck Lorre & Jim Reynolds & Maria Ferrari
Directed by: Mark Cendrowski
U.S. Broadcast Premiere: October 11, 2012

Episode 4: **The Re-Entry Minimization**

When Howard returns from space, he doesn't get the hero's welcome he expected. Meanwhile, game night turns into a battle of the sexes.

Story by: Bill Prady & Jim Reynolds & Anthony Del Broccolo
Teleplay by: Chuck Lorre & Steven Molaro & Eric Kaplan
Directed by: Mark Cendrowski
U.S. Broadcast Premiere: October 18, 2012

Episode 5: **The Holographic Excitation**

The gang celebrates Halloween at Stuart's comic book store. Meanwhile Leonard and Penny discover a new spark in their relationship when he seduces her with science. And while Howard can't stop talking about space, it takes iconic astronaut BUZZ ALDRIN (guest starring as himself) to get him grounded again.

Story by: Chuck Lorre & Eric Kaplan & Jeremy Howe
Teleplay by: Steven Molaro & Steve Holland & Maria Ferrari
Directed by: Mark Cendrowski
U.S. Broadcast Premiere: October 25, 2012

Episode 6: **The Extract Obliteration**

Sheldon's tenuous relationship with renowned scientist STEPHEN HAWKING is threatened by a game of Words with Friends, while Penny secretly enrols in a class at the local college.

Story by: Chuck Lorre & Bill Prady & Steve Holland
Teleplay by: Steven Molaro & Jim Reynolds & Eric Kaplan
Directed by: Mark Cendrowski
U.S. Broadcast Premiere: November 1, 2012

Episode 7: **The Habitation Configuration**

Pressured by Bernadette, Howard comes to terms with moving out of his mother's house. Meanwhile, Sheldon, who's caught in the middle of a feud between his "girlfriend" Amy and good friend WIL WHEATON, goes to Penny for advice. *Star Trek*'s LeVAR BURTON guest stars.

Story by: Chuck Lorre & Eric Kaplan & Jim Reynolds
Teleplay by: Steven Molaro & Steve Holland & Maria Ferrari
Directed by: Mark Cendrowski
U.S. Broadcast Premiere: November 8, 2012

> **Amy:** Wow, my boyfriend is friends with Stephen Hawking and my new dandruff shampoo doesn't smell like tar. Everything really is coming up Amy.

Episode 8: **The 43 Peculiarity**

Howard and Raj try to get to the bottom of why Sheldon disappears every afternoon at 2:45. Meanwhile, Leonard and Penny wrestle with jealousy in their relationship.

Story by: Chuck Lorre & Dave Goetsch & Anthony Del Broccolo
Teleplay by: Steven Molaro & Jim Reynolds & Steve Holland
Directed by: Mark Cendrowski
U.S. Broadcast Premiere: November 15, 2012

Episode 9: **The Parking Spot Escalation**

When the university reassigns Sheldon's (unused) parking spot to Howard, the ensuing turf battle affects the whole gang.

Story by: Chuck Lorre & Eric Kaplan, & Adam Faberman
Teleplay by: Steven Molaro & Steve Holland & Maria Ferrari
Directed by: Peter Chakos
U.S. Broadcast Premiere: November 29, 2012

Episode 10: **The Fish Guts Displacement**

Sheldon plays nursemaid to a sick Amy, while Howard attempts to bond with his father-in-law on an upcoming fishing trip.

Story by: Chuck Lorre & Bill Prady & Tara Hernandez
Teleplay by: Steven Molaro & Eric Kaplan & Jim Reynolds
Directed by: Mark Cendrowski
U.S. Broadcast Premiere: December 6, 2012

Episode 11: **The Santa Simulation**

Sheldon unwillingly revisits some Christmas memories during a lively game of Dungeons & Dragons, while Penny, Bernadette and Amy try to find the perfect girl for Raj when he joins the girls for ladies' night.

Story by: Chuck Lorre & Eric Kaplan,& Steve Holland
Teleplay by: Steven Molaro & Jim Reynolds & Maria Ferrari
Directed by: Mark Cendrowski
U.S. Broadcast Premiere: December 13, 2012

Episode 12: **The Egg Salad Equivalency**

Sheldon is accused of sexual harassment at the university and winds up dragging Leonard, Raj and Howard into the fray. *Southland*'s REGINA KING guest stars as the university's director of employee relations.

Story by: Chuck Lorre & Eric Kaplan & Jim Reynolds
Teleplay by: Steven Molaro & Bill Prady & Steve Holland
Directed by: Mark Cendrowski
U.S. Broadcast Premiere: January 3, 2013

Episode 13: **The Bakersfield Expedition**

While the guys take a road trip to a comic book convention in Bakersfield dressed as characters from *Star Trek: The Next Generation*, Leonard's car is stolen. Meanwhile, the girls stay home and try to appreciate the world of comics.

Story by: Chuck Lorre & Jim Reynolds & Steve Holland
Teleplay by: Steven Molaro & Eric Kaplan & Maria Ferrari
Directed by: Mark Cendrowski
U.S. Broadcast Premiere: January 10, 2013

Episode 14: **The Cooper/Kripke Inversion**

Outraged that he's being forced to work with his university nemesis, Barry Kripke, Sheldon faces a crisis of conscience. Meanwhile, Howard and Raj spend a thousand dollars on action figures of themselves.

Story by: Chuck Lorre & Eric Kaplan & Anthony Del Broccolo
Teleplay by: Steven Molaro & im Reynolds & Steve Holland
Directed by: Mark Cendrowski
U.S. Broadcast Premiere: January 31, 2013

Episode 15: **The Spoiler Alert Segmentation**

A fight between Leonard and Sheldon drives Leonard to finally move in with Penny—not realizing how the shift will affect Penny and Amy's living arrangements. Meanwhile, Raj takes care of Mrs. Wolowitz while Howard is away.

Story by: Chuck Lorre & Eric Kaplan & Steve Holland
Teleplay by: Steven Molaro & Maria Ferrari & Adam Faberman
Directed by: Mark Cendrowski
U.S. Broadcast Premiere: February 7, 2013

Episode 16: **The Tangible Affection Proof**

While the guys try to give their significant others the perfect Valentine's Day, Raj and Stuart throw a lonely-people party at the comic book store.

Story by: Chuck Lorre & Bill Prady & Steve Holland
Teleplay by: Steven Molaro & Jim Reynolds & Tara Hernandez
Directed by: Mark Cendrowski
U.S. Broadcast Premiere: February 14, 2013

Episode 17: **The Monster Isolation**

After a terrible date, Raj vows to never leave his apartment again. Meanwhile, Penny actually impresses Sheldon with her acting skills.

Story by: Chuck Lorre & Dave Goetsch & Maria Ferrari
Teleplay by: Steven Molaro & Eric Kaplan & Steve Holland
Directed by: Mark Cendrowski
U.S. Broadcast Premiere: February 21, 2013

Leonard: I never wanted to play the cello. How do you meet girls playing the cello? "Hey, you want to come over to my house and listen to me play an instrument that sounds like a suicidal bumblebee?"

Episode 18: **The Contractual Obligation Implementation**

Back to school! Leonard, Sheldon and Howard try to advance the cause of women in science by speaking with junior high girls about their future careers, while Raj plans his date with Lucy (guest star KATE MICUCCI).

Story by: Chuck Lorre & Eric Kaplan & Steve Holland
Teleplay by: Steven Molaro & Jim Reynolds & Maria Ferrari
Directed by: Mark Cendrowski
U.S. Broadcast Premiere: March 7, 2013

Episode 19: **The Closet Reconfiguration**

When Howard finds a letter from his father, he's forced to confront his past, struggling with whether or not he should open it. And Leonard and Penny throw a "grown-up" cocktail party at the apartment.

Story by: Chuck Lorre & Jim Reynolds & Maria Ferrari
Teleplay by: Steven Molaro & Steve Holland & Eric Kaplan
Directed by: Anthony Rich
U.S. Broadcast Premiere: March 14, 2013

Episode 20: **The Tenure Turbulence**

Let the battle begin! Leonard, Sheldon and Raj fight for tenure at the university—and the competition heats up when the girls get involved!

Story by: Steven Molaro & Eric Kaplan & Maria Ferrari
Teleplay by: Chuck Lorre & Steve Holland & Jim Reynolds
Directed by: Mark Cendrowski
U.S. Broadcast Premiere: April 4, 2013

Episode 21: **The Closure Alternative**

Sheldon feels lost after one of his favorite TV shows gets canceled too soon, so Amy tries to help him get over his compulsive need for closure. Meanwhile, Raj discovers a secret about his new love interest, Lucy.

Story by: Chuck Lorre & Bill Prady & Tara Hernandez
Teleplay by: Steven Molaro & Jim Reynolds & Steve Holland
Directed by: Mark Cendrowski
U.S. Broadcast Premiere: April 25, 2013

Episode 22: **The Proton Resurgence**

Sheldon and Leonard hire Professor Proton (guest star BOB NEWHART), the host of their favorite childhood TV show, to perform. Also, Howard and Bernadette run into trouble babysitting Raj's dog.

Story by: Chuck Lorre & Jim Reynolds & Steve Holland
Teleplay by: Steven Molaro & Eric Kaplan & Maria Ferrari
Directed by: Mark Cendrowski
U.S. Broadcast Premiere: May 2, 2013

Episode 23: **The Love Spell Potential**

When the girls' trip to Vegas falls through, the guys invite them to play Dungeons & Dragons—causing Sheldon and Amy's relationship to take an unexpected turn. Meanwhile, Raj and Lucy go on a very awkward date.

Story by: Chuck Lorre & Jim Reynolds & Maria Ferrari
Teleplay by: Steven Molaro & Eric Kaplan & Steve Holland
Directed by: Anthony Rich
U.S. Broadcast Premiere: May 9, 2013

Episode 24: **The Bon Voyage Reaction**

When Leonard is offered an exciting new job opportunity overseas, Sheldon grows very jealous and Penny is thrown for a loop. Meanwhile, Raj pushes Lucy a little too far in their relationship in the sixth season finale.

Story by: Steven Molaro & Steve Holland & Tara Hernandez
Teleplay by: Chuck Lorre & Jim Reynolds & Maria Ferrari
Directed by: Mark Cendrowski
U.S. Broadcast Premiere: May 16, 2013

Season 7

Episode 1: **The Hofstadter Insufficiency**

On the one-hour seventh season premiere, Sheldon and Penny bond in Leonard's absence, but it's Sheldon's feelings that are crushed when Leonard returns from the North Sea. Guest star REGINA KING returns as Mrs. Davis, the university's director of employee relations.

Story by: Chuck Lorre & Steven Molaro & Tara Hernandez
Teleplay by: Eric Kaplan & Jim Reynolds & Steve Holland
Directed by: Mark Cendrowski
U.S. Broadcast Premiere: September 26, 2013

Episode 2: **The Deception Verification**

On the second part of the one-hour seventh season premiere, Raj gets consoled about his ex-girlfriend and Howard's relationship with his mother causes an unusual threat to his masculinity. KEVIN SUSSMAN returns as Stuart, the comic book store owner.

Story by: Chuck Lorre & Eric Kaplan & Jim Reynolds
Teleplay by: Steven Molaro & Steve Holland & Maria Ferrari
Directed by: Mark Cendrowski
U.S. Broadcast Premiere: September 26, 2013

Episode 3: **The Scavenger Vortex**

When the entire gang competes in a cutthroat scavenger hunt designed by Raj that tests their science knowledge and street smarts, it brings out the best—and worst—in everyone.

Story by: Dave Goetsch & Eric Kaplan & Steve Holland
Teleplay by: Steven Molaro & Jim Reynolds & Maria Ferrari
Directed by: Mark Cendrowski
U.S. Broadcast Premiere: October 3, 2013

Episode 4: **The Raiders Minimization**

After Amy ruins one of Sheldon's favorite movies—*Raiders of the Lost Ark*—he gets defensive, seeking revenge. Meanwhile, Leonard discovers a way to get Penny to do anything; and Raj and Stuart create online dating profiles.

Story by: Chuck Lorre & Jim Reynolds & Tara Hernandez
Teleplay by: Steven Molaro & Steve Holland & Maria Ferrari
Directed by: Mark Cendrowski
U.S. Broadcast Premiere: October 10, 2013

Episode 5: **The Workplace Proximity**

Sheldon must decide how much "Amy time" is too much after she takes a job at his university and their relationship is put to the test. Meanwhile, Howard finds himself sleeping on Raj's couch after a fight with Bernadette.

Story by: Steven Molaro & Steve Holland & Maria Ferrari
Teleplay by: Chuck Lorre & Eric Kaplan & Jim Reynolds
Directed by: Mark Cendrowski
U.S. Broadcast Premiere: October 17, 2013

Sheldon: Amy, this isn't easy to say. All relationships are difficult. But even more so when you're with a person who struggles with everyday social interactions. And frankly, who can strike people as being kind of a weirdo.

Amy: Sheldon, you're not a weirdo.

Sheldon: I wasn't speaking about me.

Episode 6: **The Romance Resonance**

Sheldon's latest scientific breakthrough makes him feel like a fraud—and threatens to haunt him forever. Meanwhile, Howard's romantic gesture to Bernadette causes Penny to step up her game with Leonard.

Story by: Eric Kaplan & Jim Reynolds & Tara Hernandez
Teleplay by: Steven Molaro & Steve Holland & Maria Ferrari
Directed by: Mark Cendrowski
U.S. Broadcast Premiere: October 24, 2013

Episode 7: **The Proton Displacement**

Sheldon feels slighted when Professor Proton (recurring guest star BOB NEWHART) seeks advice from Leonard instead of him, and he seeks revenge by befriending a rival science TV host, BILL NYE (guest starring as himself). Meanwhile, Raj gets jealous when Howard crashes girls' night.

Story by: Chuck Lorre & Maria Ferrari & Anthony Del Broccolo
Teleplay by: Steven Molaro & Eric Kaplan & Jim Reynolds
Directed by: Mark Cendrowski
U.S. Broadcast Premiere: November 7, 2013

Episode 8: **The Itchy Brain Simulation**

Leonard tries to keep Sheldon from overreacting when a past mistake comes to light, but Sheldon punishes Leonard by making him "walk a mile in his shoes." Meanwhile, Penny confronts Raj's ex-girlfriend, Lucy.

Story by: Steven Molaro & Bill Prady & Jim Reynolds
Teleplay by: Eric Kaplan & Steve Holland & Maria Ferrari
Directed by: Mark Cendrowski
U.S. Broadcast Premiere: November 14, 2013

Episode 9: **The Thanksgiving Decoupling**

An upset Sheldon protests when the entire gang drags him to Mrs. Wolowitz's house for Thanksgiving. Meanwhile, Penny and Leonard must deal with a mistake from her past.

Story by: Eric Kaplan & Steve Holland & Maria Ferrari
Teleplay by: Steven Molaro & Jim Reynolds & Jeremy Howe
Directed by: Mark Cendrowski
U.S. Broadcast Premiere: November 21, 2013

Sheldon: Leonard, do you think I'm funny?
Leonard: No. Do you?
Sheldon: I think I'm hysterical.
Leonard: I take it back. That was funny.

Bernadette: Aww, Raj did the dishes.
Howard: How do you know I didn't do them?
Bernadette: Because once when all the knives were dirty, you cut a bagel with your keys.

Episode 10: **The Discovery Dissipation**

Leonard and Amy help Sheldon cope with the shame he's feeling after his accidental contribution to science is disproved. Meanwhile, Raj must stay with Howard and Bernadette for a week. IRA FLATOW guest stars as himself.

Story by: Eric Kaplan & Jim Reynolds & Maria Ferrari
Teleplay by: Steven Molaro & Steve Holland & Adam Faberman
Directed by: Mark Cendrowski
U.S. Broadcast Premiere: December 5, 2013

Episode 11: **The Cooper Extraction**

While Sheldon is away in Texas, everyone gathers to decorate the apartment Christmas tree and imagines what their lives would be like if they had never met Sheldon.

Story by: Steven Molaro & Eric Kaplan & Maria Ferrari
Teleplay by: Jim Reynolds & Steve Holland & Tara Hernandez
Directed by: Mark Cendrowski
U.S. Broadcast Premiere: December 12, 2013

Episode 12: **The Hesitation Ramification**

When Penny's big acting break on *NCIS* is a bust, Leonard struggles to help her, which results in Penny asking Leonard a bold relationship question. Meanwhile, Sheldon tries to learn how to be funny, and Raj tries to work on his "game" before talking to girls.

Story by: Dave Goetsch & Jim Reynolds & Tara Hernandez
Teleplay by: Steven Molaro & Steve Holland & Maria Ferrari
Directed by: Mark Cendrowski
U.S. Broadcast Premiere: January 2, 2014

Episode 13: **The Occupation Recalibration**

When Sheldon is forced to take a vacation, he tries to relax, but instead spends a lot of time with Penny after she quits her job. Meanwhile, Leonard struggles to be supportive of Penny, and Bernadette seeks Stuart's help in replacing one of Howard's comic books.

Story by: Eric Kaplan & Maria Ferrari & Tara Hernandez
Teleplay by: Steven Molaro & Jim Reynolds & Steve Holland
Directed by: Mark Cendrowski
U.S. Broadcast Premiere: January 9, 2014

Bernadette: Well, while they're acting like teenagers we could do something grown-up.

Amy: Ooh, you mean like a museum?

Penny: Yes, like a museum, but anything else!

Episode 14: **The Convention Conundrum**

After the guys can't get Comic-Con tickets, Sheldon decides to hold his own convention and winds up spending a wild night with JAMES EARL JONES (guest starring as himself). Meanwhile, the girls see if they can act like "grown-ups." *Star Wars* icon CARRIE FISHER makes a cameo appearance as well.

Story by: Eric Kaplan & Jim Reynolds & Adam Faberman
Teleplay by: Steven Molaro & Dave Goetsch & Steve Holland
Directed by: Mark Cendrowski
U.S. Broadcast Premiere: January 30, 2014

Episode 15: **The Locomotive Manipulation**

Love is in the air when Amy convinces Sheldon to join her (as well as Howard and Bernadette) for a romantic weekend in Napa Valley to celebrate Valentine's Day. Meanwhile, Leonard and Penny must rush Raj's dog to the vet.

Story by: Jim Reynolds & Steve Holland & Tara Hernandez
Teleplay by: Steven Molaro & Eric Kaplan & Maria Ferrari
Directed by: Mark Cendrowski
U.S. Broadcast Premiere: February 6, 2014

Episode 16: **The Table Polarization**

When Leonard buys a dining room table, it causes Sheldon to reevaluate the changes in his life. Meanwhile, Wolowitz is offered a chance to go back to space, and Bernadette struggles with whether or not to encourage him.

Story by: Steven Molaro & Maria Ferrari & Tara Hernandez
Teleplay by: Chuck Lorre & Jim Reynolds & Steve Holland
Directed by: Gay Linvill
U.S. Broadcast Premiere: February 27, 2014

Episode 17: **The Friendship Turbulence**

After the insults fly, Bernadette tries to broker the peace between Howard and Sheldon by having the two travel together to Houston in an attempt to improve their friendship. Meanwhile, Penny is offered an embarrassing movie role, and Raj asks Amy to write to a woman on his behalf.

Story by: Steven Molaro & Eric Kaplan & Tara Hernandez
Teleplay by: Jim Reynolds, & Steve Holland & Maria Ferrari
Directed by: Mark Cendrowski
U.S. Broadcast Premiere: March 6, 2014

Episode 18: **The Mommy Observation**

When Sheldon visits his mom in Houston, he is forced to confront a new reality. Meanwhile, Raj's "Murder Mystery" party starts some fights within the gang.

Story by: Jim Reynolds & Maria Ferrari & Steve Holland
Teleplay by: Steven Molaro & Eric Kaplan & Anthony Del Broccolo
Directed by: Mark Cendrowski
U.S. Broadcast Premiere: March 13, 2014

Episode 19: **The Indecision Amalgamation**

While Raj is wracked with guilt over dating two women at the same time and Penny is wrestling with whether to take a role in a cheesy movie, Amy must help Sheldon through the even greater hell of choosing between two gaming systems.

E=mc²

Story by: Bill Prady & Eric Kaplan & Jim Reynolds
Teleplay by: Steven Molaro & Dave Goetsch & Steve Holland
Directed by: Anthony Rich
U.S. Broadcast Premiere: April 3, 2014

Episode 20: **The Relationship Diremption**

Sheldon faces a personal crisis after deciding he's wasting his time with String Theory. Meanwhile, a double date between Raj, Emily and the Wolowitzes ends in embarrassment for Howard.

Story by: Steven Molaro & Bill Prady & Jim Reynolds
Teleplay by: Chuck Lorre & Eric Kaplan & Steve Holland
Directed by: Mark Cendrowski
U.S. Broadcast Premiere: April 10, 2014

Episode 21: **The Anything Can Happen Recurrence**

Leonard tries to help Sheldon free his mind by reinstating "Anything Can Happen Thursday," but when Sheldon tries to be spontaneous, it leads to unexpected friction between Penny, Amy and Bernadette. Meanwhile, Raj seeks Howard's help in preparing for a date with Emily.

Story by: Steven Molaro & Eric Kaplan & Adam Faberman
Teleplay by: Jim Reynolds & Steve Holland & Tara Hernandez
Directed by: Mark Cendrowski
U.S. Broadcast Premiere: April 24, 2014

Episode 22: **The Proton Transmogrification**

May the "Fourth" Be With You! Professor Proton helps Sheldon cope with grief, while Leonard turns a relationship milestone into a competition with Penny. Meanwhile Amy and Bernadette make a "*Star Wars* Day" gift for the guys.

Story by: Jim Reynolds & Maria Ferrari & Jeremy Howe
Teleplay by: Steven Molaro & Eric Kaplan & Steve Holland
Directed by: Mark Cendrowski
U.S. Broadcast Premiere: May 1, 2014

Episode 23: **The Gorilla Dissolution**

A horrible day at work prompts Penny to evaluate her life choices—including taking a big step with Leonard. Meanwhile, Howard and Bernadette struggle to care for Mrs. Wolowitz, and Raj gets relationship advice from Sheldon.

Story by: Chuck Lorre & Jim Reynolds & Jeremy Howe
Teleplay by: Steven Molaro & Steve Holland & Eric Kaplan
Directed by: Peter Chakos
U.S. Broadcast Premiere: May 8, 2014

Episode 24: **The Status Quo Combustion**

With his entire world changing around him, Sheldon is forced to confront an uncertain future and considers a major move in the seventh season finale. Meanwhile, Raj and Emily take it to the next level, and Mrs. Wolowitz's injury is a major headache for Howard and Bernadette.

Story by: Eric Kaplan & Jim Reynolds & Jeremy Howe
Teleplay by: Steven Molaro & Steve Holland & Tara Hernandez
Directed by: Mark Cendrowski
U.S. Broadcast Premiere: May 15, 2014

Season 8

Episode 1: **The Locomotion Interruption**

In the eighth season premiere, Leonard and Amy take an unexpected road trip to Arizona to pick up Sheldon. Meanwhile, Penny interviews for a job at Bernadette's company, and Howard is "weirded out" by Stuart's close relationship with Mrs. Wolowitz. STEPHEN ROOT guest stars as Bernadette's boss, Dan.

Story by: Jim Reynolds & Maria Ferrari & Tara Hernandez
Teleplay by: Steven Molaro & Steve Holland & Eric Kaplan
Directed by: Mark Cendrowski
U.S. Broadcast Premiere: September 22, 2014

Episode 2: **The Junior Professor Solution**

When Sheldon is forced to teach a class, Howard surprises everyone by taking it. Meanwhile, the tension between Penny and Bernadette gives Amy a chance to play both sides.

Story by: Steven Molaro & Eric Kaplan & Steve Holland
Teleplay by: Jim Reynolds & Maria Ferrari & Tara Hernandez
Directed by: Mark Cendrowski
U.S. Broadcast Premiere: September 22, 2014

Amy: I can't believe our first date was five years ago tonight.

Sheldon: I know. Do you think I should start watching *The Flash* TV show?

Episode 3: **The First Pitch Insufficiency**

Howard is nervous when NASA asks him to throw out the first pitch at a Los Angeles Angels game for National Space Day. Also, Leonard and Penny try to prove Sheldon wrong after he claims that he and Amy are a superior couple.

Story by: Chuck Lorre & Jim Reynolds & Anthony Del Broccolo
Teleplay by: Steven Molaro & Steve Holland & Maria Ferrari
Directed by: Mark Cendrowski
U.S. Broadcast Premiere: September 29, 2014

Episode 4: **The Hook-Up Reverberation**

Raj's honesty about his past comes back to bite him after his girlfriend, Emily (recurring guest star LAURA SPENCER), gives Penny the cold shoulder. Meanwhile, the guys consider becoming part-owners of Stuart's comic book store.

Story by: Steve Holland & Maria Ferrari & Tara Hernandez
Teleplay by: Steven Molaro & Eric Kaplan & Jim Reynolds
Directed by: Mark Cendrowski
U.S. Broadcast Premiere: October 6, 2014

Episode 5: **The Focus Attenuation**

Amy and Bernadette accuse Penny of being a "buzzkill" after she gets an email from work during their Vegas weekend. Meanwhile, the guys try to invent something cool, but only come up with new ways to procrastinate.

Story by: Jim Reynolds & Maria Ferrari & Adam Faberman
Teleplay by: Steven Molaro & Eric Kaplan & Steve Holland
Directed by: Mark Cendrowski
U.S. Broadcast Premiere: October 13, 2014

Episode 6: **The Expedition Approximation**

Sheldon and Raj test whether they could survive a dark-matter research expedition in a salt mine by simulating the conditions in a steam tunnel deep underground. Meanwhile, Leonard and Penny seek advice from Wolowitz and Bernadette after they fight about money.

Story by: Steven Molaro & Dave Goetsch & Tara Hernandez
Teleplay by: Jim Reynolds & Steve Holland & Maria Ferrari
Directed by: Mark Cendrowski
U.S. Broadcast Premiere: October 20, 2014

Episode 7: **The Misinterpretation Agitation**

The guys try to help Penny out of an awkward work dilemma when a smitten doctor shows up at her door after her flirtatious sales techniques work a little too well. Meanwhile, Amy and Bernadette argue over whether or not female scientists should play up their sexuality.

Story by: Chuck Lorre & Eric Kaplan & Jim Reynolds
Teleplay by: Steven Molaro & Steve Holland & Maria Ferrari
Directed by: Mark Cendrowski
U.S. Broadcast Premiere: October 30, 2014

Episode 8: **The Prom Equivalency**

When the gang re-creates a high school prom night on the roof of the guys' apartment building, Sheldon feels pressure to participate in all the typical romantic traditions.

Story by: Jim Reynolds & Steve Holland & Jeremy Howe
Teleplay by: Steven Molaro & Eric Kaplan & Maria Ferrari
Directed by: Mark Cendrowski
U.S. Broadcast Premiere: November 6, 2014

Episode 9: **The Septum Deviation**

When Leonard gets minor surgery on his nose, Sheldon is the one in need of sympathy. Meanwhile, Raj's parents' impending divorce causes Howard and Bernadette to work on their own marriage.

Story by: Steven Molaro & Bill Prady & Maria Ferrari
Teleplay by: Eric Kaplan & Steve Holland & Tara Hernandez
Directed by: Anthony Rich
U.S. Broadcast Premiere: November 13, 2014

Episode 10: **The Champagne Reflection**

While Sheldon says a tearful good-bye to the final instalment of *Fun with Flags*, Leonard, Howard and Raj search for something significant in a dead professor's research. And Bernadette is shocked to learn of her coworkers' true feelings from Penny.

Story by: Steven Molaro & Tara Hernandez & David Saltzberg, Ph.D.
Teleplay by: Jim Reynolds & Steve Holland & Dave Goetsch
Directed by: Mark Cendrowski
U.S. Broadcast Premiere: November 20, 2014

Penny: *(about Bernadette)* Come on, she's not that bad.
Dan: Oh, yeah? At the company picnic she yelled at me and my grandson for losing the three-legged race. He still calls her "that mean kid with the big boobies."

Episode 11: **The Clean Room Infiltration**

Leonard and Howard turn to Raj for help in dealing with a work emergency when they nearly come to blows after blaming each other for a potential disaster at the university. Amy throws an authentic Victorian Christmas party, while Sheldon seeks revenge on her for making him celebrate the holidays.

Story by: Maria Ferrari & Tara Hernandez & Jeremy Howe
Teleplay by: Eric Kaplan & Jim Reynolds & Steve Holland
Directed by: Mark Cendrowski
U.S. Broadcast Premiere: December 11, 2014

Episode 12: **The Space Probe Disintegration**

When the guys finally agree to do something the girls like, it leads to a confrontation between Leonard and Sheldon.

Story by: Bill Prady & Eric Kaplan & Jim Reynolds
Teleplay by: Steven Molaro & Steve Holland & Maria Ferrari
Directed by: Mark Cendrowski
U.S. Broadcast Premiere: January 8, 2015

Episode 13: **The Anxiety Optimization**

In the hopes of achieving a scientific breakthrough, Sheldon invites his friends to challenge him and make him miserable. Meanwhile, Wolowitz invents an embarrassing game about Raj.

Story by: Eric Kaplan & Maria Ferrari & Adam Faberman
Teleplay by: Jim Reynolds & Steve Holland & Tara Hernandez
Directed by: Mark Cendrowski
U.S. Broadcast Premiere: January 29, 2015

Episode 14: **The Troll Manifestation**

After Leonard and Sheldon co-publish a physics paper, they must defend themselves against criticism from an online bully. Also, girls' night finds Penny, Amy and Bernadette confronting embarrassing moments from their pasts.

Story by: Steven Molaro & Eric Kaplan & Tara Hernandez
Teleplay by: Jim Reynolds & Steve Holland & Maria Ferrari
Directed by: Mark Cendrowski
U.S. Broadcast Premiere: February 5, 2015

Episode 15: **The Comic Book Store Regeneration**

Howard receives some shocking news as everyone prepares for the reopening of Stuart's comic book store. Penny teaches Sheldon how to "let it go," but can't follow her own advice after she learns something infuriating about Amy. Also, Leonard and Raj think they spot Nathan Fillion at a restaurant.

Story by: Jim Reynolds & Maria Ferrari & Jeremy Howe
Teleplay by: Steven Molaro & Eric Kaplan & Steve Holland
Directed by: Mark Cendrowski
U.S. Broadcast Premiere: February 19, 2015

Episode 16: **The Intimacy Acceleration**

When the gang hears about an experiment designed to make participants fall in love, Sheldon and Penny put it to the test as a joke. Meanwhile, Leonard, Amy, Raj and Emily spend the evening trying to escape a room with a "zombie." And Bernadette and Howard run into trouble at the airport after returning from the funeral for Mrs. Wolowitz.

Story by: Dave Goetsch & Eric Kaplan & Tara Hernandez
Teleplay by: Steven Molaro & Jim Reynolds & Steve Holland
Directed by: Mark Cendrowski
U.S. Broadcast Premiere: February 26, 2015

Episode 17: **The Colonization Application**

A trip to the pet store ends in a fight when Amy learns that Sheldon has applied for a one-way mission to colonize Mars. Also, Leonard surprises Penny with a very "adult" purchase; and Raj is caught snooping in Emily's apartment.

Story by: Dave Goetsch & Jim Reynolds & Tara Hernandez
Teleplay by: Steven Molaro & Eric Kaplan & Maria Ferrari
Directed by: Mark Cendrowski
U.S. Broadcast Premiere: March 5, 2015

Episode 18: **The Leftover Thermalization**

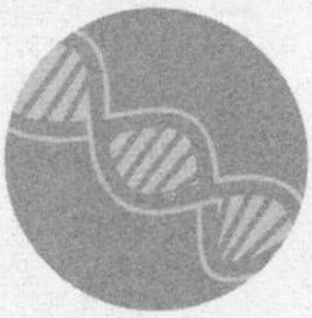

Friction ensues when a magazine fails to mention Leonard in an article about the paper he co-wrote with Sheldon. And a blackout at Mrs. Wolowitz's home leads to a final family dinner in her honor.

Story by: Steven Molaro & Maria Ferrari & Jeremy Howe
Teleplay by: Eric Kaplan & Jim Reynolds & Steve Holland
Directed by: Mark Cendrowski
U.S. Broadcast Premiere: March 12, 2015

Episode 19: **The Skywalker Incursion**

When Leonard and Sheldon are invited to speak at UC Berkeley, they take a detour to try to sneak onto George Lucas's Skywalker Ranch to meet one of their idols. Back in Pasadena, Howard and Bernadette battle over the fate of his *Doctor Who* TARDIS, while Raj and Amy offer to settle the dispute with a game of Ping-Pong.

Story by: Jim Reynolds & Tara Hernandez & Jeremy Howe
Teleplay by: Steven Molaro & Steve Holland & Maria Ferrari
Directed by: Mark Cendrowski
U.S. Broadcast Premiere: April 2, 2015

Episode 20: **The Fortification Implementation**

When Sheldon and Amy build a blanket fort, they come to a big crossroads in their relationship. And Wolowitz is shocked when a man claiming to be the half brother he never knew he had shows up at his front door. And, when Penny is invited to appear on WIL WHEATON's podcast, she and Leonard have a huge on-air argument.

Story by: Jim Reynolds & Saladin K. Patterson & Tara Hernandez
Teleplay by: Steven Molaro & Steve Holland & Maria Ferrari
Directed by: Mark Cendrowski
U.S. Broadcast Premiere: April 9, 2015

Episode 21: **The Communication Deterioration**

When Raj is asked to create a message in case a NASA mission discovers alien life, the guys fight over what he should do. Meanwhile, Penny is torn between auditioning for a movie or keeping her successful pharmaceutical sales job.

Story by: Dave Goetsch & Steve Holland & Jeremy Howe
Teleplay by: Steven Molaro & Eric Kaplan & Jim Reynolds
Directed by: Mark Cendrowski
U.S. Broadcast Premiere: April 16, 2015

Episode 22: **The Graduation Transmission**

Wolowitz questions his engineering abilities when he and Sheldon can't get a drone to fly. Meanwhile, a canceled flight nearly prevents Leonard from giving the commencement address at his former high school. And Raj pits his parents against each other when his father cuts him off financially.

Story by: Chuck Lorre & Dave Goetsch & Anthony Del Broccolo
Teleplay by: Steven Molaro & Steve Holland & Eric Kaplan
Directed by: Anthony Rich
U.S. Broadcast Premiere: April 23, 2015

Episode 23: **The Maternal Combustion**

Personalities collide and sparks fly when Sheldon and Leonard's mothers finally meet. Meanwhile, Howard decides to "man up" and do his fair share of the housework—but not without a little help from his friends.

Story by: Steven Molaro & Tara Hernandez & Jeremy Howe
Teleplay by: Chuck Lorre & Jim Reynolds & Maria Ferrari
Directed by: Anthony Rich
U.S. Broadcast Premiere: April 30, 2015

Episode 24: **The Commitment Determination**

In the eighth season finale, Sheldon presses Leonard and Penny to choose a date for their wedding, while dealing with dramatic changes in his own relationship with Amy.

Story by: Chuck Lorre & Jim Reynolds & Maria Ferrari
Teleplay by: Steven Molaro & Steve Holland & Eric Kaplan
Directed by: Mark Cendrowski
U.S. Broadcast Premiere: May 7, 2015

The Skywalker/Spock Cosmology

The show has shown a great deal of love for two of the greatest science fiction movie franchises of all time, *Star Wars* and *Star Trek*.

Star Trek

Penny gave Sheldon a napkin signed by Leonard Nimoy, and he hugged her for the first time:

Sheldon: *(stunned, then reading)* "To Sheldon, live long and prosper. Leonard Nimoy."

Penny: He came into the restaurant. Sorry the napkin's dirty. He wiped his mouth with it.

Sheldon: *(even more excited)* I possess the DNA of Leonard Nimoy?

Penny: Yeah, yeah. I guess. But you see, he signed it.

Sheldon: *(crazed)* Do you realize what this means? All I need is a healthy ovum and I can grow my own Leonard Nimoy! *

Season 2, Episode 11: The Bath Item Gift Hypothesis

Sheldon explained his rules for Rock-Paper-Scissors-Lizard-Spock:

Sheldon: Scissors cuts paper, paper covers rock, rock crushes lizard, lizard poisons Spock, Spock smashes scissors, scissors decapitates lizard, lizard eats paper, paper disproves Spock, Spock vaporizes rock and, as it always has, rock crushes scissors.

Season 2, Episode 8: The Lizard-Spock Expansion

** This is quite possibly my favorite moment of the entire series.*

Sheldon revealed he had vowed eternal hatred for Wil Wheaton ever since 1995, when he traveled ten hours by bus to a sci-fi convention in Jackson, Mississippi. He wanted to meet Wil and get him to autograph his one-sixty-fourth scale mint-in-package Wesley Crusher action figure. But even though Wil was advertised to appear, he did not show up.

Season 3, Episode 5: The Creepy Candy Coating Corollary

George Takei (and Katee Sackhoff from *Battlestar Galactica*) visited Howard in a masturbatory fantasy, giving him advice about Bernadette.

Season 4, Episode 4: The Hot Troll Deviation

Sheldon was guilt-ridden after screwing up Wolowitz's attempts to get a security clearance and dreamed he saw a Gorn.

Season 4, Episode 7: The Apology Insufficiency

Sheldon wrote a one-act play, which was adapted from a *Star Trek* fan fiction he wrote when he was eleven entitled *Where No Sheldon Has Gone Before*.

Season 4, Episode 14: The Thespian Catalyst

Leonard and Priya role-played as Kirk and Lieutenant Uhuru—she wore her brother's Uhuru Halloween costume.

Season 4, Episode 24: The Roommate Transmogrification

E=mc²

Sheldon karate-chopped Leonard on the side of the neck a la Captain Kirk after Leonard said that Amy really knew how to help a guy loosen up and have a good time. "Although, truth be told, my groin's a little worse for wear." He had accompanied her to a wedding and pulled his groin doing the hokey-pokey.

Season 5, Episode 3: The Pulled Groin Extrapolation

Wil Wheaton remembered Sheldon's story about the time he went to a convention to have Wil sign his Wesley Crusher action figure, but Wil wasn't able to make it. So at his party, Wil gave Sheldon an original mint-in-package Wesley Crusher action figure and signed it. "To Sheldon, sorry this took so long. Your friend, Wil." It was his last one, and he wanted Sheldon to have it. Sheldon then announced to the room that Wil Wheaton was his friend. Immediately after that, Brent Spiner (Mr. Data from *Star Trek: The Next Generation*) opened it and became Sheldon's new mortal enemy.

Season 5, Episode 5: The Russian Rocket Reaction

As a thank-you for all the takeout food they'd bought her over the years, Penny got Leonard and Sheldon vintage mint-in-box 1975 Mego *Star Trek* Transporters with real transporter action. Sheldon played with this using his Mr. Spock action figure and broke it. He decided to switch it with Leonard's. That night, he had a dream where the Mr. Spock action figure spoke to him. The voice? That's right—Leonard Nimoy. Sheldon called the toy "Tiny Spock" in his dream.

Spock: *(voiceover)* If I told you to jump off the bridge of the *Enterprise*, would you do it?

Sheldon: Oh, if I got on the bridge of the *Enterprise*, I would never, ever leave.

Spock: *(voiceover)* Trust me, it gets old after a while.

Season 5, Episode 20: The Transporter Malfunction

Wil Wheaton had Penny on his podcast.

Leonard: Wil's had lots of great guests—Jonathan Frakes, Brent Spiner, Michael Dorn, Gates McFadden . . . Penny: Those are *Star Trek* people.

Leonard: Yes!

Penny: *(pleased with herself)* I only figured that out because I've never heard of any of them.

Wil: I deserve that. I invited you on my show and I drove here.

Season 8, Episode 20: The Fortification Implementation

The guys played Klingon Boggle.

Season 2, Episode 7: The Panta Piñata Polarization

Sheldon was upset when he ordered a life-size cardboard Mr. Spock and got one of Zachary Quinto and not Leonard Nimoy.

Sheldon: "Live long and suck it, Zachary Quinto!"

Season 5, Episode 13: The Recombination Hypothesis

Star Wars

Leonard told Penny he loved her for the first time when she quoted Yoda to him.

Season 3, Episode 19: The Wheaton Recurrence

Sheldon spent the day with James Earl Jones. Sheldon found James at his favorite sushi restaurant. Then they went on a Ferris wheel, got ice cream and even went to a strip club. Later, James pranked Carrie Fisher by ringing her doorbell and then running off. They finished the evening in a steam room.*

James Earl Jones: Why don't you and your friends come to Comic-Con with me?

Sheldon: Really?

James Earl Jones: Of course. And San Diego is right across the border from my favorite city on Earth: Tijuana—where I'm taking you every night.

Sheldon: *(to himself)* Aye-yi-yi.

James Earl Jones: Aye-yi-yi. Bang! Bang! *(finger pistols)*

Season 7, Episode 14: The Convention Conundrum

Leonard told Penny she could send in an online video audition for the new *Star Wars* movie *(Star Wars: The Force Awakens)*. In real life, people were actually able to submit online audition videos. We also get to see part of Wolowitz's audition video.

Season 7, Episode 12: The Hesitation Ramification

Penny got Sheldon to do yoga with her because he thought she said "Yoda."

Season 7, Episode 13: The Occupation Recalibration

** James and Carrie appeared as themselves in the episode.*

When Bob Newhart's character, Arthur Jeffries, died, his funeral was on *Star Wars* Day. Bob appeared to Sheldon in a dream dressed as Obi Wan Kenobi and even wielded a lightsaber. They sat in a Dagobah Swamp set. LucasFilms got involved to help re-create the lightsaber effects, as well as the effects used in the Luke/Obi-Wan Kenobi scene from *The Empire Strikes Back* that made Bob look like a ghost.

Season 7, Episode 22: The Proton Transmogrification

Howard made matching lightsaber belt buckles for him and Raj.

Season 7, Episode 7: The Proton Displacement

When Sheldon tried to run onto Skywalker Ranch, the security guard called for "Code A-A 23." A-A 23 refers to the detention block on the first Death Star where Princess Leia was being detained and interrogated.

Leonard: I don't think George Lucas put his headquarters in the middle of nowhere because he wanted people dropping in.

Sheldon: Yoda's swamp was in the middle of nowhere. Tatooine was in the middle of nowhere. Hoth was in the middle of nowhere. That's code, Leonard. He wants us to drop in.

Season 8, Episode 19: The Skywalker Incursion

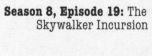

Penny: I'm just thinking about the day I met you and Leonard.

Sheldon: It was a Monday afternoon. You joined us for Indian food.

Penny: Can you believe it's been eight years?

Sheldon: And you're still eating our food.

BAZINGA!™